D1298323

THE BOOK OF INTEREST
AND MONEY

THE BOOK OF INTEREST AND MONEY

A Compendium of Everything You'll Ever Need to Calculate Yields, Rates of Interest, and Rates of Return on Investments, Loans, Mortgages, and Insurance Policies

Thomas M. Carrington, Ph.D.

1817

Harper & Row, Publishers, New York
BALLINGER DIVISION
Grand Rapids, Philadelphia, St. Louis, San Francisco
London, Singapore, Sydney, Tokyo, Toronto

International Standard Book Number: 0–88730–394–3

Library of Congress Catalog Card Number: 89–45772

Printed in the United States of America

Library of Congress Cataloging-in-Publication Data

Carrington, Thomas M., 1931–
　　The book of interest and money: a compendium of everything you'll
　　ever need to know to calculate yields, rates of interest, and rates
　　of return on investments, loans, mortgages, and insurance policies /
　　Thomas M. Carrington.
　　　　　　p.　　　　　cm.
　　　ISBN 0–88730–394–3
　　　1. Interest—Tables.　I. Title.
　　HG1626.C37　1990
　　332.8'2–dc20
　　　　　　　　　　　　　　　　　　　　　　　　　　　89–45772
　　　　　　　　　　　　　　　　　　　　　　　　　　　　　CIP

90　91　92　93　HC　9　8　7　6　5　4　3　2　1

CONTENTS

TABLES

PREFACE

Whom is this book for? The book can be of value to anyone living in the United States as well as to persons living in other countries.

The book can be beneficial to the businessperson, investor, lender, borrower, salesperson, broker, appraiser, management consultant, financial planner, financial analyst, investment counselor, portfolio manager, accountant, lawyer, corporate treasurer, banker, person in government, engineer, student, or consumer.

This book can be put to good use by anyone

- Dealing in real estate, or buying a home or other type of real estate that requires financing.
- Lending money to borrowers.
- Issuing securities.
- Investing money in capital market investments (such as stocks, bonds, and mortgages) or in money market instruments (such as treasury bills, commercial paper, and bankers' acceptances).
- Buying an insurance policy or contract.
- Who will be receiving pension or retirement benefits.
- Borrowing money from a bank, savings and loan, or other type of financial institution or funding source.
- Purchasing an automobile, boat, or other large ticket item on credit.
- Depositing money in a money market account or savings account, or anyone purchasing certificates of deposit.

Both simple interest and compound interest penetrate all areas of the financial spectrum, including investments, investment banking, commercial banking, corporate finance, insurance, and real estate and mortgage banking. Interest plays an important part not only in the business function of finance but also in other business functions such as production and marketing.

Anyone who does not understand the different aspects of interest does not truly have an adequate understanding of the world of business. Such individuals can find themselves in a weakened negotiating position if they are unable to identify alternatives and determine the relative attractiveness of options that might be available.

Knowledge is power. Where money is concerned, just one interest-related idea for investing money or for borrowing money might be worth hundreds of dollars, or even hundreds of thousands of dollars if substantial funds are involved.

The book is divided into two parts. Part I is concerned with examples and explanatory material that treat real world borrowing and investing situations. Part II deals with the use of financial calculators in providing solutions to additional real-world borrowing and investing problems. Examples of how to use financial calculators to construct compound interest tables are also furnished.

This book has been written for a wide audience because of the nature of investing, borrowing, and interest. The concepts it discusses are universal. They pervade the activities of businesses, individuals, and governments not only in this country but in other nations as well.

Because the intent is to provide a publication capable of serving the requirements of many people, readers may wish to pick and choose which parts of the book are applicable to their areas of interest and need. The detailed presentation in the Table of Contents provides readers an opportunity to do this.

Readers engaged in real estate activities, for example, will find it to their advantage to look at the material dealing with real estate and the calculations of debt service, debt service-coverage ratio, remaining principal balances, or balloon payments, and such measures as return on equity (cash on cash return) and return on total capital. A view of real estate ownership benefits such as cash flow, appreciation, and equity buildup is provided as well.

People who are in the field of insurance will be well served by concentrating on the book areas that discuss how the determination of present value is made for ordinary annuities, annuities due, deferred annuities, and lump sum payments.

The attention of businesspeople, corporate treasurers, commercial bankers, and savings and loan and other financial intermediary personnel should be directed to the discussions concerning the ascertainment of effective borrowing and lending rates and the concept of borrower opportunity cost.

Accountants, financial planners, financial analysts, and management consultants will be interested in all phases and aspects of compound interest because of the broad applications of their work.

The treatment of zero coupon bonds and premium, discount, and par bonds should be an attraction for investors, securities brokerage personnel, investment counselors, mutual fund and other portfolio managers, and persons operating in the investment banking field.

Federal and state government personnel working in the fields of real estate, insurance, securities, and banking regulation will encounter discussions of compound interest applicable to mortgages and real estate investments, insurance annuities, securities investments, and the borrowing and lending of money.

A lawyer working in the field of securities or real estate will find whole chapters devoted to these specialities. An attorney concerned with workmen's compensation cases or with prejudgment and post-judgment interest may wish to focus on calculations relating to annuity present values or the determination of lump sum future values.

Engineers should be aware that the growth equation is a powerful tool that can be employed to provide answers for nonmonetary growth variables, just as it can be used for furnishing compounded monetary growth solutions.

Undergraduate or graduate students majoring in finance, economics, statistics, computer science, marketing, management, or accounting will find that this book can be of value in their college course work. After their graduation, the book can continue to be of help for many years.

Consumers will find the material dealing with the determination of monthly payments for financed purchases such as homes, automobiles, and boats to be useful. Some consumers may be surprised to learn how much total interest they will have to pay on loans they currently may be contemplating.

A section treating the solution of real-world investing and borrowing problems, as well as the construction of compound interest tables using financial calculators, is included for persons who have an interest in this area. However, this portion may be passed over by those who are not interested in the use of financial calculators. Readers can always come back to this section at a later date if they wish.

One objective in writing this book was to give a comprehensive presentation of compound interest in an easy-to-understand manner. Another reason for writing the book was to provide readers with a chance to gain an in-depth look into the use of compound interest as it relates to the borrowing and investing of money. That material is here for the taking. However, the extent to which each reader chooses to take advantage of this opportunity is, of course, a personal matter. Bear in mind, however, that fresh ideas in investing and borrowing techniques come from those who have a solid background in fundamentals, not just an ability to press keys on a calculator or computer keyboard.

A special effort has been made to make the material in this book easy to understand. Also, an endeavor has been made to combine a number of useful ideas into one publication so that the book can be read now and kept for use as a valuable future reference.

A word of caution: Prospective readers of this book would be doing themselves a disservice by quickly thumbing through the pages and then concluding that the material might not be as easy as some of the reading that they might like to do. This is a case when looks are deceiving. Presentation tools such as equations are enhancements to learning and understanding, not deterrents. Equations have something to say just as words do; they are, in fact, nothing more than an abbreviated form of words. However, readers not comfortable with symbols can pass over the equations. It is well to remember that sometimes the appearance of easy reading can be achieved only by a decision to omit substance.

An exciting and valuable adventure awaits you as a reader of this book. Enjoy the experience of adding to your knowledge and use the information in the book to your benefit.

ACKNOWLEDGMENTS

It would be difficult for the author to mention all of the publications and seminars which have contributed to his exposure over the years to the topic of investments. However, it should be mentioned that the author was stimulated in this area by the work of L. W. Ellwood, M.A.I.

T. M. Carrington

PART I
INVESTING, BORROWING, AND INTEREST

1 SOME USEFUL OBSERVATIONS REGARDING COMMON STOCKS

Although the main thrust of this book is not equities, it would still be difficult to talk about investing without mentioning common stocks. Several related items about which investors may be uncertain or about which they may have questions are discussed.

DO YOU REALLY UNDERSTAND THE DOW JONES INDUSTRIAL AVERAGE?

In listening to news reports on radio and television, in reading newspaper accounts regarding the price movements of common stocks, and in hearing some investor conversations, it becomes apparent that there is some misunderstanding concerning the Dow Jones Industrial Average (DJIA).

For example, if the DJIA were to go up five to six points, should that rise be termed a "rally"? If the DJIA were to experience an upward move of 10 to 12 points, should that movement be labeled a "soaring market"?

The questions above may be phrased in another manner. If, on the average each of the 30 common stocks in the DJIA were to undergo an increase of $\frac{1}{8}$ point (12.5 cents) per share, would that constitute a rally? Would an average climb of $\frac{1}{4}$ point (25 cents) per share be referred to as a soaring market?

If the DJIA divisor should decline to 0.3 in the future, what would a movement of 100 points in the Average mean? The following discussion regarding the DJIA will enable the reader to answer all of the above questions.

The Dow Jones Industrial Average is a ratio based on 30 common stocks that are listed on the New York Stock Exchange. The numerator of the DJIA is the sum of the per-share prices of the 30 common stocks that are used in calculating the Average. One would expect the denominator to be 30 because there are 30 stocks whose prices are averaged; however, stock splits and stock dividends have played a role over the years in reducing the denominator. The denominator is now less than 0.7.

The number in the numerator of the DJIA represents dollars. The same may be said for the value of the Average. In everyday usage, however, the term *dollars* is usually omitted when referring to the Average. Increases and decreases in the DJIA generally are spoken of as *points of change*, instead of as dollars of change. No particular units are ascribed to the denominator.

If, for the moment, the supposition is made that there are only three stocks in the DJIA with each security selling for $40 per share, the DJIA would be 40 (dollars).

$$\text{DJIA} = \frac{40 + 40 + 40}{3}$$
$$= 40$$

If one of the stocks had a two-for-one split, the DJIA might be erroneously calculated as 33.3 (dollars).

$$\text{DJIA} = \frac{40 + 40 + 20}{3}$$
$$= 33.3$$

The drop in the DJIA would be misleading because the only thing that has happened is that one of the equities has had a stock split. In order to maintain the Average at 40 after the split, the denominator, or divisor, has to be changed to 2.5.

$$\text{DJIA} = \frac{40 + 40 + 20}{2.5}$$
$$= 40$$

Assume that the sum of the per-share prices of the 30 stocks in the Average is $1,750. Using a denominator of 0.7, the calculation of the Average gives

$$DJIA = \frac{1,750}{0.7}$$
$$= 2,500$$

If each stock in the Average were to go up one dollar per share, the numerator would increase by 30 (dollars) to 1,780. The DJIA would increase 43 points, from 2,500 to 2,543 (i.e., 1,780 ÷ 0.7).

If each stock in the Average declined one dollar per share, the numerator would decline from 1,750 to 1,720. The DJIA would fall 43 points, from 2,500 to 2,457 (i.e., 1,720 ÷ 0.7).

While, for instance, an advance of 43 points in the DJIA would mean that on the average each stock in the DJIA experienced an upward movement of one dollar per share, in reality not all of the 30 stocks may have acted in the same manner. Some securities might have increased two or three dollars per share while other stocks might have declined two or three dollars per share. Other equities in the Average may have undergone no change at all, or just a slight change. The important thing would be that the numerator showed a net increase of 30 (dollars) after the prices of all 30 stocks had been added together.

Since, in the example, an average movement of one dollar per share in the price of each of the 30 stocks is associated with a change of 43 points in the DJIA, an increase of 15 points in the DJIA means that, on the average, each of the 30 stocks increased 35 cents ($\frac{15}{43} \times \$1.00$) per share. A decrease of 28 points in the DJIA indicates that, on the average, each of the 30 stocks declined 65 cents ($\frac{28}{43} \times \$1.00$) per share.

With the DJIA at 2,500, an increase of 43 points would be equivalent to a rise of 1.7 %while a drop of 43 points would constitute a decline of 1.7 %. A 15-point advance in the DJIA from the 2,500 level would be a gain of 0.6 %and a 28-point decline from 2,500 would be a loss of 1.1 %.

It may be noted that when the Dow Jones Insdustrial Average fell a stunning 508 points on October 19, 1987, the divisor was 0.766. This means that $1.00 of average change in each of the 30 stocks in the DJIA would have caused a change in the DJIA of 39.16 points (30 ÷ 0.766). Therefore, the decline of 508 points in the DJIA indicated that, on the average, each of the 30 stocks experienced a drop of $12.97 ($\frac{508}{39.16} \times \$1.00$). The 508-point decline of the DJIA from 2,246.74 to 1,738.74 represented a one-day drop of 22.6 %.

As stock splits and stock dividends on the 30 stocks in the DJIA are declared in the future, the divisor will continue to decline. As this happens, a larger number of DJIA points will be needed to reflect an average change of one dollar (either upward or downward) in each of the 30 stocks. For example, a divisor of 0.6 would create a movement of 50 points (30 ÷ 0.6) in the DJIA, and a divisor of 0.5 would drive the DJIA 60 points (i.e., 30 ÷ 0.5) up or down. Thus one effect of a declining divisor is to create the illusion of greater volatility.

PRICE-EARNINGS RATIO AND DIVIDEND YIELD OF THE DOW JONES INDUSTRIAL AVERAGE (DJIA)

Just as it is possible to compute the price-earnings (P-E) ratio and dividend yield for a common stock, it is possible to do the same for the DJIA. The adjustments used to calculate the P-E ratio and the dividend yield are similar to the adjustment made in figuring the price level of the DJIA.

Make the supposition that the price level of the Average is $2,500, the sum of the prices per share of the 30 stocks in the Average is $1,750, and the divisor is 0.7 ($1,750 ÷ 0.7 = $2,500). Make the additional supposition that the yearly earnings per share of the 30 stocks in the Dow Jones Industrial Average total $128.

Because the sum ($1,750) of the prices per share of the 30 stocks in the DJIA is divided by 0.7 in order to arrive at the price level of $2,500 for the Average, the sum ($128) of the annual earnings per share of the 30 stocks in the DJIA is also divided by 0.7 to get the earnings level for the Average; in this case, the DJIA earnings become $182.86. The division of the price level of $2,500 by the adjusted earnings of $182.86 produces the price-earnings ratio, or P-E ratio, of 13.7 for the DJIA.

The P-E ratio for the DJIA can also be obtained by dividing the sum of the per-share prices of the 30 stocks by the sum of the yearly earnings per share of the 30 stocks. The computation would be $1,750 ÷ $128 = 13.7.

The procedure for getting the dividend yield for the Dow Jones Industrial Average requires that the yearly dividends per share of the 30 stocks in the Average be totaled. Assume that this amount comes to $57. The dividends are adjusted by dividing the sum of $57 by 0.7, producing the quotient of $81.43. If $81.43 is divided by the assumed DJIA price level of $2,500, the dividend yield for the DJIA is found to be 3.26%.

The dividend yield for the DJIA may also be found by dividing the sum of the annual dividends per share of the 30 stocks in the Average by the sum of the per-share prices of the 30 stocks. When $57 is divided by $1,750, the yield of 3.26% is obtained.

CAN YOU HANDLE STOCK SPLITS
AND STOCK DIVIDENDS?

The declaration by a company of a stock split or a relatively large stock dividend is usually interpreted by investors to mean that the firm is experiencing success in its operations. In the case of stock splits it is not uncommon to find cash dividends being either initiated or increased at the time a split is declared.

The effect of a stock split or a stock dividend is to have a declaring firm issue or make a distribution of additional shares to its stockholders. Some examples examining the number of additional shares required by certain stock splits and stock dividends as well as the cost basis of the shares, will be presented next. Also, Table 1–1 gives the percentage increase in shares for selected stock splits.

Suppose that a company declares a two-for-one split. A stockholder's holdings would increase by 100 %. For each 100 shares owned, the equity holder would be given an additional 100 shares so that total holdings would become 200 shares. If the shareholder's cost basis for 100 shares is $60 per share or $6,000, the cost basis after the split will be $30 per share ($6,000 ÷ 200 shares).

Shareholders who are participants in a three-for-one stock split will see their shares increase by 200 percent. Each 100 shares of stock that each holder owns prior to the split will become 300 shares after the split. If the 100 shares of pre-split stock cost $120 per share, the cost basis of the stock after the split will be $40 per share (i.e. , $12,000 ÷ 300 shares).

A firm may declare a stock split that is less than 100%. A three-for-two split increases a stockholder's holdings 50%. For each share owned, the person receives an additional one-half share. For instance, a holding of 22 shares before the split will become 33 shares after the split. A four-for-three split increases share holdings by $33\frac{1}{3}\%$. The ownership of 90 shares before the split will grow to 120 shares after the split.

Table 1–1. Percentage Increase in Shares from Stock Splits.

Stock Split	Percentage Increase
4 for 1	300 Percent
3 for 1	200 Percent
2 for 1	100 Percent
3 for 2	50 Percent
4 for 3	33.3 Percent

If a shareholder held a stock over an extended period of time and participated in a three-for-one split, a two-for-one split, and then a three-for-two split, the stockholder would own nine shares for each share originally purchased. One share would become three shares after the first split. After the second split, the three shares would have become six shares. The third split would add another three shares, thereby raising the total number of shares to nine. An original purchase of 120 shares, for instance, would become 1,080 shares (120 shares × 9). If the original 120 shares cost $2,160 ($18 per share), the cost per share after the three stock distributions would be $2 ($2,160 ÷ 1,080 shares).

Suppose that an equity owner receives a stock dividend of 5% on 80 shares of common stock that were purchased for a total of $3,120, or $39 per share. The new cost basis of the 80 original shares plus the 4 shares obtained from the stock dividend will be $37.14 per share ($3,120 ÷ 84 shares).

An investor owns 170 common shares of a company. The shares cost $8,712.50, which is $51.25 per share. The firm has declared a stock dividend of 10%; the cost basis of the new total holding of 187 shares of stock is $46.59 per share ($8,712.50 ÷ 187 shares).

REVERSE STOCK SPLIT

When a firm is experiencing severe financial difficulties, the price of its common stock may drop to a very low level. In such an event the company may declare a reverse stock split in order to raise the price of the stock.

Assume a situation where a stock has declined to $2 per share. If a five-for-one reverse split were declared, a shareholder would own only one share after the split for every five shares held prior to the split. In this case a holding of 60 shares would be reduced to 12 shares, and the ownership of 100 pre-split shares would become 20 shares post-split. The expectation would be for the stock to trade around $10 per share (5 × $2) after the split became effective.

YIELD ON COMMON STOCKS BASED ON DIVIDENDS

The return that a common stock provides to its holder may be in the form of dividend income, appreciation in share value, or a combination of income and capital appreciation.

Suppose that a company pays a quarterly dividend of 45 cents per share and that the price per share is $52. What annual rate of return does the dividend provide?

The annual dividend would be $1.80 (i.e., 4 times the quarterly rate of $0.45). The annual yield on the stock based on the dividend of $1.80 would be 3.46%($1.80 ÷ $52).

Instead of paying a dividend each quarter, it may be that a firm sends dividends to its shareholders only twice a year. For a semiannual dividend of 60 cents per share and a per-share price of $21, the annual dividend yield would be 5.71%($1.20 ÷ $21).

PRICE-EARNINGS RATIOS AND YIELD ON COMMON STOCKS BASED ON EARNINGS

The yield on a common stock may be computed on the basis of earnings just as it can be calculated on the basis of dividends. Because earnings are usually the source of dividends, the earnings yield may be viewed as the source of the dividend yield.

It is common to see a portion of a firm's earnings being paid out in the form of dividends. However, it is rare to see a situation where the dividend yield is consistently equal to the earnings yield because that would imply, of course, that the total amount of earnings was being paid out as dividends.

On occasion, a company's dividend yield may exceed its earnings yield. In this case the supposition can be made that the firm either is anticipating a reversal of its earnings picture or has expectations of reducing or eliminating the dividend at some future point.

The retention by a company of part or all of its earnings tends over time to increase the firm's book value. This enhancement of book value can be transformed into capital appreciation for stockholders if, for instance, the concern is sold on the basis of book value.

An increase in book value could also translate into higher market prices for a company's shares. An equity owner could then realize capital appreciation through a liquidation of the stock position.

Assume that a firm has annual earnings of $6 per common share. If the market value of the stock is $66 per share, what is the earnings yield?

$$\text{E-P Ratio} = \frac{\text{Earnings Per Share}}{\text{Price Per Share}}$$

$$= \frac{\$6}{\$66}$$
$$= 0.09$$

The earnings-price ratio (E-P ratio) would be 0.09 and the yield of the stock based on earnings would be 9%(0.09 × 100).

The price-earnings ratio (P-E ratio) on the same $66-per-share stock would be 11.

$$\text{P-E Ratio} = \frac{\text{Price Per Share}}{\text{Earnings Per Share}}$$
$$= \frac{\$66}{\$6}$$
$$= 11$$

The P-E ratio is equal to $\frac{1}{\text{E-P ratio}}$; in this case, $\frac{1}{0.09} = 11$. Obviously, the E-P ratio is also equal to $\frac{1}{\text{P-E ratio}}$; here, $\frac{1}{11} = 0.09$. In other words, the E-P ratio is the reciprocal of the P-E ratio.

2 UNDERSTANDING HOW THE DISCOUNT FEATURE AFFECTS YOUR INTEREST YIELD ON TREASURY BILLS AND OTHER SHORT TERM INVESTMENTS

Interest is the shadow of debt. Where there is debt, there is interest—billions of dollars' worth of it being paid every year around the world in many different currencies.

The interest that arises from the creation of debt or the rental of money may take the form of an actual payment or actual receipt of funds, or it may appear as accounting accrual entries. The money that a borrower owes to a lender for the use of the lender's funds is considered to be interest expense. The money that a lender generates by loaning funds to a borrower is viewed as being interest income.

A given debt appearing on the liability side of a borrower's balance sheet can be found on the asset side of a lender's balance sheet. Thus an interest payment (or expense accrual) and an interest receipt (or income accrual) may be looked upon as being opposite sides of the same transaction.

GENERAL INTEREST EQUATION

In dealing with simple interest, there is a relationship between amount of interest, principal, rate of interest, and period of interest accumulation.

This equation can be used to facilitate the determination of one factor if the other three factors are known. The general interest equation is

$$I = PRT$$

where the symbols are

- I amount of interest
- P principal amount
- R annual rate of interest, expressed as a decimal
- T time over which interest accrues or accumulates, expressed as a fraction of a year

Some applications of this equation are given below.

Example—Obtaining the Interest Expense on a Bank Loan

A borrower makes a $3,500 bank loan for 120 days. The loan is made at an annual rate of 13%. What will be the amount of the interest expense?
  The amount of interest would be

$$I = PRT$$
$$= (\$3,500)(0.13)(120/360)$$
$$= \$151.67$$

or

$$I = PRT$$
$$= (\$3,500)(0.13)(120/365)$$
$$= \$149.59$$

or

$$I = PRT$$
$$= (\$3,500)(0.13)(120/366)$$
$$= \$149.18$$

  Three different sums are provided as answers in the above example. Which sum is correct? Any one of the sums could be correct. The acceptable answer would depend upon how many days the borrower and the lender agree to use to represent the total number of days in a year. A choice is normally made between using 360 days or 365 days in the denominator of the time fraction.

No year actually has just 360 days; the use of a 360-day year provides a measure of convenience. For example, the use of a monthly interest period of 30 days would represent $^{30}/_{360}$, or $^{1}/_{12}$, of a year. A quarterly period of 90 days would be $^{90}/_{360}$, or $^{1}/_{4}$, of a year, and a semiannual interest period of 180 days would encompass $^{180}/_{360}$, or $^{1}/_{2}$ year.

An agreement might be made between the borrower and the lender to use a time denominator of 366 days during a leap year, when February contains 29 days instead of 28 so that the actual number of days in the year increases from 365 to 366.

In the case of the $3,500 loan, the differences in the yearly bases of 360 days, 365 days, and 366 days produce only small differences in the amounts of interest. This can be seen when comparing the interest amounts of $151.67, $149.59, and $149.18, respectively.

However, where large sums of money are involved, the selection of a time base can produce meaningful differences in the amounts of interest. Consider a situation where a business borrows $50 million from a bank for 180 days at an interest rate of 12% per year. The amounts of interest using time bases of 360 days, 365 days, and 366 days would be

$$
\begin{aligned}
I &= PRT \\
&= (\$50,000,000)(0.12)(180/360) \\
&= \$3,000,000
\end{aligned}
$$

and

$$
\begin{aligned}
I &= PRT \\
&= (\$50,000,000)(0.12)(180/365) \\
&= \$2,958,904
\end{aligned}
$$

and

$$
\begin{aligned}
I &= PRT \\
&= (\$50,000,000)(0.12)(180/366) \\
&= \$2,950,820
\end{aligned}
$$

The major differences in amounts of interest occur when comparing yearly bases of 360 days against 365 days (a difference of \$41,096), and 360 days against 366 days (a difference of \$49,180).

A lengthening of the 180-day maturity period would serve to increase the differences between the interest amounts, as would an increase in the interest rate or an increase in the amount of principal.

Calculations made to investigate the effect of changes in each of these factors separately on computed amounts of interest will be left to the reader. Here, a comparison of the difference in amounts of interest using time bases of 360 days and 365 days will be looked at as the loan amount, the interest rate, and the maturity of the borrowing are all increased at the same time.

$$I = PRT$$
$$= (\$60,000,000)(0.13)(270/360)$$
$$= \$5,850,000$$

and

$$I = PRT$$
$$= (\$60,000,000)(0.13)(270/365)$$
$$= \$5,769,863$$

The variance of \$80,137 (\$5,850,000 − \$5,769,863) in interest may be contrasted with the differential of \$41,096 obtained when the loan amount was \$50,000,000, the interest rate was 12%, and the loan maturity was 180 days.

Since the amount of interest expense decreases as the time denominator, or time base, increases, it is advantageous for a borrower to negotiate for as many days in the time denominator as possible. On the other hand, it is to the lender's advantage when a smaller time base is used because this reduced number produces a larger amount of interest income.

The foregoing discussion has centered around the use of different time bases when computing interest for fractional parts of a year. When the interest computation is for an entire year, the time numerator might be 360 days, 365 days, or 366 days. For a numerator containing the exact or actual number of days in one year, the time fraction could be $365/360$, $365/365$, $366/360$, $366/365$, or $366/366$. For a time numerator based on a one-year interest period containing 360 days, the possible time fraction combinations would include $360/360$, $360/365$, and $360/366$.

Because time numerators and denominators influence calculated amounts of interest, it is important that the borrower and the lender reach an understanding at the outset of the transaction regarding how the interest will be computed.

Example—Determining the Interest Earned on a Bank Savings Deposit

Suppose that a depositor puts $2,000 in a bank savings account for 60 days. The rate of interest is 7.75% per annum (i.e., per year). What sum of interest will the deposit earn if a time base of 360 days is used?

$$I = PRT$$
$$= (\$2,000)(0.0775)(60/360)$$
$$= \$25.83$$

The deposit will earn interest of $25.83.

Example—Seeking the Early Withdrawal Penalty on a Certificate of Deposit

Make the assumption that an individual purchases a $10,000 12-month certificate of deposit from a savings institution. The interest rate is 8.5% per annum, and the time base is 360 days.

Assume further that the certificate purchaser withdraws the money after holding the certificate for five months. If the penalty for early withdrawal is the forfeiture of interest for 90 days, what will be the amount of the penalty?

$$I = PRT$$
$$= (\$10,000)(0.085)(90/360)$$
$$= \$212.50$$

The buyer of the certificate will forfeit earned interest of $212.50. Assuming 153 days in the five-month period, the purchaser would earn total interest of $148.75 ($361.25 − $212.50).

ACCRUED INTEREST ON BONDS

Simple interest is used when determining amounts of accrued interest on bonds purchased between interest payment dates. Two popular types of bonds are U.S. government bonds and corporate bonds. Two differences are observed when calculating accrued interest on these two types of securities.

First, in the case of U.S. government bonds the denominator of the time fraction is twice the number of days in the coupon period, while 360 days is utilized for corporate bond calculations.

Second, in U.S. government bond computations, the exact number of elapsed days in the interest period is placed in the numerator of the time fraction. However, corporate bond calculations make the supposition that all months falling within the interest period contain 30 days.

The interest period for both types of securities is assumed to begin on the last interest payment date and is presumed to end on the day preceding settlement and delivery.

The above points may be illustrated with examples. Consider bonds having a par value (face amount) of $50,000 that pay interest of 10% (coupon rate). The securities are to be delivered for settlement on September 9. The last interest payment date is June 15. What amount of accrued (accumulated) interest is due on the bonds?

Example — Finding Accrued Interest on U.S. Government Bonds

The number of days the bonds are held by the seller since the last interest payment day is 86 days. Assume a coupon period of 182 days.

June 15 through June 30	16 days
Month of July	31 days
Month of August	31 days
September 1 through September 8	8 days
Total	86 days

$$I = PRT$$
$$= (\$50,000)(0.10)\left(\frac{86}{(2)(182)}\right)$$
$$= \$1,181.32$$

The buyer will pay accrued interest of $1,181.32 to the seller of the U.S. government bonds.

Example—Figuring Accrued Interest on Corporate Bonds

The number of days the bonds are held by the seller since the last payment date is 84 days.

June 15 through June 30	16 days
Month of July	30 days
Month of August	30 days
September 1 through September 8	8 days
Total	84 days

$$I = \frac{PR}{2}$$

$$= (\$50,000)\left(\frac{0.07}{2}\right)$$

$$= \$1,166.67$$

The seller will be due accrued interest of $1,166.67 on the corporate bonds.

Example—Computing the Semiannual Interest Payment on a Bond

A $1,000 bond with a 7% coupon rate provides its holder with semiannual interest payments. How much interest is the bondholder paid each half year?

$$I = \frac{PR}{2}$$

$$= (\$1,000)\left(\frac{0.007}{2}\right)$$

$$= \$35.00$$

For each bond owned, the investor receives semiannual income of $35.00.

EXPLAINING DISCOUNT

There is no difference in the way that a nominal annual rate of interest is applied to an amount of principal and the manner in which an annual discount rate is applied to a sum of principal. However, what is done with the amount of interest after it is calculated can present a situation that warrants the use of the term *discount*. Consider the following examples.

Case I

If a nominal annual rate of 6 percent is applied to a principal of $100 for one year, the amount of interest will be $6.00.

$$\begin{aligned} I &= PRT \\ &= (\$100)(.06)\left(\frac{360}{360}\right) \\ &= \$6.00 \end{aligned}$$

Case II

If an annual discount rate of 6 percent is applied to a principal of $100 for one year, the amount of interest will still be $6.00 because the calculation is done exactly as the computation in Case I. In Case I a borrower receives $100 from a lender and pays the lender $6.00 interest one year later. The borrower has the full use of $100 for one year. The borrower incurs a borrowing cost of 6 percent, and the lender has an earning rate of 6 percent, calculated by rearranging the general interest equation.

$$\begin{aligned} R &= \frac{I}{PT} \\ &= \frac{\$6.00}{(\$100)\left(\frac{360}{360}\right)} \\ &= .06, \text{ or 6 percent} \end{aligned}$$

The supposition will be made in Case II that a borrower pays a lender interest of $6 at the beginning of the year, or at the time that the borrower receives $100 of principal from the lender. Because the lender receives $6 from the borrower at the same time the lender gives $100 to the borrower, the lender in effect gives the borrower only $94. (The same would be true if the borrower gave nothing to the lender and the lender just withheld $6 out of the $100.) The practice of deducting interest (the discount) from the par, face value, or full amount of a borrowing at the time the borrowing occurs (in advance) gives rise to expressions such as discount investment, discount loan, discount borrowing, and discount lending.

Under this Case II scenario the borrower's borrowing rate and the lender's earning rate would both be 6.38 percent.

$$R = \frac{I}{PT}$$
$$= \frac{\$6.00}{(\$94)\left(\frac{360}{360}\right)}$$
$$= .0638, \text{ or } 6.38 \text{ percent}$$

Case III

When a nominal annual rate of 6 percent is applied to a principal of $100 for one semiannual period, the amount of interest is $3.00.

$$I = PRT$$
$$= (\$100)(.06)\left(\frac{180}{360}\right)$$
$$= \$3.00$$

Case IV

By applying an annual discount rate of 6 percent to a $100 principal for one semiannual period, an interest amount of $3.00 also emerges since the interest in this case is figured just as in Case III. Case III assumes that a borrower pays a lender $3.00 in interest one semiannual period after the borrower receives $100 from the lender. On a yearly basis of 360 days, the borrower has a borrowing cost of 6 percent and the lender has a lending rate of 6 percent.

$$R = \frac{I}{PT}$$

$$= \frac{\$3.00}{(\$100)\left(\frac{180}{360}\right)}$$

$$= .06, \text{ or } 6 \text{ percent}$$

For Case IV, assume that a borrower receives $100 from a lender and at the same time pays the lender $3.00 for interest expense for one semiannual period. The borrower's net proceeds thus become $97. The (360-day) annual borrowing and lending rates are

$$R = \frac{I}{PT}$$

$$= \frac{\$3.00}{(\$97)\left(\frac{180}{360}\right)}$$

$$= .0619, \text{ or } 6.19 \text{ percent}$$

As far as a 360-day year is concerned, the rate of 6.19% in the Case IV example is a more true rate than 6 percent. The 6.19 percent rate reflects a recognition of the discounted principal amount, whereas the 6 percent rate does not give consideration to a reduced amount of principal. Rate adjustments to reflect a 365-day year are discussed in the Treasury bill example in this chapter.

Calculations similar to those done for the semiannual borrowing term may also be done for other borrowing periods of less than a year.

Example—Ascertaining the Interest Rate on a Discount Loan

Assume that a lender loans $15,000 to a borrower for 90 days at a rate of 10% per year. The time base is 360 days. The amount of interest is determined to be $375.

$$I = PRT$$
$$= (\$15,000)(0.10)(90/360)$$
$$= \$375.00$$

If the above loan is a discount loan, the lender will deduct $375 from the loan proceeds at the time the loan is made. The rate of interest based on a 360-day year will be more than 10% per year because the borrower will receive only $14,625 of principal instead of $15,000.

The interest rate can be found by solving the general interest equation for R, putting in for P the actual principal available to the borrower.

$$I = PRT$$

$$R = \frac{I}{PT}$$

$$= \frac{\$375}{(\$14,625)(90/360)}$$

$$= \frac{\$375}{\$3,656.25}$$

$$= 0.1026, \text{ or } 10.26\%$$

The equation shows that it costs $375 to borrow $14,625 for 90 days. The interest rate for 90 days is 0.02564 (i.e., $375 ÷ $14,625), or 2.564%. In order to express the interest rate on an annual basis, it is necessary to multiply the 90-day rate by 4 since there are four 90-day periods in a 360-day year. The multiplication of 2.564% by 4 gives an annual interest rate of 10.26%.

The interest rate of 10.26% can be approximated by treating the discount loan as a type of debt that offers the lender a chance for interest to be earned on interest (compound interest).

Assume that the interest amount of $375 in the example above earns interest itself for 90 days at an annual rate of 10%. The amount of interest is $9.38 as shown below.

$$I = PRT$$

$$= (\$375)(0.10)(90/360)$$

$$= \$9.38$$

When the 90-day interest on principal of $375 is added to the 90-day interest on interest of $9.38, the total becomes $384.38. The multiplication of $384.38 by 4 (four 90-day periods in a 360-day year) renders a product of $1,537.52. If $1,537.52 is divided by the principal amount of the loan ($15,000), an interest rate of 10.25% is obtained.

Example—Calculating the Yield and Discount Rate on Treasury Bills

The discount concept is also used when dealing with some types of short term financial instruments, such as U.S. treasury bills. Suppose that treasury bills with a face value of $40,000 and a maturity of 136 days are bought by an investor at 95.814% of par value. What are the yield and discount rate on the bills?

$$I = PRT$$

$$R = \frac{I}{PT}$$

$$= \frac{\$1,674.40}{(\$38,325.60)(136/360)}$$

$$= 0.1156, \text{ or } 11.56\%$$

The investor will receive $40,000 for the treasury bills if they are held to maturity. Since $38,325.60 (95.814% × $40,000) is paid for the bills, the investor will earn $1,674.40 in interest over a period of 136 days. On the basis of a 360-day year, the yield is 11.56%.

The discount rate on the 136-day treasury bills purchased at a price of 95.814% of par would be 11.08% per year. Since the discount is $4.186 for each $100 of face value, the discount would be 4.186% for a period of 136 days. To express the discount rate on the basis of a 360-day year, it is necessary to multiply 4.186% by $^{360}/_{136}$, which gives the figure of 11.08%.

A quick approach to getting the yield on the treasury bills would be to use the computation below.

$$\left(\frac{4.186}{95.814}\right) \times \left(\frac{360}{136}\right) = 0.1156, \text{ or } 11.56\%$$

For the discount rate the following calculation would be used.

$$\left(\frac{4.186}{100}\right) \times \left(\frac{360}{136}\right) = 0.1108, \text{ or } 11.08\%$$

The treasury bill yield is based on purchase price, while the treasury bill discount rate is based on par value.

Calculations involving longer term securities such as treasury bonds are based on a 365-day year instead of a 360-day year. To approximate the so-called coupon equivalent yield, or bond equivalent yield, the treasury bill yield of 11.56% would be multiplied by $365/360$. The result would be a rate of 11.72%.

The calculation for the coupon equivalent yield would be

$$R = \frac{I}{PT}$$

$$= \frac{\$1,674.40}{(\$38,325.60)\left(\frac{136}{365}\right)}$$

$$= .1173, \text{ or } 11.73\% \text{ (rounding difference of } 0.01\%)$$

or

$$\frac{(4.186)}{(95.814)} \times \frac{(365)}{(136)} = .1173, \text{ or } 11.73\%$$

Suppose that in this example the purchase price of 95.814% of par is unknown, but the annual discount rate of 11.08% is known. The purchase price as a percentage of par may be found as follows.

$$I = PRT$$

$$= (100)(.1108)\left(\frac{136}{360}\right)$$

$$= 4.186$$

$$\frac{\text{Discount}}{\text{Par}} = \frac{4.186}{100} = 0.04186, \text{ or } 4.186 \text{ percent}$$

$$\text{Purchase Price} = \text{Par} - \text{Discount}$$

$$= 100 \text{ percent} - 4.186 \text{ percent}$$

$$= 95.814 \text{ percent (of par)}$$

Example—Determining the Interest Rate on Commercial Paper

Another example utilizing the discount concept may be examined. Assume that a company sells $1 million of 30-day commercial paper (that is, promissory notes) at a rate of 12% per annum. What is the firm's interest-rate cost based on its proceeds?

$$I = PRT$$
$$= (\$1,000,000)(0.12)(30/360)$$
$$= \$10,000$$

At the time of sale of the paper, the net proceeds to the company would be $1,000,000 minus the interest cost of $10,000, or a total of $990,000.

The company's interest cost based on its proceeds and a 360-day year would be 12.12% as indicated below.

$$I = PRT$$
$$R = \frac{I}{PT}$$
$$= \frac{\$10,000}{(\$990,000)(30/360)}$$
$$= 0.1212, \text{ or } 12.12\%$$

(This discussion does not consider the cost of any bank credit lines that might be required to back the commercial paper.)

Example—Evaluating the Cost of, and Yield on, Bankers' Acceptances

Another short term financial instrument that is handled on a discount basis is the bankers' acceptance. Take the example that an investor buys 150-day bankers' acceptances having a face value of $100,000. The acceptances are quoted to yield $7\frac{1}{2}\%$ on a discount basis. How much will the purchase cost the investor, and what will be the yield based on the purchase price?

The general interest equation will provide an answer regarding the amount of the discount (interest).

$$I = PRT$$
$$= (\$100,000)(0.075)(150/360)$$
$$= \$3,125.00$$

The purchase price of the acceptances is $96,875 ($100,000 − $3,125), which is 96.875% of par. The yield based on the purchase price is found to be 7.74%.

$$I = PRT$$

$$R = \frac{I}{PT}$$

$$= \frac{\$3,125}{(\$96,875)(150/360)}$$

$$= 0.0774, \text{ or } 7.74\%$$

The bond equivalent yield may be approximated as indicated.

$$(7.74\%)\left(\frac{365}{360}\right) = 7.85\%$$

3 A WALK INTO THE EXCITING WORLD OF COMPOUND INTEREST

Example—Showing the Difference Between Simple Interest and Compound Interest

If $1,000 were placed in a savings account and allowed to earn simple interest at the annual rate of 6%, compounded annually, the total interest earned on the $1,000 deposit at the end of the 100 years would be $6,000.

If, however, the $1,000 were put into a savings arrangement so that the funds earned interest at the yearly rate of 6%, compounded annually, the total interest earnings would amount to $338,302 at the end of 100 years. Why is there a difference in the two amounts of earned interest?

While simple interest involves the calculation of interest on principal, compound interest encompasses the computation of interest on principal plus interest on interest.

Another example can be used to illustrate this point. It may be remembered in discussing this example that a person who is obtaining a loan from a financial institution is a borrower. The financial institution is the lender in this case.

On the other hand, a person who deposits money in a money market account or savings account or who buys certificates of deposit is in the position of a lender. This person is loaning funds to the recipient, whether it be a bank, savings and loan, or other type of financial institution. In this instance the financial institution is the borrower or the other side of the transaction.

Example — Explaining Simple and Compound Interest Dissimilarities

Assume that on its savings accounts Bank One pays an annual rate of 6%simple interest, while Bank Two pays a stated or nominal annual interest rate of 6% compounded annually. If $3,000 is deposited by a customer in each bank for two years, how much interest will each deposit have earned by the end of two years?

At Bank One $3,000 is deposited at the beginning of year one. The amount of interest that the deposit earns at the end of the first year is $180.00.

$$I = PRT$$
$$= (\$3,000)(0.06)\left(\frac{365}{365}\right)$$
$$= \$180$$

At the end of the second year, the $3,000 deposit at Bank One again earns $180 for the depositor (lender).

A sum of $3,000 is also deposited in a savings account at Bank Two at the start of year one. The earned interest at the end of the first year is $180. Since Bank Two pays annually compounded interest, the $180 of earned interest is added to the depositor's initial deposit of $3,000 so as to produce a new principal balance of $3,180 as the second year commences. At the end of the second year at Bank Two, the depositor earns interest of $190.80.

$$I = PRT$$
$$= (\$3,180)(0.06)\left(\frac{365}{365}\right)$$
$$= \$190.80$$

At Bank One where simple interest is paid, a $3,000 deposit grows to $3,360 at the end of two years. The assumption may be made that the $180 of interest which is earned during the first year is paid out by the bank (borrower) at the end of the first year.

The $3,000 original deposit at Bank Two grows to $3,370.80 at the end of two years. In this case the supposition is made that the $180 of earned interest during the first year is not paid out at the end of the first year. Instead, the earned interest remains in the account and is converted or folded into principal. The Bank Two deposit demonstrates one way in which interest on interest can be earned. The compounding occurs internally, or within the original investment.

A lender who loans a sum of money to a borrower over a particular time frame expects to recover the principal amount of the loan plus some interest income for the rental of the funds. The lender looks for a return of the investment as well as a return on the investment.

In the general interest equation $I = PRT$, the focus is on the calculation of interest on principal, which is the return on investment. No provision is made to show a return of investment. Because of the way in which simple interest is defined, the equation also does not have to contain a provision for the computation of interest on interest.

The basic expression used in compound interest calculations provides for the return of investment and the return on investment (which includes interest on principal as well as interest on interest).

Consider the total amount of money returned to the lender after the deposit earns simple interest at a rate R for a time T on a principal P.

$$P + PRT$$

The initial P above represents the return of investment. The PRT term is taken from the general interest equation ($I = PRT$) and stands for the return on investment (interest on principal only).

The expression $P + PRT$ may be rewritten as $P(1 + RT)$. For compound interest, the interest rate (R) is adjusted for the number of compounding periods in a year (m), and recognition is given to the duration of the compounding or the total number of compounding periods (n). The expression becomes $P(1 + R/m)^n$.

COMPOUND INTEREST EQUATION

The formula $S = P(1 + i)^n$ is the basic equation for calculating compound interest. The equation may also be written as $S = P(1 + R/m)^n$, indicating that $i = R/m$. If P is given the value of 1 (e.g., $1.00), the equation $S = P(1 + i)^n$ can be shortened to $S = (1 + i)^n$, or $S = (1 + R/m)^n$. In any of these forms the compound interest equation permits finding the amount to which an initial sum will grow at compound interest over a given number of periods. The quantity S comprises the elements of principal, interest on principal, and interest on interest.

The symbols for the compound interest equation are defined below.

S the amount to which an initial sum will grow at compound interest
P the initial amount of principal
i the periodic rate of interest
R the nominal annual rate of interest
m the number of compounding periods per year
n the total number of compounding periods

The growth symbol S takes on whatever units P has. Unless stated otherwise, the principal amount P is assumed to be in dollars. However, it is also possible for P to be in some other monetary unit such as French francs, West German marks, British pounds, or Japanese yen, or even something that is nonmonetary in nature such as population, bushels of wheat, tons of steel, or automobiles.

The exponent (n) of the base $(1 + i)$ in the compound interest equation represents the total number of compounding periods. Where compounding exceeds a year, the value for n is obtained by multiplying the number of compounding periods per year m by the total number of years over which the compounding is to occur.

COMPOUNDING PERIODS

Usually compounding periods are daily, monthly, quarterly, semiannual, or annual. Table 3–1 shows the total number of compounding periods for these compounding frequencies for one year, three years, and five years.

Table 3–1. Total Compounding Periods for Selected Compounding Frequencies.

Compounding Frequency	Total No. of Compounding Periods (1 year)	Total No. of Compounding Periods (3 years)	Total No. of Compounding Periods (5 years)
Daily	360	1,080	1,800
Daily	365	1,095	1,825
Monthly	12	36	60
Quarterly	4	12	20
Semiannual	2	6	10
Annual	1	3	5

PERIODIC INTEREST RATES

The symbol i in the equation $S = (1 + i)^n$ is the interest rate per compounding period. The periodic rate is obtained by dividing the nominal annual interest rate (R) by the number of compounding periods per year (m). The equation is $i = R/m$.

Suppose that a nominal annual interest rate (R) of 12% is to be adjusted or prepared for quarterly compounding. The equation $i = R/m$ is used to find the quarterly rate. Since there are four quarterly compounding periods per year, the substitution becomes

$$i = R/m$$
$$= 0.12/4$$
$$= 0.03, \text{ or } 3\%$$

The periodic interest rate is 3% per compounding period or per quarterly period.

The periodic rates of interest (i) for the more commonly used compounding frequencies are shown in Table 3–2. The nominal annual interest rate is taken as 8%.

Different combinations of the fraction R/m can be used to give the same i value. As an illustration, in the first line in Table 3–3, the value of i is 0.01 where the nominal annual interest rate is 12% and the compounding

Table 3–2.   Periodic Interest Rates for a Nominal Annual Rate of 8%.

Compounding Frequency	Periodic Rate of Interest ($R/m = i$)		
Daily	$\frac{0.08}{360}$	$=$	0.0002222, or 0.02222%
	or		
	$\frac{0.08}{365}$	$=$	0.0002192, or 0.02192%
	or		
	$\frac{0.08}{366}$	$=$	0.0002186, or 0.02186%
Monthly	$\frac{0.08}{12}$	$=$	0.00667, or 0.667%
Quarterly	$\frac{0.08}{4}$	$=$	0.02, or 2%
Semiannual	$\frac{0.08}{2}$	$=$	0.04, or 4%
Annual	$\frac{0.08}{1}$	$=$	0.08, or 8%

Table 3–3.   Similar Periodic Interest Rates.

Compounding Frequency	R Nominal Annual Interest Rate, as a Decimal	m Compounding Periods Per Year	R/m	i Periodic Interest Rate, as a Decimal
Monthly	0.12	12	$\frac{0.12}{12}$	0.01
Quarterly	0.04	4	$\frac{0.04}{4}$	0.01
Semiannual	0.02	2	$\frac{0.02}{2}$	0.01
Annual	0.01	1	$\frac{0.01}{1}$	0.01
Monthly	0.18	12	$\frac{0.18}{12}$	0.015
Quarterly	0.06	4	$\frac{0.06}{4}$	0.015
Semiannual	0.03	2	$\frac{0.03}{2}$	0.015
Annual	0.015	1	$\frac{0.015}{1}$	0.015

frequency is monthly. The same i value of 0.01 is produced in the second line by using a nominal annual interest rate of 4% and a quarterly compounding frequency. Two additional R/m combinations are used in lines three and four to give an i value equal to 0.01.

EFFECTIVE INTEREST RATES

An effective annual rate of interest is produced when a periodic interest rate is compounded for one year. Effective interest rates also may be determined for periods exceeding a year. Effective annual rates will be considered first, and effective rates for time horizons greater than a year will be treated subsequently.

In order to find the effective annual interest rate, it is necessary to resort to the equation $S = (1 + R/m)^n$. For quarterly compounding for one year and a nominal annual interest rate of 12%, the equation becomes

$$S = (1 + 0.12/4)^4$$
$$= (1 + 0.03)^4$$
$$= 1.1255$$

A principal amount of $1.00 will grow to $1.1255 when it is compounded on a quarterly basis for one year at a nominal annual interest rate of 12%. One dollar of the $1.1255 is a return of the beginning principal. The remaining $0.1255 represents the interest on principal plus the interest on interest. The interest on principal is $0.12, and the interest on interest is $0.0055.

A return of $0.1255 on $1.00 for one year is equivalent to an interest rate of 12.55%. Therefore, the effective annual rate of interest of a nominal annual interest rate of 12% compounded quarterly is 12.55%.

The compounding process involved in the quarterly compounding of the 12% rate may be examined step by step by considering the four quarterly periods (Q1 through Q4). The beginning of Q1 is the starting point or the point at which the compounding of $1.00 commences. The end of the fourth period (Q4) is the point at which the compounding ceases.

When the quarterly interest rate of 3% is applied to a principal of $1.00 at the end of compounding period one (Q1), an interest amount of $0.03 is obtained. This interest on principal earns interest itself (interest on interest) for three quarterly periods (Q2, Q3, and Q4). Interest on interest is computed at the end of each of these three quarterly periods. While the first amount of interest on principal is earned at the end of Q1, it is not until the end of Q2 that the first sum of interest on interest is earned.

The next computation of interest on principal is made at the end of quarterly period two (Q2). This three-cent interest amount earns interest itself (interest on interest) over two periods (Q3 and Q4). The calculations of interest on interest over these two periods are assumed to occur at the end of Q3 and at the end of Q4.

Figure 3–1. Time Line.

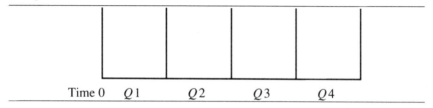

Time 0   Q1   Q2   Q3   Q4

The third calculation of interest on principal ($1.00 times 3% or 0.03) takes place at the end of Q3. This interest amount of three cents earns interest (interest on interest) over quarterly period four (Q4). The interest on interest is figured at the end of Q4.

The last computation of interest on principal happens at the end of the final quarterly period (Q4). Because the compounding in this case stops at the end of Q4, there is no opportunity for this sum of interest on principal to earn interest itself.

The combined amount of interest on principal and interest on interest may be found as shown in this quarterly interest schedule.

Quarter 1	($0.03) $\times$ $(1+0.03)^3$	=	$0.0328
Quarter 2	($0.03) $\times$ $(1+0.03)^2$	=	0.0318
Quarter 3	($0.03) $\times$ $(1+0.03)$	=	0.0309
Quarter 4	($0.03)	=	0.0300
Totals	$0.12		$0.1255

The total amount of interest on principal plus interest on interest is $0.1255. The interest on principal of $0.03 at the end of each of the quarterly periods Q1, Q2, Q3, and Q4 amounts to $0.12. Therefore, the interest on interest totals $0.0055. It is the interest on interest of 0.55% that is responsible for the variation between the nominal annual rate of interest (12.00%) and the effective annual rate of interest (12.55%).

The more frequent the compounding, the greater the effective annual interest rate becomes for a given nominal annual interest rate. This can be seen in the examples that follow, where effective annual rates of interest are calculated for different compounding frequencies. The nominal annual rate of interest is taken as 8%.

Annual Compounding.

$$S = (1 + R/m)^n$$
$$= (1 + 0.08/1)$$
$$= 1.08$$

effective annual rate $= 1.08 - 1 = 0.08$, or 8.00%

Semiannual Compounding.

$$S = (1 + R/m)^n$$
$$= (1 + 0.08/2)^2$$
$$= 1.0816$$

effective annual rate $= 1.0816 - 1 = 0.0816$, or 8.16%

Quarterly Compounding.

$$S = (1 + R/m)^n$$
$$= (1 + 0.08/4)^4$$
$$= 1.0824$$

effective annual rate $= 1.0824 - 1 = 0.0824$, or 8.24%

Monthly Compounding.

$$S = (1 + R/m)^n$$
$$= (1 + 0.08/12)^{12}$$
$$= 1.0830$$

effective annual rate $= 1.0830 - 1 = 0.0830$, or 8.30%

Daily Compounding (365 days)

$$S = (1 + R/m)^n$$
$$= (1 + 0.08/365)^{365}$$
$$= 1.083278$$

effective annual rate $= 1.083278 - 1 = 0.083278$, or 8.3278%

Continuous Compounding.   The growth of a principal of one unit for one year is

$$S = e^R$$
$$= 1 + R + R^2/2! + R^3/3! + R^4/4! + \cdots + R^N/N!$$

where

e $=$ the constant 2.71828
R $=$ the nominal rate of interest, as a decimal
$N!$ $=$ (i.e., N factorial) $= 1 \times 2 \times 3 \times \cdots \times N$

By substituting a nominal annual interest rate of 8%, the equation gives

$$S = e^{(0.08)}$$
$$= 1 + 0.08 + \frac{(0.08)^2}{1 \times 2} + \frac{(0.08)^3}{1 \times 2 \times 3} + \frac{(0.08)^4}{1 \times 2 \times 3 \times 4} + \cdots$$
$$= 1 + 0.08 + 0.0032 + 0.0000853 + 0.0000017 + \cdots$$
$$= 1.083287$$

effective annual rate $= 1.083287 - 1 = 0.083287$, or 8.3287%

(The equation may be carried out as many terms as desired.)

The above calculations bear out the statement that the more frequent the compounding, the larger the effective annual interest rate becomes for a given nominal annual rate of interest. Annual compounding has only one compounding period per year, which is the minimum number that a compounding frequency may have for a time frame of one year. So, for a given nominal annual interest rate, annual compounding has an effective annual interest rate lower than that of any other compounding frequency.

When a specific nominal annual interest rate is chosen for compounding, it is, of course, an uncompounded rate at the time that it is selected. The effective annual interest rate for an annual compounding frequency is equal to the nominal annual rate, because annual compounding in effect does not undergo any compounding. Since the only payment of interest during the year is made at the end of the year, there is no opportunity for this amount of interest to be compounded in the given year of payment. However, these statements do not affect the fact that the particular annual interest payment under discussion may be compounded in subsequent yearly interest periods.

Continuous compounding represents the most frequent type of compounding. For a given nominal annual interest rate, continous compounding provides the highest effective annual interest rate. Therefore, for a given nominal annual interest rate, the effective annual rates for all other compounding frequencies lie between the effective annual interest rate for annual compounding (lower limit) and the effective annual interest rate for continuous compounding (upper limit).

The effective annual interest rates have been calculated for various compounding frequencies and for different nominal annual interest rates in Table 3–4. It may be noticed that for a nominal annual rate of 10%, for example, the effective annual interest rate is 10% for annual compounding and 10.5171% for continuous compounding. The effective annual rates for the other compouding frequencies lie between these two rates. As the compounding increases for these other frequencies from semiannual to daily compounding, the effective annual rate of interest also increases.

Table 3–4. Effective Annual Interest Rates (Percents).

Nominal Annual Interest Rate	Compounding					
	Continuous	Daily	Monthly	Quarterly	Semiannual	Annual
1	1.0050	1.0050	1.0046	1.0038	1.0025	1.0000
2	2.0201	2.0201	2.0184	2.0151	2.0100	2.0000
3	3.0455	3.0453	3.0416	3.0339	3.0225	3.0000
4	4.0811	4.0808	4.0742	4.0604	4.0400	4.0000
5	5.1271	5.1267	5.1162	5.0945	5.0625	5.0000
6	6.1837	6.1831	6.1678	6.1364	6.0900	6.0000
7	7.2508	7.2501	7.2290	7.1859	7.1225	7.0000
8	8.3287	8.3278	8.3000	8.2432	8.1600	8.0000
9	9.4174	9.4162	9.3807	9.3083	9.2025	9.0000
10	10.5171	10.5156	10.4713	10.3813	10.2500	10.0000
11	11.6278	11.6260	11.5719	11.4621	11.3025	11.0000
12	12.7497	12.7475	12.6825	12.5509	12.3600	12.0000
13	13.8828	13.8802	13.8032	13.6476	13.4225	13.0000
14	15.0274	15.0243	14.9342	14.7523	14.4900	14.0000
15	16.1834	16.1798	16.0755	15.8650	15.5625	15.0000
16	17.3511	17.3470	17.2271	16.9859	16.6400	16.0000
17	18.5305	18.5258	18.3892	18.1148	17.7225	17.0000
18	19.7217	19.7164	19.5618	19.2519	18.8100	18.0000
19	20.9250	20.9190	20.7451	20.3971	19.9025	19.0000
20	22.1403	22.1336	21.9391	21.5506	21.0000	20.0000
21	23.3678	23.3603	23.1439	22.7124	22.1025	21.0000
22	24.6077	24.5994	24.3597	23.8825	23.2100	22.0000
23	25.8600	25.8509	25.5864	25.0609	24.3225	23.0000
24	27.1249	27.1149	26.8242	26.2477	25.4400	24.0000
25	28.4025	28.3916	28.0732	27.4429	26.5625	25.0000
26	29.6930	29.6810	29.3334	28.6466	27.6900	26.0000
27	30.9964	30.9834	30.6050	29.8588	28.8225	27.0000
28	32.3130	32.2988	31.8881	31.0796	29.9600	28.0000
29	33.6427	33.6274	33.1826	32.3089	31.1025	29.0000
30	34.9859	34.9693	34.4889	33.5469	32.2500	30.0000
31	36.3425	36.3246	35.8069	34.7936	33.4025	31.0000
32	37.7128	37.6935	37.1367	36.0489	34.5600	32.0000
33	39.0968	39.0761	38.4784	37.3130	35.7225	33.0000
34	40.4948	40.4725	39.8321	38.5859	36.8900	34.0000
35	41.9068	41.8830	41.1980	39.8676	38.0625	35.0000
36	43.3329	43.3075	42.5761	41.1582	39.2400	36.0000
37	44.7735	44.7464	43.9665	42.4577	40.4225	37.0000
38	46.2285	46.1996	45.3693	43.7661	41.6100	38.0000
39	47.6981	47.6673	46.7847	45.0835	42.8025	39.0000
40	49.1825	49.1498	48.2126	46.4100	44.0000	40.0000
50	64.8721	64.8157	63.2094	60.1807	56.2500	50.0000
60	82.2119	82.1222	79.5856	74.9006	69.0000	60.0000
70	101.3753	101.2403	97.4557	90.6125	82.2500	70.0000
80	122.5541	122.3594	116.9425	107.3600	96.0000	80.0000
90	145.9603	145.6880	138.1780	125.1873	110.2500	90.0000
100	171.8282	171.4567	161.3035	144.1406	125.0000	100.0000

COMPOUNDING AN EFFECTIVE ANNUAL INTEREST RATE

An effective annual interest rate may be compounded if desired, just as a nominal rate of interest may be subjected to compounding. When, for example, a nominal annual rate of 12% undergoes semiannual compounding for one year, the effective annual rate of interest of 12.36% is obtained.

$$S = (1 + R/m)^n$$
$$= (1 + 0.12/2)^2$$
$$= (1 + 0.06)^2$$
$$= 1.1236$$

effective annual rate $= 1.1236 - 1 = 0.1236$, or 12.36%

If the nominal annual rate of 12% were compounded for, say, four years on a semiannual basis, the figure of 1.5938 (or 1.593848) would emerge as the total amount. After subtracting an assumed beginning principal of 1 (e.g., \$1.00), the difference would be 59.38% of the original principal. The effective rate over the life of the investment is therefore 59.38%.

$$S = (1 + R/m)^n$$
$$= (1 + 0.12/2)^8$$
$$= (1 + 0.06)^8$$
$$= 1.5938$$

effective rate $= 1.5938 - 1 = 0.5938$, or 59.38%

The same figure of 1.5938 also can be gotten by compounding on an annual basis for four years the effective annual interest rate (12.36%) in the form shown.

$$S = (1 + \text{effective annual rate})^n$$
$$= (1.1236)^4$$
$$= 1.5938$$

effective rate $= 1.5938 - 1 = 0.5938$, or 59.38%

The compounding in the first method may be viewed as being

Table 3–5. Effective Interest Rates: (Percents).

Nominal Annual Interest Rate	End of Year 1	End of Year 2	End of Year 3	End of Year 4	End of Year 5
		Monthly Compounding			
2	2.0184	4.0776	6.1784	8.3215	10.5079
4	4.0742	8.3143	12.7272	17.3199	22.0997
6	6.1678	12.7160	19.6681	27.0489	34.8850
8	8.3000	17.2888	27.0237	37.5666	48.9846
10	10.4713	22.0391	34.8182	48.9354	64.5309
12	12.6825	26.9735	43.0769	61.2226	81.6697
14	14.9342	32.0987	51.8266	74.5007	100.5610
16	17.2271	37.4219	61.0957	88.8477	121.3807
18	19.5618	42.9503	70.9140	104.3478	144.3220
20	21.9391	48.6915	81.3130	121.0915	169.5970
		Quarterly Compounding			
2	2.0151	4.0707	6.1678	8.3071	10.4896
4	4.0604	8.2857	12.6825	17.2579	22.0190
6	6.1364	12.6493	19.5618	26.8986	34.6855
8	8.2432	17.1659	26.8242	37.2786	48.5947
10	10.3813	21.8403	34.4889	48.4506	63.8616
12	12.5509	26.6770	42.5761	60.4706	80.6111
14	14.7523	31.6809	51.1069	73.3986	98.9789
16	16.9859	36.8569	60.1032	87.2981	119.1123
18	19.2519	42.2101	69.5881	102.2370	141.1714
20	21.5506	47.7455	79.5856	118.2875	165.3298
		Semiannual Compounding			
2	2.0100	4.0604	6.1520	8.2857	10.4622
4	4.0400	8.2432	12.6162	17.1659	21.8994
6	6.0900	12.5509	19.4052	26.6770	34.3916
8	8.1600	16.9859	26.5319	36.8569	48.0244
10	10.2500	21.5506	34.0096	47.7455	62.8895
12	12.3600	26.2477	41.8519	59.3848	79.0848
14	14.4900	31.0796	50.0730	71.8186	96.7151
16	16.6400	36.0489	58.6874	85.0930	115.8925
18	18.8100	41.1582	67.7100	99.2563	136.7364
20	21.0000	46.4100	77.1561	114.3589	159.3742
		Annual Compounding			
2	2.0000	4.0400	6.1208	8.2432	10.4081
4	4.0000	8.1600	12.4864	16.9859	21.6653
6	6.0000	12.3600	19.1016	26.2477	33.8226
8	8.0000	16.6400	25.9712	36.0489	46.9328
10	10.0000	21.0000	33.1000	46.4100	61.0510
12	12.0000	25.4400	40.4928	57.3519	76.2342
14	14.0000	29.9600	48.1544	68.8960	92.5415
16	16.0000	34.5600	56.0896	81.0639	110.0342
18	18.0000	39.2400	64.3032	93.8778	128.7758
20	20.0000	44.0000	72.8000	107.3600	148.8320

$$(1.06)^2(1.06)^2(1.06)^2(1.06)^2 = (1.06)^8$$

which is just the same as the second method below.

$$(1.1236)(1.1236)(1.1236)(1.1236) = (1.1236)^4$$

If simple interest were computed on $1.00 at a nominal annual rate of 12% for one semiannual period (180 days) with a time base of 360 days, the interest would amount to $0.06.

$$
\begin{aligned}
I &= PRT \\
&= (\$1.00)(0.12)(180/360) \\
&= \$0.06
\end{aligned}
$$

Over a time interval of four years, or eight semiannual periods, the interest would total $0.48 ($0.06 times 8).

The simple interest figure of $0.48 for eight semiannual periods may be compared with the corresponding compound interest total of $0.5938. The interest on a principal of $1.00 is $0.48 in both cases. The difference of $0.1138 between the total amount of compound interest and the amount of simple interest is due to interest on interest. Simple interest provides no interest on interest, while compound interest does.

Table 3–5 sets forth effective rates of interest for various periods of time and for selected nominal annual interest rates. Values are shown for monthly, quarterly, semiannual, and annual compounding frequencies.

4 WHAT EVERY BORROWER AND LENDER SHOULD KNOW

TIME VALUE OF MONEY

In discussing effective interest rates, it became apparent that as the compounding frequency increases, the effective annual interest rate becomes greater. This statement has implications for both borrowers and lenders. Borrowers can promote their best interests by seeking to make their periodic interest payments as seldom as possible, whereas lenders should try to collect their periodic interest receipts as often as possible for a given nominal annual interest rate.

The expression *the time value of money* refers to the fact that time is worth money. Funds held by either a borrower or a lender can be used to generate earnings with the passage of time.

Lenders can earn interest on interest either internally (within the original investment) or externally (outside of the original investment). For example, if depositors (lenders) place money in a bank savings account where the interest is being compounded, they would have a chance to earn interest on their unpaid interest payments internally. If, on the other hand, the lenders were receiving periodic payments from a borrower, the lenders would have to reinvest the paid interest payments externally, or outside of the original investment, if they wanted to earn interest on the interest payments. The lenders could decide that they wanted to spend the periodic interest payments that they were receiving from the borrower. In that event the lenders would forfeit their chance to earn interest on interest. Their return would be restricted to interest on principal.

INTERNAL COMPOUNDING—QUARTERLY COMPOUNDING FREQUENCY

If a depositor (lender) were earning a nominal annual rate of 9% compounded quarterly for one year on a bank savings account or other savings arrangement, the internal compounding (i.e., the accumulation of interest on interest within the original investment) could be shown as in this growth schedule for a $1,000 principal amount. The base $(1 + R/m)$ in the compound interest formula would be $(1 + 0.09/4)$ or (1.0225). That is, the quarterly interest rate would be 2.25%.

Quarter 1	($1,000.0000)(1.0225)	=	$1,022.5000
Quarter 2	($1,022.5000)(1.0225)	=	$1,045.5062
Quarter 3	($1,045.5062)(1.0225)	=	$1,069.0301
Quarter 4	($1,069.0301)(1.0225)	=	$1,093.0833

The lender would receive a total of $1,093.0833 (or $1,093.08) from the savings account at the end of one year. Of this amount, $1,000 would be a return of the investment. The remaining $93.0833 would consist of interest on principal of $90 (9% of $1,000) and interest on interest of $3.0833.

It can be observed that the depositor (lender) is earning an annual rate of 9% on the principal of $1,000, as well as an interest rate of 9% on the quarterly interest payments of $22.50 which are converted into principal at the end of each quarterly period. The total earnings of $93.0833 on an initial principal of $1,000 provide the lender with an effective annual interest rate or earning rate of 9.30833% although the nominal annual interest rate is only 9%.

$$S = (1 + R/m)^n$$
$$= (1 + 0.09/4)^4$$
$$= 1.0930833\%$$

effective annual rate $= 1.0930833 - 1 = 0.0930833$, or 9.30833%

When this rate is applied to the $1,000 principal, it may be seen that the growth amount is $1,093.0833.

$$S = P(1 + R/m)^n$$
$$= \$1,000(1.0930833)$$
$$= \$1,093.0833$$

What is the borrower's (bank's) borrowing rate in this example of internal compounding? In internal compounding, the borrower shoulders the responsibility of paying the lender both interest on principal and interest on interest. As interest payments are converted into principal, the borrower pays interest on these increments of principal as well as on the lender's initial deposit of $1,000. Because the borrower agrees to quarterly interest payments (and quarterly compounding) instead of annual interest payments (and annual compounding), the effective annual borrowing rate is 9.30833% instead of just 9%. For a deposit of $1,000 from the lender for one year, the borrower incurs an interest cost of $93.0833.

EXTERNAL COMPOUNDING—QUARTERLY COMPOUNDING FREQUENCY

Consider an example of external compounding or compounding outside of the original investment where both lender and borrower positions will be examined.

Figure 4-1.   Time Line.

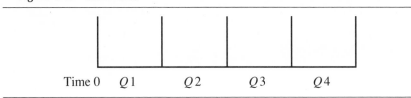

Time 0 $Q1$ $Q2$ $Q3$ $Q4$

Assume that a borrower makes a one-year loan for $1,000 from Banker Q at a nominal annual interest rate of 9%. Banker Q requires the borrower to make interest payments of $22.50 each at the end of quarterly periods Q1 through Q4. The principal of $1,000 is due at maturity or at the end of Q4.

On the same day, the same borrower also makes a one-year loan for $1,000 from Banker A at a nominal annual rate of 9%. The total amount of interest of $90 as well as the principal of $1,000 is due at the end of the year (i.e., at the end of Q4).

For both loans, the principal, the nominal annual interest rate, and the amount of interest on principal are the same. Also, the loan maturities extend over the same time horizon (one year). However, it would still be incorrect to say that the two loans are identical.

The Banker A loan allows the borrower to retain possession of the total amount of interest on principal until maturity, permitting the borrower to earn money on the $90 for one year if desired. For one year, the borrower's position as far as interest payments are concerned is the same as it was before the loan was made. The interest expense of $90 on a principal of $1,000 results in a cost to the borrower of 9%. Banker A's interest income of $90 on an investment of $1,000 for one year gives an earning rate or lending rate of 9%.

In contrast, the borrower incurs an opportunity cost in the loan from Banker Q by forfeiting in stages the chance to earn interest on portions of the $90. The opportunity cost may be viewed as shown below.

The supposition is made that the borrower could invest quarterly portions ($22.50) of the $90 at a nominal annual rate of 9% or a quarterly rate of 2.25%. Also, Banker Q can, if desired, reinvest the interest payments in another investment and actually earn interest on interest at an annual rate of 9% on the basis of the same quarterly schedule by which the borrower incurs an opportunity cost. Although the borrower pays the lender interest on principal, the borrower is not obligated to the lender for the payment of interest on interest. The lender earns interest on interest outside of the original investment or loan.

In this example, the borrower's opportunity cost is allowed to equal the interest on interest earned externally by the lender. This amount is displayed in the following quarterly interest schedule.

Quarter 1	($22.5000) $\times$ $(1.0225)^3$	=	$24.0532
Quarter 2	($22.5000) $\times$ $(1.0225)^2$	=	23.5239
Quarter 3	($22.5000) $\times$ (1.0225)	=	23.0062
Quarter 4	($22.5000)	=	22.5000
Totals	$90.0000		$93.0833

The first $22.50 payment of interest on principal, which is paid at the end of the first quarter, is assumed to earn interest itself over Q2, Q3, and Q4. The second payment of interest on principal occurs at the end of Q2, and this $22.50 amount is compounded at the periodic interest rate of 2.25% (9% annual rate) over Q3 and Q4. While the third payment of interest on principal earns interest itself over the fourth quarter, the payment which takes place at the end of Q4 has no opportunity to earn interest.

On the Banker Q loan, the borrower incurs an actual interest cost of $90 ($22.50 per quarter times 4 quarters) plus an opportunity cost of $3.0833 ($93.0833 minus $90). Banker Q receives income of $90 plus reinvestment income of $3.0833. Thus the borrower experiences a borrowing rate of 9.30833% and the lender (Banker Q) an earning rate of 9.30833%. Recall that the effective annual interest rate for a nominal annual interest rate of 9% compounded quarterly for one year is 9.30833%.

The compounding for the borrower assumes an investment rate or opportunity rate of 9% and the external compounding for the lender (Banker Q) presumes a reinvestment rate of 9%. The same effective annual interest rate of 9.30833% was found for both internal compounding and external compounding (Banker Q loan) because of this assumption that the rate of interest on principal and the rate of interest on interest were both 9%.

The supposition is made in internal compounding that interest on principal is converted into principal at the end of each interest period. Therefore, in internal compounding the rate of interest on interest is always assumed to be the same as the rate of interest on principal. In external compounding, the assumption can be made that the rate of interest on interest is the same as the rate of interest on principal or that the two rates are different.

It might be pointed out that the borrower's investment rate or opportunity rate in external compounding is independent of the lender's reinvestment rate. Neither party is responsible to the other for the generation of interest on interest. The borrower's investment rate may be assumed to be the same as or different from the lender's reinvestment rate. In turn, either one or both of these interest-on-interest rates may be equal to or different from the interest rate used to calculate interest on principal.

EXTERNAL COMPOUNDING WITH DISSIMILAR INTEREST ON PRINCIPAL AND INTEREST ON INTEREST RATES

Suppose now that the borrower's investment rate is 6% instead of 9%. For quarterly compounding, this gives a periodic rate for calculating interest on interest of 1.5%. The annual rate for computing interest on a $1,000 principal amount is still assumed to be 9% and, therefore the quarterly payments continue to be $22.50. The compounding of the quarterly interest payments from the borrower's point of view is shown in this schedule.

Quarter 1	($22.5000) × $(1.015)^3$	=	$23.5278
Quarter 2	($22.5000) × $(1.015)^2$	=	23.1801
Quarter 3	($22.5000) × (1.015)	=	22.8375
Quarter 4	($22.5000)	=	22.5000
Totals	$90.0000		$92.0454

The total interest cost of $92.0454 on a principal amount of $1,000 gives the borrower an effective annual borrowing rate of 9.20454%. The same effect can be described instead by a modified nominal annual rate.

CALCULATION OF THE MODIFIED NOMINAL ANNUAL RATE

The calculation of the modified nominal annual interest rate follows. For this situation we have already calculated S for the borrower, the quantity that represents principal, interest on principal, and the opportunity cost of interest on interest. Substituting this value into the compound interest equation, we solve for R, which is now the modified nominal annual interest rate.

$$P(1 + R/m)^n = S$$
$$1,000(1 + R/4)^4 = 1,092.0454$$
$$(1 + R/4)^4 = \frac{1,092.0454}{1,000} = 1.0920454$$
$$(1 + R/4)^2 = \sqrt{1.0920454} = 1.04501$$
$$(1 + R/4) = \sqrt{1.04501} = 1.02226$$
$$R/4 = 0.02226$$
$$R = 0.08904, \text{ or } 8.904\%$$

The borrower's modified annual rate would be equal to the nominal annual rate only if the opportunity rate were the same as the rate of interest on principal. (Similarly, a modified nominal annual rate for the lender of 9% would imply a reinvestment rate of 9%, in conjunction with the rate of 9% on principal).

The combination of a 9% rate for interest on principal and a 6% opportunity rate for the borrower thus serves to change (reduce in this case) the nominal annual interest rate of 9%.

The modified nominal annual interest rate of 8.904% can be thought of as a rate of interest on principal of 8.904% and an opportunity rate for the borrower of 8.904%.

Testing the Modified Nominal Annual Rate

A rate of 8.904% for a principal of $1,000 produces quarterly interest payments of $22.26 and thus a quarterly interest rate of 0.02226 or 2.226%. Using this information we can construct a quarterly interest schedule.

Quarter 1	($22.2600) × (1.02226)^3	=	$23.7799
Quarter 2	($22.2600) × (1.02226)^2	=	23.2620
Quarter 3	($22.2600) × (1.02226)	=	22.7555
Quarter 4	($22.2600)	=	22.2600
Totals	$89.0400		$92.0574

The combination of an interest on principal rate of 8.904% and a borrower investment rate (lender reinvestment rate) of 8.904% gives a total interest-on-principal and interest-on-interest amount of $92.0574, which represents an effective annual rate of 9.20574%. Compare this with the amount of $92.0454, corresponding to an effective annual interest rate of 9.20454%, which was obtained by using the combination of a 9% rate for interest on principal and a 6% borrower investment rate (lender reinvestment rate). Apparently, the dollar amounts vary by a little over one cent, causing the effective rates to differ by slightly more than 0.001%. Actually, the difference is due solely to rounding. The dollar amounts and the effective annual interest rates for the two interest rate combinations should be the same.

INTERNAL COMPOUNDING—SEMIANNUAL COMPOUNDING FREQUENCY

Without repeating the sequence of calculations that has been done for quarterly compounding, the results alone will be stated for semiannual compounding so that effective annual interest rates may be compared for these two compounding frequencies under the conditions of internal and external compounding. We will use the example of a loan principal of $1,000 and a nominal annual interest rate of 9%, which are the same quantities used in doing the calculations for quarterly compounding.

Under the condition of internal compounding for a quarterly compounding frequency, it was found that the lender had an effective annual earning rate of 9.30833%. The borrower's effective annual borrowing rate was also 9.30833%. For semiannual compounding, the lender's effective earning rate and the borrower's effective borrowing rate would be lower, specifically 9.2025%. This is in line with expectations, since effective annual interest rates increase with an increase in the compounding frequency and, conversely, decrease with a decrease in the compounding frequency.

EXTERNAL COMPOUNDING—SEMIANNUAL COMPOUNDING FREQUENCY

The same effective annual interest rates would apply to the borrower and to the lender where the compounding is external, so long as the investment rate for the borrower and the reinvestment rate for the lender are both assumed to be equal to the interest rate (9%) used to compute interest on principal. That is, the effective annual rates still would be 9.30833% (quarterly compounding) and 9.2025% (semiannual compounding).

By using quarterly external compounding, a rate of 9% for interest on principal, and an interest-on-interest rate of 6% for the borrower and for the lender, the effective annual interest rate (borrowing rate and lending rate) was determined to be 9.20454%. The same type of calculation using semiannual compounding instead of quarterly compounding produces an effective annual rate of 9.135% for the borrower and for the lender. It is noticed again that the effective annual interest rate obtained with semiannual compounding is lower than the rate provided by quarterly compounding.

COMPARABLE NOMINAL ANNUAL INTEREST RATES

In cases where the interest-on-interest rate is assumed to be the same as the interest-on-principal rate, a nominal annual interest rate with a given compounding frequency can be found that is comparable to another nominal annual interest rate having a different compounding frequency. The following example is used to illustrate the point.

Assume that it is desired to find the nominal annual interest rate R with semiannual compounding that matches a nominal annual interest rate of 13% with quarterly compounding. The following method may be used. Using the expression $(1 + R/m)^n$, we have

$$(1 + R/2)^2 = (1 + 0.13/4)^4 = 1.136476$$
$$1 + R/2 = \sqrt{1.136476} = 1.066056$$
$$R/2 = 0.066056$$
$$R = 0.1321, \text{ or } 13.21\%$$

The nominal annual interest rate of 13.21% with semiannual compounding is equivalent to the nominal annual rate of 13% with quarterly compounding. The interest-on-interest rate in the case of the 13.21% nominal annual rate is assumed to be 13.21%. The 13% nominal annual rate carries the supposition that the interest-on-interest rate is 13%.

It may be seen that both of these nominal annual interest rates produce the same effective annual interest rate of 13.65%.

$$S = (1 + R/m)^n$$
$$= (1 + 0.1321/2)^2$$
$$= 1.1365$$

effective annual rate $= 1.1365 - 1 = 0.1365$, or 13.65%

and

$$S = (1 + R/m)^n$$
$$= (1 + 0.13/4)^4$$
$$= 1.1365$$

effective annual rate $= 1.1365 - 1 = 0.1365$, or 13.65%

LOAN ROLL OVERS OR RENEWALS

It is possible to generate an effective annual interest rate that exceeds the nominal annual interest rate in two ways.

The first method was demonstrated in the foregoing examples dealing with the payment of interest at intervals between the time that a loan is made and the time of maturity. The payments of interest were made at periods less than one year.

The second way of producing an effective annual rate greater than the nominal annual rate is to have a roll over, or a renewal of a loan or a debt at periods less than one year, with interest payments being made each time that maturity occurs.

From a compounding standpoint, a one-year loan requiring quarterly interest payments would be the same as a loan with a quarterly maturity that was being renewed each quarter over a period of one year. Of course, the quarterly loan maturities would carry the supposition that interest payments were being made at each maturity. Under the conditions outlined, the effective annual interest rates for these two types of debt would be the same.

Example—Figuring a Borrower's Effective Annual Interest Rate for a Loan Being Rolled Over

During the past year a certain borrower has had a recurring need for short term funds. The borrower has rolled over quarterly loans at a nominal annual rate of 11.25%. Interest payments have been made at each quarterly maturity.

If it is assumed that the borrower's opportunity rate is also 11.25% what is the effective annual borrowing rate based on a 360-day year?

$$S = (1 + R/m)^n$$
$$= (1 + 0.1125/4)^4$$
$$= (1.0281)^4$$
$$= 1.1172$$

effective annual rate $= 1.1172 - 1 = 0.1172$, or 11.72%

The borrower's effective annual rate is 11.72%. This would also have been the borrower's effective rate if a one-year loan had been made which required quarterly interest payments. (The lender's effective annual earning rate for the two types of loans also would be 11.72%, if it were presumed that the reinvestment rate was 11.25%).

Example—Computing a Commercial Paper Issuer's Effective Annual Borrowing Rate on Roll Overs

Suppose that a company (issuer) sells its commercial paper (i.e., promissory notes) over the course of one year by doing monthly roll overs. That is, each month when its paper matures, the firm turns around and reissues or resells commercial paper on the same day for another month. This is continued each month for a one-year period.

The commercial paper is sold on a discount basis, which means that the interest is given to the lender (buyer) at the time of sale. What is the issuer's effective annual borrowing rate for a 360-day year if an annual discount rate of 12% adjusts to a rate of 12.12% based on actual proceeds to the issuer? (See the commercial paper example in Chapter 2 for the calculation of the 12.12% rate.)

$$S = (1 + R/m)^n$$
$$= (1 + 0.1212/12)^{12}$$

$$= (1.0101)^{12}$$
$$= 1.1282$$

effective annual rate $= 1.1282 - 1 = 0.1282,$ or 12.82%

The effective annual rate is 12.82%.

NEGOTIATING THE FREQUENCY OF INTEREST PAYMENTS

With respect to the timing of simple interest payments, the most unfavorable type of borrowing that a borrower can make is a discount loan, because the total amount of discount (interest) is due at the time that the borrowing occurs. A borrower's opportunity cost is realized immediately since there is no lag between the time that a loan is made and the time that interest is due.

In viewing the lender's position regarding the timing of simple interest receipts, a discount loan is the most advantageous type of loan (investment) that the lender can make. With such a loan, the lender can reinvest immediately, if desired, the borrower's total payment of interest on principal.

Having made the foregoing statements concerning discount loans, the following discussion excludes these discount obligations and considers only interest-bearing debts requiring either the total payment of interest on principal at loan maturity or the partial payment of interest at points falling beyond the start of a loan.

For a given nominal annual interest rate, the lowest effective annual interest rate occurs when interest payments are made annually. The highest effective annual interest rate is provided by continuous interest payments. From a theoretical standpoint, the optimal interest payment arrangement for a borrower would be annual payments while the optimal arrangement for a lender would be continuous interest payments.

For a given nominal annual interest rate, a borrower in an actual negotiating situation would be moving from annual interest payments to more frequent payments. That is, the borrower would first try to get the lender to agree to having annual interest payments (assuming a loan with a maturity of one year or longer). If that were not acceptable to the lender, the borrower would next negotitate for semiannual payments and then for quarterly payments.

Needless to say, continuous interest payments are impracticable. However, for a given nominal annual interest rate, a lender would move in the negotiations with a borrower from the concept of continuous payments to less frequent payments. The lender would first try to get the borrower to accept, say, quarterly payments and then semiannual payments.

For a shorter term loan, one being made for perhaps six months, the borrower would negotitate first to have the interest payable at maturity, then for a quarterly or some other more frequent arrangement. The lender, however, for the same given nominal annual rate of interest, might opt first to get monthly payments and then quarterly payments of interest. The lender's last choice would be to have the interest payable at maturity (semiannually).

5 PUTTING THE POWERFUL GROWTH CONCEPT TO WORK

OVERVIEW OF THE COMPOUND INTEREST TABLES

It is desired now to pursue the use of compound interest tables. The reader should turn to Appendix D in the back of the book and examine the compound interest tables presented there. Included in the compound interest set are four tables. These tables are for monthly, quarterly, semiannual, and annual compounding at a nominal annual rate of 8%.

Tables for just one rate of interest are included. A reader who can use the compound interest tables for one rate of interest should be able to use tables for any other interest rate. If other tables had been included, all of them would have had the same format or arrangement as the 8% tables. For those persons desiring them, separate volumes of compound interest tables are available in many bookstores. Alternatively, Chapter 14 of this book explains how to construct compound interest tables using financial calculators.

The first table to be found in the compound interest set is the table for monthly compounding. At the extreme left side of the page, space is provided for the total number of compounding periods n. In this table this time space contains months and years.

The other three tables have similar time spaces. However, instead of months, the quarterly table carries the designation quarters while the semiannual table has the label half years. The annual table lists years only in the time space. (Although the time space is actually the first column of the tables, the use of the word *column* is reserved for the six functions of $1.00.)

Six major columns in the monthly table carry the headings of Column 1 through Column 6. The tables for quarterly, semiannual, and annual compounding also contain these same six columns.

The use of each column of the compound interest tables is indicated below. The various columns will be discussed in more detail in this and the next three chapters.

Column 1: Determination of the future value or amount to which a known single payment will grow (Future Value of a Lump Sum).

Column 2: Determination of the future value or amount to which a series of known equal payments will grow (Future Value of an Annuity).

Column 3: Determination of the size of a series of equal payments required to reach a known future value (Payment Size of an Annuity When Total Future Value is Known).

Column 4: Finding the present value or worth of a known single payment to be made in the future (Present Value of a Lump Sum).

Column 5: Finding the present value or worth of a series of known equal payments to be made in the future (Present Value of an Annuity).

Column 6: Finding the size of a series of equal future payments when their present value is known (Payment Size of an Annuity When Total Present Value is Known).

COLUMN 1 OF THE COMPOUND INTEREST TABLES: FUTURE VALUE OF A LUMP SUM

The amount to which a lump sum of one unit (e.g., $1.00) will grow is the concern of Column 1. Therefore, Column 1 entails the use of the equation $S = P(1 + i)^n$. Since P is assigned the value of unity, the equation is reduced to $S = (1 + i)^n$.

The assumption made in Column 1 is that a lump sum deposit of one unit is made at the beginning of the first compounding period. There is no other deposit of principal during any other period. (It is emphasized that the deposit is made at the start, not at the end of the first period.)

An entry can be found in Column 1 of the quarterly compounding table for a nominal annual rate of 8% that permits one to find, for example, the value of

$$\left(1 + \frac{0.08}{4}\right)^{20} \quad \text{or} \quad (1 + 0.02)^{20}$$

The time space at the extreme left side of the table is scanned until 20 quarters, or 5 years, is found. By moving to the right, the figure 1.4859 is encountered in Column 1. This number means that a lump sum deposit of $1.00 made at the beginning of quarter one (compounding period one) will grow to $1.4859 by the end of 20 quarters (20 compounding periods). Therefore, if a $1.00 deposit will grow to $1.4859, a $100 deposit, for instance, will grow to $148.59 ($100 times 1.4859).

Figure 5–1. Time Line.

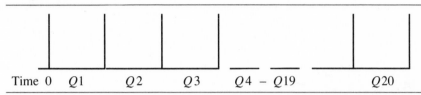

| Time 0 | Q1 | Q2 | Q3 | Q4 – Q19 | Q20 |

The figure $148.59 consists of the initial deposit or principal amount of $100 plus accumulated interest of $48.59. The depositor receives a return of investment ($100) plus a return on investment ($48.59). An analysis of the compounding is given in the following example.

Example—Calculating the Growth of a Lump Sum Deposit

Make the assumption that a depositor places a $100 savings deposit with a bank for five years at a nominal annual rate of interest of 8% compounded quarterly. To what amount would the $100 grow at the end of five years?

The deposit of $100 is made at the beginning of the first quarter or compounding period (Q1). At the end of the first quarter, interest is computed for one quarter and is added to the period's starting principal amount of $100. A similar procedure is repeated for each period for a total of 20 compounding periods. At the end of the twentieth quarter (Q20), the depositor will receive the $100 deposit plus the interest accumulated on that deposit.

The equation $S = P(1 + R/m)^n$ is used to find the growth of the $100 deposit over a 20-quarter or five-year period.

$$S = \$100(1 + 0.08/4)^{20}$$
$$= \$100(1 + 0.02)^{20}$$
$$= \$100(1.4859)$$
$$= \$148.59$$

The growth of the $100 deposit at the end of each quarter is shown in this quarterly compounding schedule for 20 quarters (5 years), where the nominal annual interest rate is 8% and the periodic or quarterly interest rate is 2%.

```
 1 ($100.0000)(1.02) = $102.0000
 2 ($102.0000)(1.02) = $104.0400
 3 ($104.0400)(1.02) = $106.1208
 4 ($106.1208)(1.02) = $108.2432
 5 ($108.2432)(1.02) = $110.4081
 6 ($110.4081)(1.02) = $112.6162
 7 ($112.6162)(1.02) = $114.8686
 8 ($114.8686)(1.02) = $117.1659
 9 ($117.1659)(1.02) = $119.5093
10 ($119.5093)(1.02) = $121.8994
11 ($121.8994)(1.02) = $124.3374
12 ($124.3374)(1.02) = $126.8242
13 ($126.8242)(1.02) = $129.3607
14 ($129.3607)(1.02) = $131.9479
15 ($131.9479)(1.02) = $134.5868
16 ($134.5868)(1.02) = $137.2786
17 ($137.2786)(1.02) = $140.0241
18 ($140.0241)(1.02) = $142.8246
19 ($142.8246)(1.02) = $145.6811
20 ($145.6811)(1.02) = $148.5947
```

The final effective rate of 48.59% may be found in another way by using the effective annual interest rate. This rate is developed in Table 5.1.

The total interest amount of $8.2432 for one year for a principal of $100 gives an effective annual interest rate of 8.2432%.

The annual compounding of the effective annual interest rate of 8.2432% gives effective rates at the end of each intermediate year.

$$2 \text{ years} \quad (1.082432)^2 = 1.1716, \text{ or } 17.16\%$$
$$3 \text{ years} \quad (1.082432)^3 = 1.2681, \text{ or } 26.81\%$$
$$4 \text{ years} \quad (1.082432)^4 = 1.3726, \text{ or } 37.26\%$$
$$5 \text{ years} \quad (1.082432)^5 = 1.4859, \text{ or } 48.59\%$$

The two-year compounded rate of 17.16% compares with the eight-quarter calculation of $117.1659 or a compounded rate of 17.17%. The

Table 5–1. Total Interest on a $100 Deposit During the First Year, in Dollars.

End of Quarter	Interest Payment on Principal	Interest on Interest in Quarter 2	Interest on Interest in Quarter 3	Interest on Interest in Quarter 4	Total Interest
1	2.00	0.04	0.0408	0.0416	2.1224
2	2.00	—	0.0400	0.0408	2.0808
3	2.00	—	—	0.0400	2.0400
4	2.00	—	—	—	2.0000
Totals	8.00				8.2432

three-year rate of 26.81% above corresponds to the 12-quarter figure of $126.8242 or a rate of 26.82%. The four-year compounded rate of 37.26% would be set against the 16-quarter computation of $137.2786 or a rate of 37.28%. The five-year compounded rate of 48.59% may be contrasted with the 20-quarter calculation of $148.5947 or a compounded rate of 48.59%. The related pairs of compounded rates differ only because of some variance due to rounding.

AVERAGE EFFECTIVE RATES

The longer the period over which compounding occurs, the larger the average effective interest rate per year becomes. This increase can be seen in Table 5–2.

Table 5–2. Average Effective Rates.

Compounding Period	Effective Rate	Average Effective Rate per Year
2 years	17.16%	8.58%
3 years	26.81%	8.94%
4 years	37.26%	9.32%
5 years	48.59%	9.72%

Each of the average effective rates per year may be contrasted with the nominal annual interest rate of 8%.

The following examples illustrate the use of the growth concept.

Example—Seeking the Effective Annual Interest Rate Paid on a Bond Margin Account

A bondholder maintains a bond margin account in which there are monthly debits of interest expense. If a nominal annual interest rate of 8% is being charged, what is the investor's effective annual borrowing rate on the account?

$$
\begin{aligned}
S &= (1 + R/m)^n \\
&= (1 + 0.08/12)^{12} \\
&= (1 + 0.00667)^{12} \\
&= 1.0830
\end{aligned}
$$

effective annual rate $= 1.0830 - 1 = 0.0830$, or 8.30%.

Use of the Column 1 formula provides an effective annual rate of 8.30%.

Where $n = 12$ months or 1 year, the monthly compound interest table for an 8% nominal annual rate shows a factor of 1.0830. This value coincides with the formula amount and provides the same effective rate of 8.30%.

Example—Finding the Amount of Post-Judgment Interest Imposed by a Judge on a Defendant

A lawyer has informed a client that their judicial appeal has been lost and that damages of $106,000 plus post-judgment interest for two years at the rate of 10% compounded annually will have to be paid by the client. How much post-judgment interest will this litigant have to pay?

$$
\begin{aligned}
S &= P(1 + R/m)^n \\
&= (\$106,000)(1 + 0.10/1)^2 \\
&= (\$106,000)(1.21) \\
&= \$128,260
\end{aligned}
$$

$$\text{interest} = \$128,260 - \$106,000 = \$22,260$$

Post-judgment interest of \$22,260 must be paid.

Example—Choosing Between Effective Annual Interest Rates on Savings Deposits

As in any deposit arrangement, it is necessary that the depositor understand the assumptions that underlie the interest computations.

Allow the assumption to be made that one financial institution pays an annual rate of 8.40% compounded quarterly on one-year savings deposits. Another financial intermediary pays a yearly rate of 8.35% compounded daily on deposits left for one year. Which nominal rate offers a depositor the higher effective interest rate?

The 8.40% nominal rate compounded quarterly is equivalent to an effective annual interest rate of 8.67%.

$$
\begin{aligned}
S &= (1 + R/m)^n \\
&= (1 + 0.0840/4)^4 \\
&= (1 + 0.0210)^4 \\
&= 1.0867
\end{aligned}
$$

effective annual rate $= 1.0867 - 1 = 0.0867$, or 8.67%

The nominal yearly rate of 8.35% compounded daily is the equivalent of an effective annual rate of 8.83%.

$$
\begin{aligned}
S &= (1 + R/m)^n \\
&= (1 + 0.0835/360)^{365} \\
&= (1 + 0.0002319)^{365} \\
&= 1.0883
\end{aligned}
$$

effective annual rate $= 1.0883 - 1 = 0.0883$, or 8.83%

It is important to notice in this last calculation that the value of m (360 days) is different from the value of n (365 days). If 365 days were used for both values, the effective annual rate would be 8.71% instead of 8.83%.

The 8.35% nominal annual rate would be chosen because it provides a higher effective annual rate (either 8.83% or 8.71%) than does the 8.40% nominal yearly rate (8.67% effective annual rate).

Example — Evaluating the Effect of An Escalator Clause on a Lessee's Rent

A lessee (tenant) has an escalator clause in a five-year rental contract that requires the payment of annual increases of 3.5% in the monthly rent. If the beginning rent per month is $2,150, how much will the lessee's monthly rent be during the fifth year of the lease?

The lessee will experience four annual increases in the monthly rent. They will occur at the beginning of the second, third, fourth, and fifth years.

$$
\begin{aligned}
S &= P(1 + R/m)^n \\
&= (\$2,150)(1 + 0.035/1)^4 \\
&= (\$2,150)(1.1475) \\
&= \$2,467
\end{aligned}
$$

At the beginning of the fifth year, the lessee will be paying a rental rate of $2,467 per month.

Example — Estimating a Future Salary

The income of an individual is $36,000 per year at the present time. This person expects to receive salary increases of approximately 6.5% in each of the next three years. What is the estimate of this person's level of income at the end of three years?

$$
\begin{aligned}
S &= P(1 + R/m)^n \\
&= (\$36,000)(1 + 0.065/1)^3 \\
&= (\$36,000)(1.2079) \\
&= \$43,484
\end{aligned}
$$

This person should be making $43,484 a year if the estimated annual salary increases are realized.

Example—Obtaining a Customer's Effective Annual Borrowing Rate on a Retail Charge Account

A customer maintains a balance in a charge account at a department store throughout the year because of frequent purchases. The retailer applies an interest rate of 1.5% per month to unpaid customer balances. What effective rate of interest is the customer paying on the account?

A monthly rate of 1.5% produces a nominal annual interest rate of 18% (i.e., 1.5% times 12).

$$S = (1 + R/m)^n$$
$$= (1 + 0.18/12)^{12}$$
$$= 1.1956$$

effective annual rate $= 1.1956 - 1 = 0.1956$, or 19.56%

The customer's effective annual borrowing rate is 19.56%.

Example—Figuring the Growth in a Dutch Company's Guilder Dividend

An investor in Amsterdam is receiving an annual dividend of two guilders per share on the stock of a firm. This equity owner figures that the Dutch company will probably raise its dividend 5.5% in each of the next three years. At the end of three years, to what amount will the dividend have grown?

$$S = P(1 + R/m)^n$$
$$= (2\text{guilders})(1 + 0.055/1)^3$$
$$= (2\text{guilders})(1.1742)$$
$$= 2.35\text{guilders}$$

The anticipation is that the future dividend will be 2.35 guilders.

Example—Ascertaining the Expected Growth in Yen in the Sales of a Japanese Firm

A Japanese computer company in Tokyo has experienced an increase in its total sales over the past two years that amounts to growth at an annual rate of 15% compounded quarterly. Sales were 1.3 billion yen last year. If the growth continues for another two years at this same rate, what will be the size of the firm's sales at the end of the second year?

$$S = P(1 + R/m)^n$$
$$= (1.3\text{billion yen})(1 + 0.15/4)^8$$
$$= (1.3\text{billion yen})(1.3425)$$
$$= 1.75\text{billion yen}$$

If growth expectations are met, the Japanese company will have sales of 1.75 billion yen at the end of the second year.

Example—Determining the Purchase Price in British Pounds of a Painting Whose Current Value is Known

Ten years ago a British art collector bought a painting in London that today is worth 75,000 pounds. On the supposition that the painting has increased in value at a rate of 11% per year, what was the price of this art piece at the time of purchase?

$$S = P(1 + R/m)^n$$
$$P = \frac{S}{(1 + R/m)^n}$$
$$= \frac{75,000\text{pounds}}{(1 + 0.11/1)^{10}}$$
$$= \frac{75,000\text{pounds}}{2.8394}$$
$$= 26,414\text{pounds}$$

The collector paid 26,414 British pounds for the painting.

Example—Estimating the Revenue in Marks of a German Company Planning to Increase Both Product Price and Output

A firm in Frankfurt intends to expand its current annual production of 13,500 units by an annual rate of 10% compounded quarterly over the next three years.

This company also has plans to increase the selling price of each unit at a yearly rate of 7% compounded semiannually over the same three-year period. If the present price of a single unit is 128 marks, at what annual rate will the firm be generating total revenues by the end of the next three years?

Increase in Units

$$S = P(1 + R/m)^n$$
$$= (13,500)(1 + 0.10/4)^{12}$$
$$= (13,500)(1.3449)$$
$$= 18,156 \quad \text{units}$$

Production will rise to an annual rate of 18,156 units.

Increase in Price

$$S = P(1 + R/m)^n$$
$$= (128 \text{marks})(1 + 0.07/2)^6$$
$$= (128 \text{marks})(1.2293)$$
$$= 157 \text{ marks}$$

The unit price will increase to 157 marks.

Revenues at the end of the three years will be running at an annual rate of 2,850,492 marks (18,156 units at 157 marks each).

Example—Obtaining the Starting Amount of a Real Estate Portfolio

Suppose that a person owns a real estate portfolio of vacant land that today is worth $160,000. If the portfolio has increased in value at the rate of 10% per annum over the past six years, what was the beginning value of the portfolio six years ago when it as acquired?

$$P = \frac{S}{(1 + R/m)^n}$$

$$= \frac{\$160,000}{(1 + 0.10/1)^6}$$
$$= \frac{\$160,000}{1.77156}$$
$$= \$90,316$$

When the real estate portfolio was started six years ago, it had a value of $90,316 or, say, $90,300.

Example—Finding the Growth in Earnings of a Company's French Subsidiary

A company has a French subsidiary whose earnings last year were 35 million francs. If the earnings are expected to increase at the rate of 8% per year over the next seven years, what will be the subsidiary's earnings at the end of the seventh year?

$$
\begin{aligned}
S &= (1 + R/m)^n \\
&= (1 + 0.08/1)^7 \\
&= 1.7138
\end{aligned}
$$

The growth amount of 1.7138 for an initial amount (P) of 1 is also found in Column 1 of the annual compounding table for $n = 7$ years. The multiplication of 1.7138 by 35 million francs gives a value of 59.98 million francs. The French subsidiary's earnings at the end of year seven are expected to be 59,980,000 francs or, say, 60 million francs.

The actual principal value of 35 million francs could be used in the growth equation if desired so as to get the result in one calculation.

$$
\begin{aligned}
&= (35 \times 10^6 \text{francs})(1 + 0.08/1)^7 \\
&= 59.98 \times 10^6 \text{francs}
\end{aligned}
$$

Example—Ascertaining The Future Level of a Canadian Work Force (Nonmonetary Growth)

The payroll of a Canadian company currently has 210 employees. The anticipation is that this firm's labor force will grow for the next 10 years at an annual rate of 8%. How many employees will be on the payroll at the end of 10 years?

$$S = (1 + R/m)^n$$
$$= (1 + 0.08/1)^{10}$$
$$= 2.1589$$

Column 1 of the annual compound interest table shows the factor 2.1589 where $n = 10$ years. At the end of a decade, the firm anticipates having 453 persons (i.e., 2.1589 times 210) on its employment rolls.

Example — Computing the Previous Population of a Growing Area

The current population of an area is 71,000 persons. Over the last four years the annual growth rate of this community has been 2.7%. What was the population four years ago?

$$S = P(1 + R/m)^n$$
$$P = \frac{S}{(1 + R/m)^n}$$
$$= \frac{71,000}{(1 + 0.027/1)^4}$$
$$= \frac{71,000}{1.1125}$$
$$= 63,820 \text{persons}$$

The area had a population of 63,820 persons four years ago.

Example — Estimating Future Oil Production (Nonmonetary Growth)

A country is currently producing 315,000 barrels of oil per day. What will the daily level of production be five years from now, if output is expected to grow at an annual rate of 10% compounded monthly?

$$S = P(1 + R/m)^n$$
$$= (315,000 \text{barrels})(1 + 0.10/12)^{60}$$

$$= (315,000 \text{barrels})(1.6453)$$
$$= 518,270 \text{barrels}$$

Oil production will rise to 518,270 barrels per day.

LOGARITHMS

The value of $(1 + i)^n$ for a particular i and n, can be determined by the use of logarithms as well as by using compound interest tables. For some preliminary discussion concerning logarithms, see Appendix C.

Example—Seeking the Rate of Growth

If in the growth equation $S = P(1 + i)^n$ the values of S, P, and n are known, then the compound interest expression $(1 + i)^n$ can be used to secure a value for i.

A company has seen its yearly sales grow from $11 million to $19 million over the past three years. What has been the annual rate of growth of the firm's sales?

The equation $S = P(1 + i)^n$ is solved for the value of $(1 + i)^n$.

$$
\begin{aligned}
(1 + i)^n &= S/P \\
&= \frac{\$19 \times 10^6}{\$11 \times 10^6} \\
&= 1.7273
\end{aligned}
$$

The expression $(1 + i)^n$ can now be used to get the value of i. The value of n is three years.

$$
\begin{aligned}
(1 + i)^3 &= 1.7273 \\
3\log(1 + i) &= \log 1.7273 \\
3\log(1 + i) &= 0.23737 \text{(from logarithm tables)} \\
\log(1 + i) &= 0.23737/3 \\
\log(1 + i) &= 0.07912 \\
\text{antilog} 0.07912 &= 1.1998 \text{(from logarithm tables)}
\end{aligned}
$$

$$1 + i = 1.1998$$
$$i = 0.1998, \text{ or } 19.98\%$$

The company's sales over the past three years have grown at a yearly rate of approximately 20% compounded annually.

Example—Calculating the Number of Compounding Periods

A knowledge of $(1 + i)^n$ and i permits the determination of the total number of compounding periods n if the quantities for S and P are provided.

A manufacturing concern expects its earnings to show an annual growth rate of 15%. If yearly earnings are now \$2.85 per share, how many years will it take for annual earnings to reach \$5.00 per share?

The value of $(1 + i)^n$ can be secured from the equation

$$S = P(1 + i)^n$$
$$(1 + i)^n = S/P$$
$$= \$5.00/\$2.85$$
$$= 1.75$$
$$(1 + R/m)^n = 1.75$$
$$(1 + 0.15/1)^n = 1.75$$
$$n \log 1.15 = \log 1.75$$
$$n(0.0607) = 0.24304 \text{(from logarithm tables)}$$
$$n = \frac{0.24304}{0.0607}$$
$$n = 4 \text{ years}$$

It will take four years for earnings to reach \$5.00 per share.

USE OF EXPONENTS IN CALCULATING FUTURE VALUES OF A LUMP SUM (COLUMN 1 FACTORS)

When a Column 1 factor is desired for some n that does not appear in a compound interest table, it is possible to calculate the desired number using other Column 1 figures. For a given compounding frequency and a given nominal annual interest rate, all of the factors in Column 1 have the same base. For example, for a nominal annual rate of 8% and monthly compounding, the base $(1 + 0.08/12)$ applies to all of the factors in Column 1. The existence of the common base allows the use of the rule (see Appendix C) that exponents are added when there is multiplication of a common base. The exponent rules may be tested using Column 1 numbers from the monthly compound interest table for a nominal annual rate of 8%. The rule would also apply to Column 1 values for other compounding frequencies.

A base such as $(1 + 0.08/12)$ can raise the question of which value should be used in the base. Should it be 1.007, 1.0067, 1.00667, 1.006667, or a value containing a greater number of digits to the right of the decimal point? The extension of the value will depend upon the accuracy desired when considering the principal amount (P) that will be affected by the calculation. The use of two different base values with n values of 36, 84, and 120 months is shown below.

$$(1.0067)^{36} = 1.2718$$
$$(1.006667)^{36} = 1.2703$$

and

$$(1.0067)^{84} = 1.7523$$
$$(1.006667)^{84} = 1.7475$$

and

$$(1.0067)^{120} = 2.2285$$
$$(1.006667)^{120} = 2.2197$$

Since 1.006667 is a smaller value than 1.0067 (i.e., 1.006700), the quantities obtained by using 1.006667 as a base are smaller than those that are gotten by the utilization of the base 1.0067.

Where n is 24 months, the equation $S = (1 + R/m)^n$ becomes $S = (1 + 0.08/12)^{24}$ or, say, $S = (1.006667)^{24}$. The value of $(1.006667)^{24}$ is 1.1729 and, therefore the magnitude of S is 1.1729. This is the figure that appears in Column 1 for n equal to 24 months.

Column 1 also reveals that $(1.006667)^{72}$ is equal to 1.6135 for $n = 72$ months. If 1.1729 is multiplied by 1.6135 the product is 1.8925, which is the Column 1 factor where $n = 96$ months. The calculation using the base (1.006667) is

$$(1.006667)^{24} \times (1.006667)^{72} = (1.006667)^{96}$$
$$(1.1729) \times (1.6135) = 1.8925$$

More than two Column 1 figures can be multiplied together to get other Column 1 values. Consider the Column 1 factors below.

$$(1.0201)(1.0407)(1.0476)(1.0546) = 1.1729$$

The multiplication of the Column 1 values for three, six, seven, and eight months gives the Column 1 factor for $n = 24$ months, namely 1.1729. (This same technique may be used to get Column 1 factors for n values that do not appear in the tables.)

RELATIONSHIP BETWEEN FUTURE VALUES OF A LUMP SUM FOR DIFFERENT NUMBERS OF COMPOUNDING PERIODS

For a given nominal annual interest rate and for a given compounding frequency, the percentage increase will be the same in Column 1 factors for any two n values with the same interval between them. This relationship will be demonstrated for n values that have a constant difference of 12 months.

Consider monthly compounding for a nominal annual rate of 8%. (The Column 1 factors are carried out to six decimal places so as to minimize the effect of rounding.)

$$n = 60 \text{ months:} 1.489846$$
$$n = 48 \text{ months:} 1.375666$$
$$n = 36 \text{ months:} 1.270237$$
$$n = 24 \text{ months:} 1.172888$$
$$n = 12 \text{ months:} 1.083000$$

Now examine the percentage increase from $n = 48$ to $n = 60$:

$$\begin{array}{r} 1.489846 \\ -1.375666 \\ \hline 0.114180 \end{array} \div 1.375666 = 0.0830, \text{ or } 8.30\%$$

from $n = 36$ to $n = 48$:

$$
\begin{array}{r}
1.375666 \\
-1.270237 \\
\hline
\end{array}
$$

$0.105429 \div 1.270237 = 0.0830$, or 8.30%

from $n = 24$ to $n = 36$:

$$
\begin{array}{r}
1.270237 \\
-1.172888 \\
\hline
\end{array}
$$

$0.097349 \div 1.172888 = 0.0830$, or 8.30%

and from $n = 12$ to $n = 24$:

$$
\begin{array}{r}
1.172888 \\
-1.083000 \\
\hline
\end{array}
$$

$0.089888 \div 1.083000 = 0.0830$, or 8.30%

(Since the factors in Column 4 are reciprocals of the factors in Column 1 (see Chapter 7), a similar statement regarding percentage changes between factors would also apply to Column 4.)

6 USING ANNUITIES AS A MEANS OF REACHING FUTURE GOALS

Each figure in Column 1 of the compound interest tables gives the future value of a lump sum deposit of one unit made at the start of the first compounding period. The assumption is that this deposit alone is compounded to get each of the future values given in this column.

Column 2 also lists future values. However, the supposition made in this column is that each of the future values (except where $n = 1$) represents more than one deposit or payment. A series of deposits, each of one unit, is made at regular intervals. The compounding frequency is assumed to coincide with the frequency of the deposits. That is, if the deposits are made at the end of each month, then the compounding frequency is monthly. If deposits happen every six months, the compounding is semiannual.

Whereas the assumption in Column 1 is that the lump sum deposit takes place at the beginning of the first compounding period, the supposition made in Column 2 is that the deposits occur at the end of each compounding period. A series of equal payments made at regular intervals is called an annuity. When the payments are made at the end of each period, the annuity is classified as an ordinary annuity, or an annuity in arrears.

USING COLUMN 1 VALUES TO OBTAIN COLUMN 2 VALUES: RELATING THE FUTURE VALUE OF AN ANNUITY TO THE FUTURE VALUE OF A LUMP SUM

A Column 2 value for a given number of periods n, giving the future value of an annuity where each payment is one unit, may be found by taking the summation of Column 1 values (future values of a lump sum deposit of one unit) up to $n - 1$ periods plus an additional amount of 1 unit. As an

71

illustration, the monthly compounding table for a nominal annual rate of 8% shows a Column 2 value of 4.0402 when $n = 4$ months. The Column 1 factors for $n = 1$, $n = 2$, and $n = 3$ months are 1.0067, 1.0134, and 1.0201, respectively. The summation of these three Column 1 values provides a total of 3.0402. If 1 is added to 3.0402, the amount becomes 4.0402, which is the Column 2 factor for $n = 4$ months.

The following equations provide further clarification of the relationship between Columns 1 and 2. Let S^n denote the future value of a lump sum deposit of size P for a particular n. That is, $S^n = P(1 + i)^n$. Then for $P = 1$,

$$
\begin{aligned}
S &= (1 + i) \\
S^2 &= (1 + i)^2 \\
S^3 &= (1 + i)^3
\end{aligned}
$$

To get the Column 2 factor for $n = 4$ months, the future value (FV) equation is used.

$$
\begin{aligned}
FV &= S^3 + S^2 + S + 1 \\
&= (1 + i)^3 + (1 + i)^2 + (1 + i) + 1
\end{aligned}
$$

Example—Finding the Future Amount of Periodic Savings Deposits

Assume that $200 is deposited in a bank savings account at the end of each semiannual period for two years (four semiannual periods). How much money will be in the account at the end of two years, if the deposits earn interest at a nominal annual rate of 8% compounded semiannually?

For analysis purposes it will be assumed for the moment that each deposit is $1.00 instead of $200. Once the total sum to which a series of $1.00 deposits will grow is known, it is possible to multiply this sum by 200 in

Figure 6–1.   Time Line.

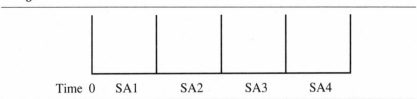

Time 0   SA1   SA2   SA3   SA4

order to determine the total amount to which a series of $200 deposits will grow.

The $1.00 deposit made at the end of the first semiannual compounding period SA1 earns compound interest for the next three compounding periods (SA2, SA3, and SA4). The deposit of $1.00 made at the end of the second semiannual compounding period (SA2) accumulates interest over two periods (SA3 and SA4). The third $1.00 deposit made at the end of SA3 earns interest for only one period (SA4). The last deposit of $1.00 occurring at the end of SA4 does not earn any interest.

The periodic interest rate (i.e., the rate per semiannual compounding period) would be $i = R/m = 0.08/2 = 0.04$.

The analysis of the deposits given above may be summarized as follows. The deposit stream is set equal to an unknown future value (FV) in the long-form equation.

$$
\begin{aligned}
FV &= S^3 + S^2 + S + 1 \\
&= 1(1 + i)^3 + 1(1 + i)^2 + 1(1 + i) + 1 \\
&= 1(1 + 0.04)^3 + 1(1 + 0.04)^2 + 1(1 + 0.04) + 1 \\
&= 1.1249 + 1.0816 + 1.0400 + 1 \\
&= 4.2465
\end{aligned}
$$

A deposit of $1.00 made at the end of each semiannual period for a total of two years (four semiannual periods) will grow to $4.2465 if the series of deposits earns interest at a nominal annual rate of 8% compounded semiannually. A total of $4 is deposited and the amount of interest earned is $0.2465. Of this latter amount, $0.24 is interest on principal and $0.0065 is interest on interest.

The amount to which a series of four deposits of $200 will grow can be found by multiplying $200 by 4.2465. The resulting product of $849.30 consists of $800 of deposits and interest of $49.30. Of the earned interest, $48 represents interest on principal and $1.30 is interest on interest.

Referring to the compound interest table in Appendix D that has semiannual compounding for a nominal annual rate of 8%, it is seen that for $n = 4$ half years, the entry in Column 2 is 4.2465. To find the future value (FV) of the four $200 deposits, it is only necessary to multiply 4.2465 by $200. It is not required that Column 1 values be summed every time it is desired to calculate the future value of an annuity. As long as there is a compounding table with the appropriate nominal rate and compounding frequency, Column 2 can be used directly. It remains only to multiply the Column 2 factor by the amount of the periodic payment.

COLUMN 2 EQUATION: FINDING THE FUTURE VALUE OF AN ANNUITY

The summation of Column 1 factors can be reduced to a single short-form equation, which is the easiest way to calculate Column 2 quantities (future values of an annuity). It is usually written

$$S_n = \frac{(1 + i)^n - 1}{i}$$

The future value ($F\,V$) of the four semiannual deposits of $1.00 was originally found as shown below.

$$F^V = 1(1 + 0.04)^3 + 1(1 + 0.04)^2 + 1(1 + 0.04) + 1$$

Substituting S_n for $F\,V$, the equation is rearranged to read

$$S_4 = 1 + (1 + 0.04) + (1 + 0.04)^2 + 1(1 + 0.04)^3$$

This series is a geometric progression because after the first term (1), each of the other terms equals the preceding term multiplied by a fixed number or progression ratio. In this case the ratio is 1.04.

The formula for the sum of a geometric progression of the form

$$S_n = a + ar + ar^2 + ar^3 + \cdots + ar^{n-1} \text{ is}$$

$$S_n = \frac{ar^n - a}{r - 1}$$

It is seen that a is the first term in the series, n is the total number of terms in the series, and r is the progression ratio. In the case of the four semiannual deposits, $a = 1$, $n = 4$, and $r = (1 + 0.04)$. The equation becomes

$$S_4 = \frac{(1)(1 + 0.04)^4 - 1}{(1 + 0.04) - 1}$$
$$= \frac{(1 + 0.04)^4 - 1}{0.04}$$
$$= \frac{0.16986}{0.04}$$
$$= 4.2465$$

Note that when $a = 1$ and $r = (1 + i)$, the sum

$$S_n = \frac{ar^n - a}{r - 1}$$

can be written as

$$S_n = \frac{(1 + i)^n - 1}{i}$$

which is the Column 2 equation.

Example — Seeking the Unknown Future Value of a Series of Deposited Cash Dividends to be Used for Landscaping a Home

The quarterly cash dividends received by an investor over the next year will be placed in a savings arrangement and will be used to landscape the investor's home. The anticipation is that the quarterly dividends of $260 will earn a yearly interest rate of 8% compounded quarterly. How much money will this person have for landscaping at the end of one year?

Column 2 of the quarterly compounding table for a nominal annual rate of 8% shows the factor 4.1216 where $n = 4$. Therefore, for quarterly amounts of $260 the future value of the dividends at the end of one year would be $1,072 (4.1216 times $260).

Example — Obtaining the Future Value of Periodic Contributions by Members of a Limited Partnership

Because of an uncertain cash flow from an income property, members of a limited partnership have agreed to make monthly contributions to a reserve fund over the next 12 months so as to make property repairs that will be required at that time.

If the monthly contribution to the fund is $2,000, and these payments can be invested so as to earn an annual rate of 8% compounded monthly, what will be the worth of the fund at the end of 12 months?

Where $n = 12$ and the nominal annual rate is 8%, Column 2 of the monthly compounding table contains a value of 12.4499. Multiplying 12.4499 by monthly payments of $2,000 each, the anticipated value of the fund at the end of 12 months is found to be $24,900.

CONVERTING THE AMOUNT OF AN ORDINARY ANNUITY TO THE AMOUNT OF AN ANNUITY DUE

In the case of an ordinary annuity, payments are made at the end of each payment period. By contrast, an annuity due (or annuity in advance) has payments that occur at the beginning of each period. It is possible to convert the amount of an ordinary annuity to the amount of an annuity due.

Figure 6–2.   Time Line.

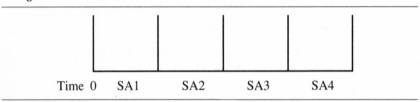

Time 0   SA1   SA2   SA3   SA4

Return to the example of four semiannual payments of $1.00, where the annual rate is 8% compounded semiannually. When a payment is made at the end of each six-month period, the series of payments may be thought of as an ordinary annuity. The future value (S_n) or (S_4), denoting four payments, of this ordinary annuity was found to be 4.2465.

$$S_4 = 1(1 + i)^3 + 1(1 + i)^2 + 1(1 + i) + 1$$
$$= 1(1 + 0.04)^3 + 1(1 + 0.04)^2 + 1(1 + 0.04) + 1$$
$$= 1.1249 + 1.0816 + 1.0400 + 1$$
$$= 4.2465 \text{ (Ordinary Annuity)}$$

For an annuity due, payments would occur at the beginning of each semiannual period. The first payment would then be compounded over four periods, the second payment over three periods, the third payment over two periods, and the fourth payment over one period. Thus the future value of the annuity due would be

$$S_4 = 1(1 + i)^4 + 1(1 + i)^3 + 1(1 + i)^2 + 1(1 + i)$$
$$= 1(1 + 0.04)^4 + 1(1 + 0.04)^3 + 1(1 + 0.04)^2 + 1(1 + 0.04)$$
$$= 1.1699 + 1.1249 + 1.0816 + 1.04$$
$$= 4.4164 \text{ (Annuity Due)}$$

The amount of the annuity due (4.4164) is found to be larger than the amount of the ordinary annuity (4.2465). The reason for this difference is that each payment of the annuity due earns interest for one more period than the corresponding payment in the ordinary annuity.

One means of obtaining the amount of an annuity due once the amount of an ordinary annuity is known is to multiply the amount of the ordinary annuity by the base $(1 + i)$. Since the base for a nominal annual interest rate of 8% compounded semiannually is $(1 + 0.04)$ the calculation would be

$$\text{Amount of Annuity Due} = \text{Amount of Ordinary Annuity} \times \text{Base}$$
$$= (4.2465)(1.04)$$
$$= 4.4164$$

If four payments of $200 each were involved, the amount of the ordinary annuity would be

$$(\$200)(4.2465) = \$849.30$$

The amount of the annuity due for payments of $200 each would be

$$(\$200)(4.4164) = \$883.28$$

ALTERNATE METHOD FOR CONVERTING AN ORDINARY ANNUITY

There is another method for converting the amount of an ordinary annuity to the amount of an annuity due. The approach is to obtain the Column 2 figure (from the appropriate compounding table) for $n + 1$, where n is the required number of payments and then subtract one from this factor. The resulting number will be the amount of an annuity due for payments of $1.00 each.

Figure 6–3   Time Line.

Time 0   SA1   SA2   SA3   SA4   SA5

Again, consider four semiannual payments of $1.00 each. It has been shown that, for a nominal annual interest rate of 8%, the amount of an annuity due would be expressed as

$$S_4 = 1(1.04)^4 + 1(1.04)^3 + 1(1.04)^2 + 1(1.04)$$
$$= 4.4164$$

For $n = 5$ semiannual periods, the amount of an ordinary annuity for five payments of $1.00 each and a base of 1.04 would be

$$S_5 = (1 + .04)^4 + 1(1.04)^3 + 1(1.04)^2 + 1(1.04) + 1$$
$$= 5.4164.$$

It can be seen that the payment stream for the amount of an ordinary annuity of five payments has the same terms as the payment stream for the amount of an annuity due of four payments, except for one non-interest-earning payment of $1.00 occurring in the fifth semiannual period. The four-payment stream does not include such a payment in any period. This $1.00 payment has to be subtracted from the stream of five payments in order to establish equality with the flow of four payments.

CONVERTING THE AMOUNT OF AN ANNUITY DUE TO THE AMOUNT OF AN ORDINARY ANNUITY

It has been stated that one means of converting an ordinary annuity to an annuity due having the same number of payments and compounding base is to multiply the ordinary annuity by the compounding base. In a previous example, an ordinary annuity of 4.2465 was multiplied by the base (1.04) to convert it to an annuity due having a value of 4.4164.

If the annuity due value of 4.4164 is divided by the base (1.04), the ordinary annuity value of 4.2465 is obtained.

AMOUNT OF A DEFERRED ANNUITY

A deferred annuity is one in which there is a passage of time before payments begin. Consider the case where a person agrees to make three annual payments after a deferred period of two years. Would there be any difference between the amount of this deferred ordinary annuity and the amount of an undeferred ordinary annuity of three annual payments?

In the case of an undeferred ordinary annuity, the three payments would be made at the end of each of the first three annual periods.

For an ordinary annuity deferred for two years, the three yearly payments would be made at the end of the third, fourth, and fifth annual periods.

The fact that there is a time delay of two years in the case of the deferred annuity before payments are made is of no consequence, since it does not affect the compounding. As shown by the payment streams, the amount of three annual payments of $1.00 each would be the same for both the undeferred annuity and the deferred annuity.

Figure 6–4.   Time Line.

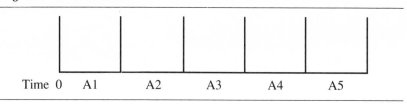

$$1(1 + i)^2 + 1(1 + i) + 1 = \text{Amount of an Undeferred Annuity}$$
$$1(1 + i)^2 + 1(1 + i) + 1 = \text{Amount of a Deferred Annuity}$$

FUTURE VALUE OF AN ORDINARY ANNUITY WHEN THE COMPOUNDING IS MORE FREQUENT THAN THE PAYMENTS

Compound interest tables for annuities generally are constructed so that the compounding frequency coincides with the frequency of the payments. However, as will be shown here and in Chapter 8, table values still can be used without adjustment to calculate annuity values in cases where the compounding frequency is greater than the frequency of the payments.

As an example, assume that an ordinary annuity has a life of one year and that the compounding frequency is quarterly whereas the frequency of $1.00 payments is semiannual. The nominal annual rate of interest is 8%.

The future value of the ordinary annuity can be obtained through the use of the relationship S_n/S_c where S_n is the future value of an ordinary annuity with a total of n compounding periods and S_c is the future value of an ordinary annuity having c compounding periods per payment period.

Column 2 of the compound interest tables where the compounding is quarterly and $n = 4$ contains a factor of 4.1216 for a nominal annual rate of 8%. Therefore, S_n is 4.1216. The same table shows a factor of 2.0200 in Column 2 for two quarterly periods. Thus the value of S_c is 2.0200. The relationship S_n/S_c may be solved as shown.

$$S_4/S_2 = 4.1216/2.0200$$
$$= 2.04$$

The future value of the annuity for $1.00 payments is $2.04.

For an ordinary annuity with a two-year life, $300 semiannual payments, and an annual rate of 8%, the future value based on quarterly compounding would be $1,275, computed as follows.

$$S_8/S_2 = 8.5830/2.0200$$
$$= 4.25$$
$$(\$300)(4.25) = \$1,275$$

This compounding of four $300 semiannual payments at a quarterly rate of 2% (annual rate of 8%) may also be found in the following way.

$$(\$300)(1.02)^6 = \$338$$
$$(\$300)(1.02)^4 = \ \ 325$$
$$(\$300)(1.02)^2 = \ \ 312$$
$$(\$300) \ \ \ \ \ \ \ \ \ \ = \ \ 300$$
$$\text{Total} = \$1,275$$

FUTURE VALUE OF AN ANNUITY DUE WHEN THE COMPOUNDING IS MORE FREQUENT THAN THE PAYMENTS

Assume that a two-year annuity due has quarterly compounding, an 8% annual rate, and $300 semiannual payments. The future value of this annuity can be computed by using the relationship S_n/PV_c, where S_n is the future value of an ordinary annuity with a total of n compounding periods and PV_c (column 5) is the present value of an ordinary annuity having c compounding periods per payment period.

$$S_8/PV_2 = 8.5830/1.9416$$
$$= 4.42$$
$$(\$300)(4.42) = \$1,326$$

The future value of the annuity is $1,326.

The quarterly compounding for this series of four payments can be viewed as follows.

$$(\$300)(1.02)^8 = \$351$$
$$(\$300)(1.02)^6 = 338$$
$$(\$300)(1.02)^4 = 325$$
$$(\$300)(1.02)^2 = 312$$
$$\text{Total} = \$1,326$$

DETERMINING PAYMENT SIZE OF AN ANNUITY WHEN THE TOTAL FUTURE VALUE IS KNOWN: RECIPROCAL RELATIONSHIP BETWEEN COLUMN 2 AND COLUMN 3

Column 3 of the compound interest tables, like Columns 1 and 2, is concerned with growth and future values. For a desired future value of one unit, the entries in Column 3 give the size of the annuity payments necessary to achieve that value. Remembering that Column 2 lists the future value of an annuity with payments of one unit each, it can be easily shown that, for a given number of periods (n), the value in Column 2 is the reciprocal of the value in Column 3. Conversely, the Column 3 figure is the reciprocal of the Column 2 figure. This relationship holds for each of the various compounding frequencies.

Consider, for example, the monthly compounding table in Appendix D. For $n = 8$, Column 2 shows a figure of 8.1892 and Column 3 contains a factor of 0.1221. The reciprocal of 8.1892 (i.e., 1/8.1892) is 0.12211205, to eight decimal places, which rounds to 0.1221. The reciprocal of 0.12211205 (i.e., 1/0.12211205) is 8.18920000. However, the reciprocal of 0.1221, to eight decimal places, is 8.19000819, which rounds to 8.1900. The small variance between the figures 8.1892 and 8.1900 is a rounding discrepancy only.

Exploring the similarities and dissimilarities of Columns 2 and 3 provides a better understanding of each of the columns. Each value in Column 2 of the tables represents the future amount to which a series of *n* equal deposits or payments of one unit will grow. Each payment is fixed at one unit. There is no deviation from this amount. The future amounts include the total value of *n* deposits made up to that point plus the accumulation of interest. There are no restrictions on these future amounts.

Each value in Column 3 of the tables gives the size of *n* equal deposits that must be made in order for the deposits plus the interest accumulated on them to total a future value of one unit. This future amount of one unit is fixed in every case. Other than the total growth limitation, there are no restrictions on Column 3 payment sizes.

The payments in Column 3, like those in Column 2, are made at the end of each period. Since the compounding also occurs at the end of each period, the compounding frequency agrees with the frequency of the payments.

Example—Accumulating a Fund for a Prospective College Student

The use of Column 3 can be illustrated by considering a case in which a grandparent wishes to build a fund that totals $6,000 at the end of four years for a grandchild who anticipates entering college at that time. How much money must the grandparent place in a savings account each Christmas for the next four years, if it is believed that the funds can earn a nominal annual rate of 8% compounded annually?

Figure 6–5   Time Line.

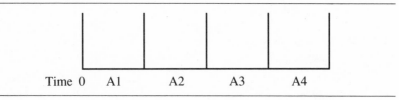

Time 0   A1   A2   A3   A4

The first payment (*X*), is made at the end of the first annual period and earns interest over three annual periods. The second payment (X_2) is made at the end of the second annual period and accumulates interest over two periods. The third payment (X_3) is made at the end of the third annual period, and accrues interest during the last annual period. Since the fourth payment (X_4) is made at the end of the last period it does not earn any interest.

The unknown size of the deposits necessary to total (with the accumulated interest) $1.00 at the end of four years can be found from the following equation. The future value (FV) of the four payments, keeping in mind that a nominal annual interest rate of 8% compounded annually is equivalent to a periodic rate of 8%, is given by

$$
\begin{aligned}
FV &= X_1(1 + i)^3 + X_2(1 + i)^2 + X_3(1 + i) + X_4 \\
&= X_1(1 + 0.08)^3 + X_2(1 + 0.08)^2 + X_3(1 + 0.08) + X_4 \\
&= X_1(1.2597) + X_2(1.1664) + X_3(1.08) + X_4
\end{aligned}
$$

Because the payments are all the same size, $X_1 = X_2 = X_3 = X_4 = X_n$. Since FV $= 1$, the equation can be rewritten as

$$
\begin{aligned}
1 &= 1.2597X_4 + 1.1664X_4 + 1.08X_4 + X_4 \\
1 &= 4.5061X_4 \\
X_4 &= \frac{1}{4.5061} \\
&= 0.2219
\end{aligned}
$$

This is the same figure that is found for $n = 4$ in Column 3 of the annual compounding interest table.

The four deposits of $0.2219 each add to a total of $0.8876. When this amount is subtracted from $1.00, the difference of $0.1124 is the accumulated interest. Of the total interest amount, $0.1065 is the amount of interest on the four deposits of $0.2219 each, and $0.0059 is the interest on interest.

A deposit of a little over 22 cents made at the end of each year for four years and earning a nominal annual interest rate of 8% compounded annually will grow to $1.00 at the end of the four years.

In order to have a future value of $6,000 at the end of the four years, it is necessary for each Christmas deposit to be $1,331.40 ($6,000 times 0.2219). If this is done, at the end of the four years the deposit total would equal $5,325.60 ($1,331.40 times 4) and the total accumulated interest on the four deposits would be $674.40 ($6,000 minus $5,325.60). The interest on the deposits would be $639.07 and the interest on interest would be $35.33.

DETERMINING PAYMENT SIZE OF AN ANNUITY WHEN THE TOTAL FUTURE VALUE IS KNOWN: COLUMN 3 EQUATION

It has already been shown that the short form formula for calculating Column 2 future values is

$$S_n = \frac{(1 + i)^n - 1}{i}$$

Since Column 3 values are reciprocals of Column 2 values, the Column 3 payment factors (X_n) can be found using the reciprocal of the equation above.

$$X_n = \frac{1}{S_n} = \frac{i}{(1 + i)^n - 1}$$

Return to the question posed earlier regarding what deposit size would be required each year with interest at a nominal annual rate of 8% compounded annually in order to have a total of $6,000 at the end of four years for a prospective college student. It has already been determined that the payment size should be $1,331.40.

Using the same deposit data in the Column 3 short-form equation (where $i = 0.08$ and $n = 4$), the substitution of values is

$$\frac{1}{S_n} = \frac{i}{(1 + i)^n - 1}$$

$$X_4 = \frac{0.08}{(1 + 0.08)^4 - 1}$$

$$= \frac{0.08}{1.3605 - 1}$$

$$= 0.2219$$

The payment size of $0.2219 for each $1.00 of future value is the same payment figure that can be seen in Column 3 of the annual compounding table for $n = 4$ years. In order to have $6,000 at the end of four years, the value of 0.2219 is multiplied by $6,000 which again gives an annual payment size of $1,331.40.

Example — Finding the Payment Size Necessary to Accumulate a Down Payment for a Home

Suppose that a working couple wishes to place enough money in a savings account each month in order to accumulate $9,000 at the end of two years for a home down payment. How much money will the couple have to place in the savings account each month, if the expectation is that the funds will earn interest at a nominal annual rate of 8% compounded monthly?

The Column 3 factor for $n = 24$ months is found to be 0.0386 in the monthly compounding interest table. A monthly deposit of almost four cents will grow with accumulated interest to $1.00 in two years. Therefore, a monthly deposit of $347.40 (0.0386 times $9,000) will grow to $9,000 at the end of two years, if the anticipated nominal interest rate of 8% is realized. The deposits would total $8,337.60 ($347.40 times 24 months), and the interest earned would be $662.40 ($9,000 minus $8,337.60).

Example — Figuring the Size of Annuity Payments Required to Purchase a Boat of Known Future Value

A boat owner has told her neighbor that in two years she intends to sell her boat for $15,000. The neighbor would like to buy the boat and would like to know how much of his semiannual bond income he would have to reinvest in order to accumulate $15,000. It is anticipated that over a two-year period the coupon income could be reinvested at a nominal annual rate of 8% compounded semiannually.

The semiannual compounding table for a nominal rate of 8% has a Column 3 factor of 0.2355 for $n = 4$. (This payment factor is based on a total future annuity value of $1.00.) The multiplication of 0.2355 by $15,000 furnishes a product of $3,533. The neighbor would therefore have to reinvest $3,533 of his bond income semiannually over the next two years (that is, in each of four semiannual periods) in order to have the reinvested amounts plus their accumulated earnings build to a total of $15,000.

Example — Calculating Sinking Fund Payments Necessary to Retire a Given Amount of Bonds in the Future

A bond sinking fund feature requires that, three years from now, a company purchase debt obligations having a face value of $4 million either in the open market at market prices or at par through a call arrangement in the indentures.

This firm has begun experiencing some slowdown in its business. Nevertheless, it does not want to risk being unable to meet its first obligation under the sinking fund requirement which will become due at the end of the third year. Therefore, the company plans to invest enough money in a savings arrangement each quarter so that these quarterly contributions plus the earnings on them will total $4 million at the end of three years. If the expectation is that earnings on contributed funds will be 8% per year compounded quarterly, what will be the size of the quarterly contributions?

The Column 3 factor for a nominal annual rate of 8% compounded quarterly is 0.0746 for $n = 12$ quarters. This indicates that the firm's quarterly contributions will have to be $298,400 (0.0746 times $4 million).

7 LEARNING HOW MUCH TO PAY TODAY FOR MONEY THAT YOU WILL RECEIVE TOMORROW

DETERMINING THE PRESENT WORTH OF A KNOWN SINGLE PAYMENT TO BE MADE IN THE FUTURE: RECIPROCAL RELATIONSHIP BETWEEN COLUMN 1 AND COLUMN 4

Column 1 of the compound interest tables lists the future value of a lump sum deposit of one unit. Each number in Column 4 stands for the present value of a lump sum deposit of one unit to be made in the future.

For corresponding n values, the figure in Column 1 is the reciprocal of the figure in Column 4. Conversely, each entry in Column 4 is the reciprocal of the corresponding entry in Column 1.

For instance, for $n = 3$ quarters in the quarterly compounding table, the figure 1.0612 is found in Column 1. The reciprocal of 1.0612 is 0.9423, which is the number that appears in Column 4. The reciprocal of 1.9423 is 1.0612. As is the case with Columns 2 and 3, rounding errors may cause slight discrepancies when converting between Columns 1 and 4.

It is easy to prove the reciprocal relationship between Columns 1 and 4. It has been shown that the formula underlying Column 1 is $S = P (1 + i)^n$. The equation states that a present value of principal P compounded at the periodic rate of interest i for a total number of compounding periods n is equal to a future value or growth amount S. The future value S includes the principal amount plus the accumulation of interest on principal and interest on interest. The equation $S = P (1 + i)^n$ becomes $S = (1 + i)^n$ when $P = 1$, as used in Column 1.

Suppose that a lump sum V^n is deposited now in an interest-bearing account. Its future value is $F V = V_n(1 + i)^n$. If it is desired that FV =

87

1, then the present value V^n will be $\frac{1}{(1+i)^n}$. These present values of one are the Column 4 values. The relationship is $V^n = \frac{1}{S}$ and $S = \frac{1}{V^n}$.

Example—Finding the Present Value of an Insurance Policy Reversion

Suppose that an individual purchases an insurance policy that will pay a lump sum, or reversion, of $10,000 ten years from now. What amount of money would this person pay now for the policy if the earning rate on the policy is assumed to be a nominal annual rate of 8% compounded annually.

Figure 7–1. Time Line.

Time 0   A1   A2   A3   A4 – A9   A10

At the beginning of the first year, the insurance buyer purchases the policy for a lump sum amount, which is unknown at the moment. This purchase amount starts earning interest at the beginning of annual period one and continues earning interest through the end of annual period ten. The earning rate is at the nominal annual rate of 8% compounded annually. The periodic interest rate is $i = R/m = 0.08/1 = 0.08$.

At the end of annual period ten the individual will receive a lump sum of $10,000 from the insurance company. This future amount will include the lump sum purchase price plus the accumulated interest on the purchase amount.

The present value factor is found to be 0.4632 for $n = 10$ years in Column 4 of the annual compounding table where the nominal annual rate is 8%. If the policyholder has to put up $0.4632 now so as to earn $1.00 ten years from now, then the purchase price will have to be 0.4632 times $10,000, or $4,632, now in order to get $10,000 ten years hence. The interest earned would be $5,368 ($10,000 minus $4,632).

The present value equation for a reversion of $1.00 in n periods would be

$$V^n = (1)\frac{1}{(1 + i)^n} \quad \text{or} \quad \frac{1}{(1 + i)^n}$$

Therefore the present value for a reversion of $1.00 in ten years for a periodic interest rate of 8% compounded annually would be

$$V^{10} = \frac{1}{(1 + 0.08)^{10}}$$

$$= \frac{1}{2.1589}$$

$$= 0.4632$$

The calculation above represents the discounting of a future value of $1.00 to a present value of $0.4632. The computation below illustrates the compounding of a present value of $0.4632 to a future value (FV) of $1.00.

$$FV = (\$0.4632)(1 + i)^n$$

$$= (\$0.4632)(1 + 0.08)^{10}$$

$$= (\$0.4632)(2.1589)$$

$$= \$1.00$$

Present value examples follow.

Example—Computing the Present Worth of a Consumer's Future Furniture Payment

A furniture store agrees to extend credit to a consumer today with the understanding that the consumer will pay $2,500 one year from now upon receipt of some money from an estate settlement.

If the furniture dealer stipulates that the future payment is to be discounted at an annual rate of 14.25% compounded semiannually, how much furniture will the consumer be allowed to buy on credit today?

$$V^n = \frac{1}{(1 + R/m)^n}$$

$$V^2 = \frac{1}{(1 + 0.1425/2)^2}$$

$$= \frac{1}{1.1476}$$

$$= 0.8714$$

The amount of $1.00 discounted at a nominal annual rate of 14.25 compounded semiannually is found to have a present worth of $0.8714, or a little more than 87 cents.

If $2,500 is multiplied by 0.8714, the product of $2,179 turns out to be the present value of $2,500, or the amount of furniture that the consumer can purchase on credit now. The interest that the customer would be paying over the one-year period would be $321 ($2,500 − $2,179).

Example—Obtaining a Merchant's Proceeds From a Discount Loan

The owner of a clothing store borrows $30,000 from a lender for six months for working capital purposes. The lender discounts the loan at an annual rate of 10.75% compounded monthly. How much money does the merchant receive at the time the loan is made?

$$V^n = \frac{1}{(1 + R/m)^n}$$

$$V^6 = \frac{1}{(1 + 0.1075/12)^6}$$

$$= \frac{1}{1.0550}$$

$$= 0.9479$$

The discounted proceeds of the loan are $28,437 (0.9479 times $30,000). The borrower's interest cost is $1,563 ($30,000 − $28,437).

ZERO COUPON BONDS

It is possible to buy bonds that carry a zero percent coupon, which is to say that there are no semiannual payments of interest or any other type of interest disbursements. The entire yield on the bonds is reflected in the discounted price from par. Column 4 of the semiannual compounding table can be used to determine prices for zero coupon bonds.

Example—Determining The Price of Zero Coupon Bonds

Take the case where an investor wishes to purchase $100,000 of zero coupon bonds having a maturity of 20 years. The investor requires an 8% yield on the securities. What price would he pay for the bonds?

In the table for semiannual compounding, Column 4 shows a present value of 0.2083 for n = 40 half-years. This factor could also be obtained using the Column 4 equation.

$$V^n = \frac{1}{(1 + R/m)^n}$$

$$V^{40} = \frac{1}{(1 + 0.08/2)^{40}}$$

$$= \frac{1}{4.8010}$$

$$= 0.2083$$

An investor would pay almost 21 cents today to receive $1.00 twenty years from now if a nominal annual rate of return of 8% compounded semiannually were set.

In order to buy bonds having a face value of $100,000, the investor would be required to pay $20,830 (0.2083 times $100,000). In 20 years the investor would receive $100,000 for the $20,830 investment.

Example—Accumulation of Interest on Zero Coupon Bonds

Assume that a $1,000 zero coupon bond has a maturity of five years and provides a nominal annual interest yield (yield to maturity) of 8% compounded semiannually. What would be the accumulation of interest during each of the five years?

The following factors are found in Column 4 of the compound interest table for which the compounding is semiannual. The number of semiannual periods is represented by n.

$n = 2$	0.9246
$n = 4$	0.8548
$n = 6$	0.7903
$n = 8$	0.7307
$n = 10$	0.6756

The present values of the bond during the five-year period would be

5 years before maturity	$1,000 × 0.6756 = $675.60
4 years before maturity	$1,000 × 0.7307 = $730.70

3 years before maturity	$1,000 × 0.7903 = $790.30
2 years before maturity	$1,000 × 0.8548 = $854.80
1 year before maturity	$1,000 × 0.9246 = $924.60

Using these data, the amount of interest accumulated during each of the five yearly periods is calculated.
During the fifth year before maturity,

$730.70 − $675.60 = $55.10

During the fourth year before maturity,

$790.30 − $730.70 = $59.60

During the third year before maturity,

$854.80 − $790.30 = $64.50

During the second year before maturity,

$924.60 − $854.80 = $69.80

During the first year before maturity,

$1,000 − $924.60 = $75.40

The sum of the interest is $324.40. This sum agrees with the figure of $324.40 obtained when the present value of the bond five years prior to maturity ($675.60) is subtracted from the value of the bond at maturity ($1,000).

The average amount of interest accumulated during each year of the 5-year period is $64.88 ($324.40 divided by 5 years).

It may be stated that the percentage increases between consecutive present values are the same even though the absolute differences between the consecutive present values increase as one proceeds from a point at 5 years prior to maturity to the point of maturity. This occurs because the calculating bases (present values) become larger as one moves toward maturity.

This point is conveniently demonstrated by examining the Column 4 factors. (These values have been calculated to six digits in order to lessen the rounding effect.)

During the fifth year before maturity, the percentage increase in the present value is 8.16%. The same is true for the other yearly increases.

$$0.730690$$
$$\underline{-0.675564}$$
$$0.055126 \div 0.675564 = 0.0816, \text{ or } 8.16\%$$

During the fourth year before maturity,

$$0.790315$$
$$\underline{-0.730690}$$
$$0.059625 \div 0.730690 = 0.0816, \text{ or } 8.16\%$$

During the third year before maturity,

$$0.854804$$
$$\underline{-0.790315}$$
$$0.064489 \div 0.790315 = 0.0816, \text{ or } 8.16\%$$

During the second year before maturity,

$$0.924556$$
$$\underline{-0.854804}$$
$$0.069752 \div 0.854804 = 0.0816, \text{ or } 8.16\%$$

During the first year before maturity,

$$1.000000$$
$$\underline{-0.924556}$$
$$0.075444 \div 0.924556 = 0.0816, \text{ or } 8.16\%$$

The effective annual rate of a nominal annual rate of 8% compounded semiannually is 8.16%.

OBSERVATIONS REGARDING THE PRESENT VALUES (PRICES) OF ZERO COUPON BONDS

Several observations may be made from Table 7–1 which displays the present values (prices) of zero coupon bonds for selected maturities and nominal annual yields. Notice that for a given yield to maturity the present values decline as maturity increases. This seems reasonable, since the longer

Table 7–1.   Present Values (Prices) of Zero Coupon Bonds (Dollars Per $100 of Bond Par Value).

Yield (Percent)	5 Years	10 Years	15 Years	20 Years	25 Years	30 Years
5	78.12	61.03	47.67	37.24	29.09	22.73
6	74.41	55.37	41.20	30.66	22.81	16.97
7	70.89	50.26	35.63	25.26	17.91	12.69
8	67.56	45.64	30.83	20.83	14.07	9.51
9	64.39	41.46	26.70	17.19	11.07	7.13
10	61.39	37.69	23.14	14.20	8.72	5.35
11	58.54	34.27	20.06	11.75	6.88	4.03
12	55.84	31.18	17.41	9.72	5.43	3.03
13	53.27	28.38	15.12	8.05	4.29	2.29
14	50.83	25.84	13.14	6.68	3.39	1.73
15	48.52	23.54	11.42	5.54	2.69	1.30
16	46.32	21.45	9.94	4.60	2.13	0.99
17	44.23	19.56	8.65	3.83	1.69	0.75
18	42.24	17.84	7.54	3.18	1.34	0.57
19	40.35	16.28	6.57	2.65	1.07	0.43
20	38.55	14.86	5.73	2.21	0.85	0.33

bondholders have to wait to collect the redemption value of their bonds, the less they will be willing to pay for the securities now. The value of V^n becomes smaller with an increasing n value in the equation $V^n = \frac{1}{(1+i)^n}$.

For a given maturity, the present value of a zero coupon bond per $100 of bond par value decreases as the yield on the bond increases. Again, as the value of $(1 + i)^n$ becomes larger (with an increasing i), the magnitude of V^n becomes smaller.

As maturity increases and as yield rises, the present values become smaller and smaller until the point is reached where a prospective issuer of zero coupon bonds would not consider it practical to issue this type of security. For instance, at a maturity of 25 years and a yield to the investor of 11%, the proceeds for the issuer from a $100 million bond offering based on par value would be only $6,880,000 (6.88%, or 0.0688, times $100 million) before the deduction of underwriting costs. During times of relatively high market rates of interest, an issuer desiring to sell zero coupon bonds would have to look to the issuance of bonds with shorter maturities in order to increase proceeds from the offering.

USING COLUMN 4 VALUES TO CALCULATE OTHER COLUMN 4 VALUES

In the discussion regarding future values of a lump sum, it was mentioned that two or more Column 1 factors can be multiplied together so as to get other Column 1 values (see Chapter 5). Since Column 4 numbers are reciprocals of Column 1 figures, two or more Column 4 factors for a given compounding frequency can be multiplied together in order to obtain other Column 4 values. When the Column 4 figures are multiplied, their n values are added in order to determine the n value to which the result of the multiplication applies.

To illustrate, consider the following Column 4 values taken from the semiannual compounding table with a nominal annual interest rate of 8%.

n	Column 4	n	Column 4
2	0.9246	10	0.6756
4	0.8548	12	0.6246
6	0.7903	14	0.5775
8	0.7307	16	0.5339

For instance, one could use $n = 2$ and $n = 4$ to find a value for $n = 6$:

$$(0.9246)\ (0.8548) = 0.7903$$
$$(n = 2)\ \ (n = 4) \quad (n = 6)$$

The value for $n = 16$ could be found in at least two different ways:

$$(0.7307)\ (0.7307) = 0.5339$$
$$(n = 8)\ (n = 8) \quad (n = 16)$$

or

$$(0.7903)\ (0.6756) = 0.5339$$
$$(n = 6)\ (n = 10) \quad (n = 16)$$

The $n = 12$ value can be gotten by putting three factors together:

$$(0.9246)\ (0.8548)\ (0.7903) = 0.6246$$
$$(n = 2)\ (n = 4)\ (n = 6) \quad (n = 12)$$

The semiannual compounding table does not contain a Column 4 value for $n = 28$ half years (14 years). However, it can be calculated using, for instance, the values for $n = 12$ and $n = 16$:

$$(0.6246) \ (0.5339) \ = \ 0.3335$$
$$(n = 12) \ (n = 16) \quad (n = 28)$$

Factors for other n values not found in Column 4 of the tables may be found in the same manner.

COMPARING SIMPLE DISCOUNT AND COMPOUND DISCOUNT

When an amount of money is discounted, the interest (discount) is deducted from the par amount of principal to arrive at the discounted amount of principal. The discount, or the amount of interest to be deducted from the par value of the principal, may be calculated using simple interest or compound interest.

Assume that a $45,000 principal amount is to be discounted at 11% for three months. What would be the discounted amount of principal using (a) simple interest and (b) compound interest? Also, what would be the effective annual rate for each method?

The simple discount on $45,000 at an annual discount rate of 11% for three months based on a 360-day year would be $1,238.

$$I = PRT$$
$$= (\$45,000)(0.11)\left(\frac{90}{360}\right)$$
$$= \$1,238$$

The discounted amount of principal would be $43,762 ($45,000 − $1,238).

The discount rate of 11% increases to 11.32% when calculated on the discounted principal of $43,762.

$$I = PRT$$
$$R = \frac{I}{PT}$$

$$= \frac{\$1,238}{(\$43,762)(\frac{90}{360})}$$

$$= 0.1132 \text{ or } 11.32\%$$

The effective annual rate for an adjusted discount rate of 11.32% would be 11.81% based on a 360-day year.

$$1 + \text{Effective annual rate} = \left(1 + \frac{R}{m}\right)^n$$

$$= \left(1 + \frac{0.1132}{360/90}\right)^4$$

$$= 1.1181$$

$$\text{Effective annual rate} = 1.1181 - 1$$

$$= 0.1181 \text{ or } 11.81\%$$

On the basis of compound interest the discount would be $1,215 and the discounted amount of principal would be $43,785, assuming monthly compounding, for example.

$$\text{Present value} = \$45,000\frac{1}{\left(1 + \frac{0.11}{12}\right)^3}$$

$$= \$45,000(0.9730)$$

$$= \$43,785$$

The effective annual rate for an annual discount rate of 11% based on compound interest with a monthly compounding frequency would be 11.57%.

$$1 + \text{Effective annual rate} = \left(1 + \frac{R}{m}\right)^n$$

$$= \left(1 + \frac{0.11}{12}\right)^{12}$$

$$= 1.1157$$

$$\text{Effective annual rate} = 1.1157 - 1$$

$$= 0.1157 \text{ or } 11.57\%$$

Assuming a quarterly compounding frequency, the discounted principal amount would be $43,796 and the effective annual rate would be 11.46%.

When simple discount is used with a given annual discount rate, the effective annual rate will increase as the discount period increases. This will occur because the adjusted annual discount rate will tend to become larger. However, when compound discount is used with a given annual discount rate, the effective annual rate will not change as the discount period changes so long as the compounding frequency remains the same.

With P in the equation $I = PRT$ as the par amount of principal and P in the equation $R = \frac{I}{PT}$ as the discounted amount of principal, these two equations can be combined with the ratio 365/360 to form an equation for calculating for simple interest the adjusted annual discount rate based on a 365-day year. For an annual discount rate of 11% and a maturity of 90 days, the equation would become

$$\frac{\text{Adjusted annual}}{\text{discount rate}} = \frac{(365)(\text{Annual discount rate})}{360 - (\text{Annual Discount Rate})(\text{Days to maturity})}$$

$$= \frac{(365)(0.11)}{(360) - (0.11)(90)}$$

$$= 0.1147 \text{ or } 11.47\%$$

(The rate of 11.47% would also be a bond or coupon equivalent yield.)

By substituting 360 days for 365 days in the previous equation, the adjusted annual discount rate for a 360-day year can be computed in one step instead of two steps as shown before.

$$\frac{\text{Adjusted annual}}{\text{discount rate}} = \frac{(360)(0.11)}{(360) - (0.11)(90)}$$

$$= 0.1131 \text{ or } 11.31\% \text{ (Rounding difference of } 0.01\%$$
$$\text{when compared with the}$$
$$\text{rate of } 11.32\%)$$

8 TAKE COMMAND OF INVESTMENTS BY KNOWING HOW TO EVALUATE FLOWS OF MONEY

In the previous chapter the focus was on determining the present value of a future lump sum payment or single amount of money. The primary thrust of the present chapter is the evaluation of a series of future payments or money flows in terms of present worth.

PRESENT VALUE OF A SERIES OF FUTURE PAYMENTS

The numbers in the fifth column of the compound interest tables are present values of payments that are to be forthcoming in the future. Each figure in Column 5 represents a series of n equal payments of one unit each to be made or to be received at the end of each period. The timing of the payments coincides with the compounding frequency.

Example—Finding the Present Value of a Series of Insurance Payments

Assume that a person contracts with an insurance company to receive $5,000 at the end of each year for the next five years. What amount of money would the person pay to the insurance company now if the earning rate on the contract is at the nominal annual interest rate of 8% compounded annually? (The periodic interest rate is $i = R/m = 0.08/1 = 0.08$.)

The objective is to find the present value of a stream of five annual receipts. This is the amount that will be given to the insurance company at the beginning of the first year as payment for the contract. The insurance company will then make five annual payments of $5,000 each to the

99

purchaser of the contract. For calculating purposes, it will be assumed initially that the five payments by the insurance company are to be $1.00 each.

The contract buyer will receive the first payment of $1.00 at the end of the first year, so the payment is discounted for one period.

The second payment of $1.00 is to be received at the end of the second year. Since the buyer has to wait two years from the beginning of the contract to receive this payment, it must be discounted for two periods.

The third payment is made by the insurance company at the end of year three. Accordingly, this payment is discounted for three years.

The fourth $1.00 payment occurs four years from the start of the contract and is discounted over four periods.

The buyer has to wait five years before receiving the fifth payment. This dollar is discounted for five periods. All discounting is done at the nominal annual rate of 8% compounded annually.

The summation of the discounted stream of $1.00 payments or receipts is given in the long-form equation below. The periodic interest rate is 8% since there is an annual compounding frequency. The present value (PV) equation would be

$$
\begin{aligned}
PV &= \frac{1}{(1+i)} + \frac{1}{(1+i)^2} + \frac{1}{(1+i)^3} + \frac{1}{(1+i)^4} + \frac{1}{(1+i)^5} \\
&= \frac{1}{(1+0.08)} + \frac{1}{(1+0.08)^2} + \frac{1}{(1+0.08)^3} + \frac{1}{(1+0.08)^4} \\
&\quad + \frac{1}{(1+0.08)^5} \\
&= \frac{1}{1.08} + \frac{1}{1.1664} + \frac{1}{1.2597} + \frac{1}{1.3605} + \frac{1}{1.4693} \\
&= 0.9259 + 0.8573 + 0.7938 + 0.7350 + 0.6806 \\
&= 3.9926
\end{aligned}
$$

The first payment of $1.00 has a discounted value of $0.9259. If $0.9259 is compounded for one period (one year in this case) at the effective peri-

Figure 8–1. Time Line.

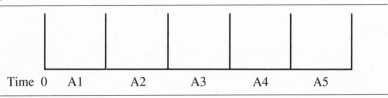

Time 0   A1   A2   A3   A4   A5

odic interest rate of 8%, an amount of $1.00 will be obtained. That is, ($0.9259)(1.08) = $1.00.

The second $1.00 payment has a present value of $0.8573, which is less than the present value of the initial payment ($0.9259). Because the wait for this payment is longer than that for the first payment, the buyer is not willing to pay as much at the start of the contract for the second receipt as for the first receipt. Note that if $0.8573 is compounded for two periods, it will have a future value of $1.00 (i.e., $0.8573 × 1.08^2 = $1.00).

The third receipt has a present value of $0.7938 whereas the fourth and fifth receipts have even lower present values of $0.7350 and $0.6806, respectively. The farther a payment is from the beginning of the contract, the lower its present value.

The third, fourth, and fifth payments will each total $1.00 when compounded over the appropriate number of periods.

$$(\$0.7938)(1.08)^3 = \$1.00$$
$$(\$0.7350)(1.08)^4 = \$1.00$$
$$(\$0.6806)(1.08)^5 = \$1.00$$

The five payments total $5.00. The buyer of the contract would be willing to pay almost $4.00 (actually, $3.9926) today in order to receive $5.00 worth of payments in the future. The difference between what the purchaser receives from the insurance contract and what the purchaser pays for the contract represents accumulated interest of $1.0074 ($5.00 minus $3.9926).

Since the present value of $1.00 payments equals $3.9926, the present value of $5,000 payments would be $19,963 ($5,000 times 3.9926). The buyer of the insurance contract would receive $25,000 (five payments of $5,000 each) after having paid $19,963 to purchase the contract. The accumulated interest earnings would amount to $5,037 ($25,000 minus $19,963).

USING COLUMN 4 VALUES TO OBTAIN COLUMN 5 VALUES: RELATING THE PRESENT VALUE OF A SERIES OF FUTURE PAYMENTS TO THE PRESENT VALUE OF A FUTURE LUMP SUM PAYMENT

For a given n in any of the compound interest tables, the Column 5 figure is a summation of the n Column 4 factors up to that point. In practice, it will be necessary to fill in any Column 4 entries that have been omitted in constructing the tables before doing the sum.

A consultation of Column 5 of the table for annual compounding shows that for $n = 5$ years the present value of a stream of $1.00 payments is 3.9927. This matches the figure of 3.9926 calculated in the preceding example. (The difference of 0.0001 is caused by rounding.)

The Column 5 present value figure of 3.9927 represents a total of the present values of the first five lump sum amounts contained in Column 4, which are 0.9259 ($n = 1$), 0.8573 ($n = 2$), 0.7938 ($n = 3$), 0.7350 ($n = 4$), and 0.6806 ($n = 5$). These are the same as the figures calculated earlier in arriving at the present value total of 3.9926.

Another look at the present value (PV) equation makes clear the point that Column 5 factors are a summation of Column 4 values.

$$PV = \frac{1}{(1 + i)} + \frac{1}{(1 + i)^2} + \frac{1}{(1 + i)^3} + \frac{1}{(1 + i)^4} + \frac{1}{(1 + i)^5}$$

The first term is the same as the Column 4 entry for $n = |:|V^1 = 1/(1 + i)$ (see Chapter 7). The second term matches $V^2 = 1/(1 + i)^2$ in Column 4 for $n = 2$. The third term corresponds to $V^3 = 1/(1 + i)^3$, the fourth term coincides with $V^4 = 1/(1 + i)^4$, and the fifth term is the same as $V^5 = 1/(1 + i)^5$. Therefore, the present value (PV) equation for $1.00 payments could be written as

$$PV = V^1 + V^2 + V^3 + V^4 + V^5$$

COLUMN 5 CONTRASTED WITH COLUMN 2: COMPARING THE PRESENT VALUE OF AN ANNUITY TO THE FUTURE VALUE OF AN ANNUITY

The discounting of payments in determining the present value of a stream of payments (Column 5 of the tables) may be contrasted with the compounding

Figure 8–2.   Time Line.

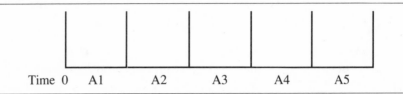

Time 0   A1   A2   A3   A4   A5

of payments in obtaining the future value of a stream of payments (Column 2 of the tables. See Chapter 6).

For payments of $1.00 each, the equations for the future value (FV) of Column 2 and the present value (PV) of Column 5 would be

$$FV = 1(1 + i)^4 + 1(1 + i)^3 + 1(1 + i)^2 + 1(1 + i) + 1$$

$$PV = (1)\frac{1}{(1 + i)} + (1)\frac{1}{(1 + i)^2} + (1)\frac{1}{(1 + i)^3} + (1)\frac{1}{(1 + i)^4}$$

$$+ (1)\frac{1}{(1 + i)^5}$$

The first term in the future value equation for Column 2 is $1(1 + i)^4$. The first payment is made at the end of the first period. The $1.00 payment is compounded over four periods, so it is multiplied by $(1 + i)^4$. The amount of compounding is determined by the amount of time between the payment and the end of the entire series of payments. In other words, the time interval over which compounding occurs spans the remaining life of the investment.

The initial term in the present value equation for Column 5 is $(1)1/(1 + i)$. The first payment of $1.00 occurs at the end of the first period and so it is discounted for only one period. The amount of discounting is governed by the amount of time between the payment and the start of the entire series of payments. Only one period is included in this first interval.

The second term in the future value equation for Column 2 is $1(1 + i)^3$. The second payment happens at the conclusion of the second period and gets compounded for three periods because there are three periods between the time the payment is made and the termination of the complete series of payments (end of the life of the investment).

The second term in the present value equation for Column 5 is $(1)1/(1 + i)^2$. The second payment occurs at the end of the second period. Since the discounting is governed by the amount of time between the payment and the beginning of the complete series of payments, the second term gets discounted over two periods.

Similar reasoning is applied to each of the remaining payments in both equations in order to determine how many times a particular payment is to be compounded (future value equation for Column 2) or by how much it is to be discounted (present value equation for Column 5). It may be remembered that it is the interval between the payment time and the time that an entire series of payments ends (the end of the last payment period) that governs the amount of compounding that a payment receives in the future value equation. The interval between the time of payment and the start of a complete series of payments determines the extent to which a payment is discounted in the present value equation.

CAPITAL BUDGETING

There are times when expenditures for plant equipment are predicated on an urgent need to make replacements because of breakdowns. In other instances a safety consideration may dictate spending for certain equipment. On most occasions, however, capital expenditures for plant and equipment are based on the expected contribution of the outlay to profitability.

Example — Estimating the Value of a Manufacturing Plant for Capital Budgeting Purposes

Assume that a company has an opportunity to purchase an existing manufacturing plant. The firm believes that the facility will be usable for another 10 years. It is felt that the plant can be run so as to generate a stabilized annual income of $120,000. Disregarding residual value, how much would the company be willing to pay now (i.e., what is the present value of this plant) if the company requires a yield of 8% per annum?

The compound interest tables can be used to find the present value of this stream of income. Column 5 for the table for annual compounding shows a figure of 6.7101 for $n = 10$ years. A stream of income of $1.00 per year for 10 years would have a present value of just over $6.71. For a plant that could generate $120,000 annually in income for ten years, the present value would be $805,212 (6.7101 times $120,000).

The company would be willing to pay about $805,000 for the purchase of the facility. By paying an amount greater than this, the firm would be earning a yield of less than 8% yearly. If the firm were able to secure the property for less than the calculated present value of $805,000, the return per year would exceed 8%.

Assuming a purchase price of approximately $805,000, the company would get an annual yield greater than 8% if the stabilized income actually turned out to be more than $120,000 per year. A realized annual income of less than the projected $120,000 would serve to reduce the yield below the annual level of 8%.

LEASING

Leasing usually involves a contract setting forth the responsibilities of the lessor (the party writing the lease) and the lessee (the party to whom the lease is given). Factors such as the lessee's current financial position, credit standing, and anticipated earning power are considered since both parties to the lease need to determine whether the lessee can service the periodic payments required by the contract. Column 5 of the compound interest tables can be used to determine the periodic payments necessary under a lease to satisfy a given rate of return for a given investment outlay.

Example—Seeking the Amount of the Monthly Payments Required by an Equipment Lease

Consider a case in which a lessor would have to pay $57,000 for a piece of equipment that could be leased to someone else over a five-year period. The equipment would be essentially worn-out at the end of five years and would have a negligible residual value. If the lessor requires an 8% annual rate of return, what would be the size of the lessee's level monthly payments?

A factor of 49.3184 is contained in Column 5 of the monthly compounding table for $n = 60$ months (five years) and a nominal annual rate of 8%. This means that 60 monthly payments of one unit each have a present value of 49.3184. The problem is to find the actual size x of 60 payments that will give a present value of $57,000. The division of $57,000 by 49.3184 gives $x = \$1,156$, which is the required size of the lessee's monthly payments. If monthly payments of less than $1,156 were agreed upon, the lessor's rate of return would drop below 8% on the outlay of $57,000.

Suppose that the lessee claimed to be unable to make monthly payments in excess of $1,000. If the lessor still wanted to meet the yield objective of 8%, a substitute piece of equipment whose cost did not exceed $49,318 ($1,000 times 49.3184) would have to be found.

FINANCING AN OIL DRILLING PROGRAM

Oil producers who have marginal production and who wish to do wildcat or highly speculative drilling usually must look to equity-type funds to support their drilling programs. In cases where an oil producer has reasonably stable production and desires to do further development drilling, the producer may find that a portion of expected future production can be pledged as a means of securing borrowed capital.

Example—Ascertaining the Present Worth of Future Oil Production Payments

Suppose that an oil producer wishes to generate cash so as to drill some new wells. The producer offers to sell to a potential financing party a portion of the income from monthly production over the next five years. Neglecting possible incentives tied to any future rise in oil prices, the lending party would get a monthly payment of $45,000. The payments would be discounted at an annual rate of 8% compounded monthly. How much cash will the oil producer get to drill the new wells if the transaction is completed?

For $n = 60$ months (5 years) and for a nominal annual rate of 8%, Column 5 of the monthly compounding table shows a factor of 49.3184 for monthly payments of $1.00. The present value of a monthly stream of $45,000 payments would be $2,219,328 (49.3184 times $45,000). This would be the amount of cash that the oil producer would receive from the financing party.

Over the 60-month period the lending party would receive $2,700,000 ($45,000 per month times 60 months). The $480,672 difference between the payment sum of $2,700,000 and the cash amount of $2,219,328 that the oil producer would receive represents the amount of interest that the producer would be paying.

PENSION OR RETIREMENT BENEFITS

There are wide varieties of pension and retirement programs. Even under the same plan the present values of the various alternatives may be different. The following discussion, although it cannot cover every case, will nevertheless enable a prospective retiree to understand better any retirement options that might be offered.

Example—Computing the Values of Various Pension or Retirement Alternatives

Column 5 (present value of an annuity) can be used as one means of deter- mining the size of payments to be made under a pension plan or retirement program. Assume that a company offers the option of early retirement to its employees at age 55 if they meet certain requirements. The firm provides several alternatives from which the employees may individually choose their pension or retirement benefits. All of the alternatives are based on the suppositions that the retiring employee will live to age 74 and that the interest rate will be taken as 8% per annum.

Suppose that under the conventional plan a retiring employee is entitled to receive monthly payments of $600 beginning at age 65 and continuing until the employee dies. However, the employee may select from among other alternatives for collecting benefits.

Assume that the present values of the other alternatives are keyed to the present value of the conventional plan. The first task would be to determine the present value of the conventional program. Because the supposition is made that the employee will live to age 74, the annuity will have an expected life of 108 months (9 years).

For $n = 108$ months and for a nominal annual rate of 8%, Column 5 of the monthly compound interest table shows a present value of 76.8125 for monthly payments of $1.00. Since the monthly payments are to be $600 instead of $1.00, the present value of the annuity is $46,088 (76.8125 times $600).

Suppose that one of the other retirement alternatives allows employees to take a lump sum in cash if they retire at age 55. (They would not receive any other payment besides the lump sum.) The single sum payment that each employee would get would be the present value of the conventional plan, which is $46,088.

Another retirement option might allow employees to receive monthly payments from age 55 to age 62, when they would qualify to receive early social security payments. The monthly payments under this program for 7 years would be $718.34. For monthly payments of $1.00, a nominal annual rate of 8%, and $n = 84$ months (7 years), Column 5 of the monthly compounding table shows a present value of 64.1593. If the actual present value of $46,088 is divided by the present value 64.1593, which is based on $1.00 monthly payments, the monthly payment amount of $718.34 is obtained. The assumption under this option is that payments from the retirement program would cease when the employee turned 62.

Still another retirement alternative might let the employee begin drawing monthly payments at age 55. The payments would continue until age 65, when the employee would qualify for regular social security payments. The employee would receive no further retirement payments after age 65. Under this program, monthly payments would be $559.17. Column 5 of the monthly compounding table reveals a present value of 82.4215 for 120 monthly payments of $1.00 at a nominal annual rate of 8%. By dividing the actual present value of $46,088 by the present value 82.4215, which is based on monthly payments of $1.00, the monthly payment sum of $559.17 is found.

Whereas present value represents one means by which retirement options might be compared, the total amount of funds payable under a plan would be another way.

If an employee were to die at the expected age of 74 under the conventional retirement plan, the total amount of funds paid out would be $64,800 ($600 per month for nine years). Should the employee live to age 80, for instance, the total retirement collection would be $108,000 ($600 per month for 15 years).

The option providing monthly payments of $718.34 for 7 years (age 55 to 62) would pay total retirement benefits of $60,341.

The alternative with a $559.17 monthly payment for 10 years (age 55 to age 65) would furnish a total payment sum of $67,100.

The total payment under the lump sum option would be equivalent to the option's present value of $46,088.

COLUMN 5 EQUATION: DETERMINING THE PRESENT VALUE OF A SERIES OF FUTURE PAYMENTS

There is a basic formula underlying the present values in Column 5, which eliminates the need to explicitly sum Column 4 figures. Recall the first example in this chapter, in which five payments are to be made on an insurance contract at the end of each of the next five years. Assuming an interest rate i, and payments of unit size, the present value of the contract was found to be

$$PV = \frac{1}{(1+i)} + \frac{1}{(1+i)^2} + \frac{1}{(1+i)^3} + \frac{1}{(1+i)^4} + \frac{1}{(1+i)^5}$$

Rearranging this equation as

$$PV = \frac{1}{(1+i)^5} + \frac{1}{(1+i)^4} + \frac{1}{(1+i)^3} + \frac{1}{(1+i)^2} + \frac{1}{(1+i)}$$

the result is a geometric progression of the form

$$S_n = a + ar + ar^2 + ar^3 + \ldots + ar^n$$

with progression ratio $r = (1 + i)$ and first term $a = 1/(1 + i)^5$. Remember (from Chapter 6) that the sum of such a series with n terms can be expressed as

$$S_n = \frac{ar^n - a}{r - 1}$$

Hence the present value equation can be written as

$$PV_5 = \frac{\frac{1}{(1+i)^5} \times (1 + i)^5 - \frac{1}{(1+i)^5}}{(1 + i) - 1}$$
$$= \frac{1 - \frac{1}{(1+i)^5}}{i}$$

Since the Column 4 value for $n = 5$ is $V^5 = 1/(1 + i)^5$, the equation becomes

$$PV_5 = \frac{1 - V^5}{i}$$

More generally, the present value of n periodic payments of one unit each (Column 5 of the compound interest tables) is represented by $a_{\overline{n}}$ (a angle n). The equation used to calculate Column 5 values is

$$a_{\overline{n}} = \frac{1 - V^n}{i}$$

or

$$a_{\overline{n}} = \frac{1 - \frac{1}{(1+i)^n}}{i}$$

where i is the periodic interest rate.

To verify the Column 5 formula, use it to calculate the present value of the insurance contract. Continue to assume that the five annual payments are $1.00 each. The nominal annual rate of interest is 8% compounded annually, so the periodic rate is $i = R/m = 0.08/1 = 0.08$. Hence

$$a_{\overline{n}|} = \frac{1 - \frac{1}{(1+i)^n}}{i}$$

$$= \frac{1 - \frac{1}{(1+0.08)^5}}{0.08}$$

$$= \frac{1 - 0.680583}{0.08}$$

$$= \frac{0.319417}{0.08}$$

$$= 3.9927$$

The present value of 3.9927 agrees with the value found for $n = 5$ in Column 5 of the table for annual compounding and also with the value found using the long form of the equation.

ANNUITIES (PRESENT VALUE)

Column 5 of the compound interest table contains figures that represent the present value of a series of periodic payments each of size one unit. Since the payments are assumed to occur at the end of each period, they constitute an ordinary annuity with level payments.

Keep in mind that the timing of the payments is the factor that distinguishes between the two main types of annuities. Both kinds of annuities involve a series of payments or receipts occurring at regular intervals. However, in an ordinary annuity (or annuity in arrears) the payments are made at the end of each period, whereas in an annuity due the payments occur at the beginning of each period.

To illustrate the difference between these two annuities, consider again the insurance contract with five annual payments of $1.00 each.

Figure 8–3.   Time Line.

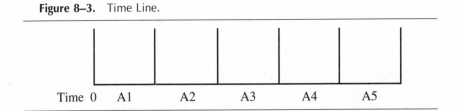

| Time 0 | A1 | A2 | A3 | A4 | A5 |

The present value (PV) of the stream of five payments made at the end of each year (the ordinary annuity) was expressed as follows for a periodic interest rate of 8%.

$$PV_o = \frac{1}{(1 + i)} + \frac{1}{(1 + i)^2} + \frac{1}{(1 + i)^3} + \frac{1}{(1 + i)^4} + \frac{1}{(1 + i)^5}$$

$$= \frac{1}{(1 + 0.08)} + \frac{1}{(1 + 0.08)^2} + \frac{1}{(1 + 0.08)^3} + \frac{1}{(1 + 0.08)^4}$$

$$+ \frac{1}{(1 + 0.08)^5}$$

$$= 0.9259 + 0.8573 + 0.7938 + 0.7350 + 0.6806$$

$$= 3.9926 \text{ (Ordinary Annuity)}$$

If the insurance company had instead agreed to make its payments at the beginning of each year, the stream of payments would be considered an annuity due and the present value would be

$$PV_d = 1 + \frac{1}{(1 + i)} + \frac{1}{(1 + i)^2} + \frac{1}{(1 + i)^3} + \frac{1}{(1 + i)^4}$$

$$= 1 + \frac{1}{(1 + 0.08)} + \frac{1}{(1 + 0.08)^2} + \frac{1}{(1 + 0.08)^3} + \frac{1}{(1 + 0.08)^4}$$

$$= 1 + 0.9259 + 0.8573 + 0.7938 + 0.7350$$

$$= 4.3120 \text{ (Annuity Due)}$$

The ordinary annuity has a present value of 3.9926, whereas the present value of the annuity due is 4.3120. Each term in the equation of the annuity due is larger than the corresponding term in the equation of the ordinary annuity because the annuity due payments are received earlier than the ordinary annuity payments. Therefore, all annuity due payments are discounted for one less period (for example, $(1 + i)^3$ is greater than $(1 + i)^2$, so $1/(1 + i)^2$ is larger than $1/(1 + i)^3$).

CONVERTING THE PRESENT VALUE OF AN ORDINARY ANNUITY TO THE PRESENT VALUE OF AN ANNUITY DUE

If the present value of an ordinary annuity is multiplied by the base $(1 + i)$, the present value of the corresponding annuity due is obtained. Thus, in the example, $(3.9926) \times (1.08) = 4.3120$.

For five annual insurance payments of $5,000 each (with the other conditions as given in the example), the present value of the ordinary annuity would be $19,963 ($5,000 times 3.9926). The present value of the annuity due would be $21,560 ($5,000 times 4.3120). The interest earned in the ordinary annuity is $5,037 ($25,000 minus $19,963), and the interest accumulated from the annuity due is $3,440 ($25,000 minus $21,560).

Example—Obtaining the Present Worth of a Series of Rental Payments (Ordinary Annuity and Annuity Due)

A retired couple pays their apartment rent for one year at the beginning of each year because they take frequent trips. The monthly rental rate is $690.

If the property owner discounts the early rental payments at an annual rate of 8% compounded monthly, what annual rental amount does the couple pay on January 1?

For $n = 12$ months, a factor of 11.4958 appears in Column 5 of the table with a nominal annual rate of 8% (monthly compounding). The multiplication of the monthly rental rate of $690 by the 11.4958 factor renders an amount of $7,932.

The quantity $7,932 is the present value of an ordinary annuity with equal payments ($690 each) occurring at the end of each month over a one-year period. If, however, the property owner requires that normal rental payments be made at the beginning rather than at the end of each month, then the ordinary annuity has to be converted or changed to an annuity due. This can be done by multiplying the ordinary annuity present value of $7,932 by the base $(1 + 0.08/12)$ to get $7,985. The couple would then have to pay $7,985 on January 1 for their year's rent.

ALTERNATE METHOD FOR CONVERTING THE PRESENT VALUE OF AN ORDINARY ANNUITY TO THE PRESENT VALUE OF AN ANNUITY DUE

An alternate method can be used to get the present value of an annuity due from the present value of an ordinary annuity. The alternate method of getting the present value of an annuity due of n payments is first to get, from the appropriate compounding table, the Column 5 value for $n - 1$ periods and then add one to this value. The resulting figure will be the present value of an annuity due of n payments, each of $1.00.

This alternative method can be demonstrated using the example of the five annual insurance payments of $1.00 each. The table for annual compounding lists, for $n = 4$ years (one less period than the number of payments), the Column 5 value 3.3121. If 1 is added to 3.3121, the total becomes 4.3121. This present value of the annuity due agrees with the value 4.3120 calculated twice before, using different methods. (The 0.0001 difference is due to rounding.)

CONVERTING THE PRESENT VALUE OF AN ANNUITY DUE TO THE PRESENT VALUE OF AN ORDINARY ANNUITY

If the present value of an annuity due is known, the present value of the corresponding ordinary annuity can be found by dividing the annuity due by the base $(1 + i)$. In the insurance example, 4.3120 is the present value of the annuity due and the base is 1.08. The division is $4.3120 \div 1.08 = 3.9926$, which is the present value of the ordinary annuity.

PRESENT VALUE OF A DEFERRED ANNUITY

A deferred annuity is an annuity in which the series of payments does not commence until after the expiration of a certain period of time. The present value can be calculated for a deferred annuity.

Suppose that a person will receive payments of $1,200 at the end of each of four years. However, the payments will be deferred for two annual periods (starting now). The first of the four payments will be made at the end of the third year. What is the present value of this deferred anuity, assuming a nominal annual rate of 8% compounded annually?

The payments will be deferred during the first two periods (A1 and A2). The payments will begin at the end of the third annual period (A3) and will continue through the end of year six (A6). The present value of

Figure 8–4.   Time Line.

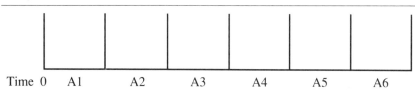

Time 0   A1   A2   A3   A4   A5   A6

the deferred annuity can be determined by finding the present value of an ordinary annuity for six years and then subtracting the present value of an ordinary annuity for two years.

According to Column 5 of the annual compounding table, the present value of an ordinary annuity of $1.00 payments for six years ($n = 6$) is 4.6229. This value includes annual payments at the ends of periods A1 through A6. For the present value of an ordinary annuity of $1.00 payments for two years ($n = 2$), Column 5 shows a figure of 1.7833. This value includes the two annual payments at the ends of A1 and A2. THe difference between the two present values is 2.8396 (4.6229 minus 1.7833).

The present value of the deferred annuity for $1.00 payments made at the ends of annual periods A3 through A6 is 2.8396. Since each of the four payments is actually $1,200, the present value of the deferred annuity is $3,407.52 (2.8396 times $1,200). Contrast the present value of an undeferred annuity of four annual payments of $1,200: from Column 5, $1,200 \times 3.3121 = 3,974.52$.

PRESENT VALUE OF A DEFERRED ANNUITY (ALTERNATE METHOD)

There is an alternative method for finding the present value of a deferred annuity. The first step is to find the present value of an ordinary annuity for the number of periods for which there are payments. Since there are four annual payments in our example, we look in Column 5 of the table for annual compounding and find that, for $n = 4$, the present value is 3.3121 for a series of payments of $1.00 each occurring at the end of annual periods A1 through A4.

The present value figure 3.3121, representing annual payments at the end of periods A1 through A4, has to be adjusted to reflect four annual payments made at the end of periods A3 through A6. The worth, or present value, of four payments made over periods A3 through A6 will be less than the worth of four payments made over periods A1 through A4 because of the delay involved in the receipt of the funds.

The shift from the interval A1–A4 to the interval A3–A6 can be accomplished by multiplying the A1–A4 present value factor 3.3121 by the present value of a lump sum of $1.00 to be received at the end of two years. In the annual compounding table, the present value of a lump sum for $n = 2$ is shown as 0.8573 in Column 4. The multiplication of 3.3121 by

0.8573 provides an adjusted present value factor of 2.8395. This figure differs (because of rounding) by only 0.0001 from the factor of 2.8396 computed by the first method.

Taking into account the fact that the payments are $1,200 each, the present value of an ordinary annuity of four annual payments deferred for two annual periods is $3,407.40 (2.8395 times $1,200). This figure compares with the value of $3,407.52 obtained using the first method. The difference of 0.0001 in the factors accounts for the 12-cent variation in the present values.

PRESENT VALUE OF AN ORDINARY ANNUITY WHEN THE COMPOUNDING IS MORE FREQUENT THAN THE PAYMENTS

In Chapter 6 is was shown that the future value of an annuity can be calculated from compound interest table values without adjustment when the compounding is more frequent than the payments. The present value of an annuity may also be computed using table factors without adjustment in instances where the compounding frequency exceeds the frequency of the payments.

Suppose that a one-year ordinary annuity has $1.00 semiannual payments and that the nominal annual interest rate is 8% compounded quarterly.

The present value of the ordinary annuity may be found by using the relationship PV_n/S_c where PV_n is the present value of an ordinary annuity having a total of n compounding periods and S_c is the future value of an ordinary annuity having c compounding periods per payment period.

Column 5 of the compound interest tables (quarterly compounding) shows a figure of 3.8077 where $n = 4$ and the nominal annual rate is 8%. This gives PV_n a value of 3.8077.

In the same table Column 2 contains a factor of 2.0200 for two quarterly periods and S_c takes on the value 2.0200.

The relationship PV_n/S_c becomes

$$PV_4/S_2 = 3.8077/2.0200$$
$$= 1.89$$

The present value of the annuity for $1.00 payments is $1.89.

The present value of a two-year ordinary annuity having $500 semiannual payments and quarterly compounding would amount to $1,813, computed as follows.

$$PV_8/S_2 = 7.3255/2.0200$$
$$= 3.626$$
$$(\$500)(3.626) = \$1,813$$

The discounting for this two-year annuity having four $500 semiannual payments and a quarterly interest rate of 2% (8% annual rate) would be as shown.

$$(\$500)\left(\frac{1}{1.02^2}\right) = \$481$$

$$(\$500)\left(\frac{1}{1.02^4}\right) = 462$$

$$(\$500)\left(\frac{1}{1.02^6}\right) = 444$$

$$(\$500)\left(\frac{1}{1.02^8}\right) = 427$$

Total $1,814
(rounding difference of $1)

PRESENT VALUE OF AN ANNUITY DUE WHEN THE COMPOUNDING IS MORE FREQUENT THAN THE PAYMENTS

A two-year annuity due has $500 semiannual payments, quarterly compounding, and a nominal annual interest rate of 8%. The computation of the present value of this annuity can be made by employing the relationship PV_n/PV_c where PV_n is the present value of an ordinary annuity having a total of n compounding periods and PV_c is the present value of an ordinary annuity with c compounding periods per payment period.

$$PV_8/PV_2 = 7.3255/1.9416$$
$$= 3.773$$
$$(\$500)(3.773) = \$1,887.$$

The discounting for the $500 semiannual payments is reflected in the following figures.

$$(\$500) \qquad\qquad = \$500$$

$$(\$500)\frac{1}{(1.02)^2} = \$481$$

$$(\$500)\frac{1}{(1.02)^4} = \ \ 462$$

$$(\$500)\frac{1}{(1.02)^6} = \ \ 444$$

Total $\$1,887$

9 ALL ABOUT BONDS—PREMIUM, DISCOUNT, AND PAR BONDS

The combination of a Column 5 value (present value of an ordinary annuity) and a Column 4 value (present value of a lump sum) from the compound interest tables can be used to compute the present value of a bond. A table for semiannual compounding is used since bonds generally have semiannual interest payments and semiannual compounding. Before looking at an example in which the compound interest tables are used in obtaining the present value of a bond, some general observations will be made concerning these securities. (Zero coupon bonds are discussed separately in Chapter 7.)

The present value or price of a bond usually depends upon the quantities in the stream of interest payments (determined by amount of principal and rate of interest) and the redemption price, as well as the length of this flow of benefits. The quality of the benefits is reflected in the yield to maturity, which in turn affects the present value of the security. The price of a bond in general thus becomes a composite of the factors of quantity, quality, and maturity. (See the discussion regarding par bonds and maturity.)

BASIS POINT

A basis point is $\frac{1}{100}$ of one percent, so that in an interval of one percent there are 100 basis points. A basis point measures absolute change, not relative change. If, for example, the yield on a bond were to increase from 10% to 10.75%, the percentage increase would be 7.5%. The absolute change would be three-fourths of one percent, or 75 basis points. If the yield on a bond moved from 9.41% to 9.64%, the absolute increase would amount to

119

23 basis points. A movement in yield from 11.36% to 10.22% would involve an absolute decline of 114 basis points.

TYPES OF BOND YIELDS

Bonds may have several yields. The coupon yield is the yield provided by the interest payments for one year based on the par or face value of the bond.

$$\text{coupon yield} = \frac{\text{annual interest income}}{\text{par value}}$$

The current yield, on the other hand, is based on the current market value.

$$\text{current yield} = \frac{\text{annual interest income}}{\text{present value}}$$

A bond with a face value of $100 and interest payments of $8 per year ($4 per semiannual period) would carry a coupon yield of 8%. If this bond is currently selling for $95 (95% of par or face value), the current yield would be 8.42% ($8 ÷ $95).

The yield to maturity of a bond takes into consideration bond discounts and bond premiums in addition to coupon payments (i.e., interest payments). If the purchase price of a bond is the same as the redemption price (that is, the price at which the issuer of the bond buys it back at maturity), the yield to maturity is equal to the coupon yield. In this case there would be no discount and no premium. If a bond is purchased at a price lower than the redemption value of the security, there is a discount, and the yield to maturity would exceed the coupon yield. A purchase price at a level greater than the redemption value of a bond indicates that there is a premium. In this instance the yield to maturity of the security would be less than the coupon yield.

BOND DISCOUNTS AND PREMIUMS

Why do bond discounts and bond premiums exist? Assume that a bond with an 8% coupon yield is sold by an issuer at its face value of 100. The redemption value is also 100. At the time of issue, the yield to maturity is the same as the coupon yield since the selling price is equivalent to the redemption price.

Assume further that after the subject bond is issued, the general level of interest rates rises so that newly issued securities having a life similar to the remaining life of the subject bond and having credit quality comparable to that of the given bond now carry coupon yields of, say, 10%. Other things being equal, investors are not going to buy the existing bond with an 8% coupon if they can purchase a newly issued security with a 10% coupon for the same money.

The holder of the existing bond, if wanting to sell before maturity, has to deivse a way to make this security as attractive as the securities being newly issued. One method of doing this is for the holder of the existing security to offer the bond at a discount price, that is, a selling price below the redemption price.

The discount (the difference between the redemption price and the selling price) is viewed as additional income by a buyer of the existing bond. This extra yield provided by the capital discount is prorated over the remaining life of the bond. Since the discount is added to the interest income, the yield to maturity (coupon yield plus the discount effect) will exceed the coupon yield.

The basic idea of capital discount allocation to interest may be illustrated by assuming that a 10-year $1,000 bond is selling for 90%of par, or $900. This debt obligation carries a coupon of 8%, which provides yearly interest of $80 to an investor. If the $100 discount were prorated over the life of the security, the annual increment assignable to interest would be $10, and the yearly combination of coupon interest and discount would be $90. (A bond premium of $100 would produce an annual interest decrement of $10.)

When the general level of interest rates rises, the prices investors will pay for existing bonds (those available in the secondary markets) decline. Premiums may be reduced or discounts may be produced or deepened, causing yields to maturity to increase. Conversely, when there is a decline in the general level of interest rates, the prices of existing bonds rise. As a result, discounts may be lessened, or premiums may be generated or increased. As this happens, yields to maturity decrease.

If an investor is holding an existing bond with an 11% coupon yield when the coupon on newly issued securities of comparable quality and maturity drops to 9%, the holder of the existing bond should be able to sell the bond prior to maturity at a premium. A new investor coming into the market to buy bonds would be willing to pay more for an existing bond with an 11% coupon than for a newly issued security with only a 9% coupon.

The premium of a bond (the excess of the purchase price over the redemption value) is prorated over the remaining life of the security. The capital premium serves to reduce interest income. Because of this, the yield to maturity (coupon yield minus the premium effect) of a premium bond will be less than its coupon yield.

In situations where the coupon yield and the yield to maturity are both known, the yield to maturity should be checked against the coupon yield. If the yield to maturity exceeds the coupon yield, the bond will be a discount bond since the discount will be enhancing the yield to maturity. Should the yield to maturity be lower than the coupon yield, then the security will be a premium bond because the premium will be penalizing the yield to maturity.

Example—Why Bond Prices Fall When Interest Rates Rise

It has been stated that as interest rates rise bond prices decline, and as interest rates decline bond prices rise. The reason for these inverse movements can be better understood by looking at the relationship between bond prices and bond yields in equation form.

$$PV = \frac{\text{Income}}{(1 + i)^n} + \frac{\text{Reversion}}{(1 + i)^n}$$

or

$$PV = \frac{rP + \text{Reversion}}{(1 + i)^n}$$

The present value (PV) is the current or present worth of a bond of face value P. (See Chapter 7 for an explanation of determining the present value of a lump sum to be paid in the future, and Chapter 8 for determining the present value of a series of future payments.) The periodic rate of interest (i) is the yield to maturity and it would reflect semiannual compounding. The annual coupon yield is $2r$, so the rP term is the amount of semiannual interest. The reversion is the redemption value of the bond.

For simplicity, take a case where there is one semiannual period, a present value that is 100% of the par value of $100, a semiannual income of $4 (annual coupon rate of 8% of par or face value), and a reversion of $100. The yield to maturity is found to be 8% per annum compounded semiannually.

$$PV = \frac{\text{Income}}{(1 + i)^n} + \frac{\text{Reversion}}{(1 + i)^n}$$

$$PV = \frac{rP + \text{Reversion}}{(1 + i)^n}$$

$$1 + i = \frac{rP + \text{Reversion}}{PV}$$

$$i = \frac{rP + \text{Reversion}}{PV} - 1 = \frac{\$4 + \$100}{\$100} - 1 = 0.04$$

annual yield to maturity $= 2i = 0.08$ or 8%

If the present value or price of the bond is 98% of par instead of 100% of par, the yield to maturity becomes 12.24%.

$$PV = \frac{\text{Income}}{(1 + i)^n} + \frac{\text{Reversion}}{(1 + i)^n}$$

$$i = \frac{rP + \text{Reversion}}{PV} - 1$$

$$= \frac{\$4 + \$100}{\$98} - 1 = 0.0612$$

annual yield to maturity $= 2i = 0.1224$ or 12.24%

Using a premium price of 102% of par, the bond yield drops to 3.92%.

$$PV = \frac{\text{Income}}{(1 + i)^n} + \frac{\text{Reversion}}{(1 + i)^n}$$

$$i = \frac{rP + \text{Reversion}}{PV} - 1$$

$$= \frac{\$4 + \$100}{\$102} - 1 = 0.0196$$

annual yield to maturity $= 2i = 0.0392$ or 3.92%

As can be seen in the equation

$$PV = \frac{\text{Income}}{(1 + i)^n} + \frac{\text{Reversion}}{(1 + i)^n}$$

there is a direct relationship between the price (present value) of a bond and the interest income (coupon rate) of the bond. As coupon income increases, bond price increases. As income decreases, bond price decreases. The same direct relationship exists between the price of a bond and the reversion.

There is an inverse relationship, however, between bond price and yield to maturity. As the yield to maturity increases, the price (present value) of a bond decreases. Conversely, as the yield to maturity declines, the bond price or present value rises.

As shown in the foregoing examples, a drop in price from 100 to 98 on an existing bond raises the annual yield to maturity on the bond from 8% to 12.24%. A rise in bond price from 100 to 102 causes the annual yield to maturity to fall from 8% to 3.92%. In the first instance the 2%bond discount causes the annual yield to maturity to change by 4.24%. In the second case the 2% bond premium results in an absolute change in the annual yield to maturity of 4.08%.

When the statement is made that bond prices rise when interest rates fall and bond prices decline when interest rates go up, the interest rate that changes in response to changes in the general level of interest rates is the yield to maturity.

Example — Calculating the Present Value of a Bond Selling at a Premium and Purchased on a Coupon Payment Date

Assume that a bond has a remaining maturity of 15 years and a coupon rate of 12%. If the bond is priced to provide a yield to maturity of 8% what is the price (present value) of the bond?

The bond has a coupon of 12%, which means that for each $100 of bond face value an interest amount of $12 is paid per year. Since semiannual payments are assumed, there are two interest payments per year of $6 each. At the time the given bond was issued, coupon yields for debt securities of similar quality and maturity were approximately 12%. At the present time, the market interest rate for this kind of bond has dropped to 8%. Since the 12% coupon is fixed, the price of the bond moves upward in order to reflect the downward movement in interest rates.

The subject bond will provide a semiannual interest payment of $6 for each $100 of bond face value over the next 30 semiannual periods (SA1 through SA30). In addition, at maturity (end of SA30) the issuer will pay the bondholder a lump sum redemption amount, or reversion, of 100%of the face value of the bond.

The present value of the given bond can be found with the aid of the compound interest table for semiannual compounding. First, the present value of an annuity of $1.00 for $n = 30$ semiannual periods is found in Column 5 to be 17.2920. (The table uses a nominal annual interest rate of 8%.) Since the bond's semiannual interest payments per $100 of face value are $6 rather than $1.00 each, 17.2920 is multiplied by $6 to obtain $103.75. This is the present value of the interest income for $100 of face value.

Figure 9–1   Time Line.

Time 0   SA1   SA2   SA3 – SA29   SA30

Second, the present value of a $1.00 lump sum reversion to be received after 30 semiannual periods is found in Column 4 to be 0.3083. To find the present value of a lump sum future payment of $100, the number 0.3083 is multiplied by $100 to get $30.83. This is the present value of the reversion for $100 of face value.

Finally, the present values of the income and the reversion are added together. The addition of $103.75 (step one) and $30.83 (step two) gives a total bond present value of $134.58 for $100 of face value.

The premium over the redemption value is $34.58 ($134.58 minus $100). The premium amount of $34.58 would be prorated over the 15-year (30 semiannual periods) remaining life of the bond, thereby diluting each period's coupon income. The premium serves to decrease the bond's yield from 12% to 8%.

The present value of a bond could also be obtained by consulting tables that list bond values per $100 of face value. The present value of $134.58 would appear in a column for a bond having a coupon of 12%, a yield to maturity of 8%, and a remaining life of 15 years.

For every $100 of par value the given bond would have a present value of $134.58. A bond with a face value of $1,000 would have a present value of $1,345.80 ($1,000 times 134.58%). At this price, bonds with a total face value of $750,000, for example, would be worth $1,009,350 ($750,000 times 1.3458).

The present value of a bond having a coupon of 12%, a yield to maturity of 8%, and a remaining life of 15 years can also be found using the formulas underlying Column 5 and Column 4 (see Chapters 7 and 8). The Column 5 formula would be used to get the present value of the interest income.

$$a_{\overline{n}} = \frac{1 - \frac{1}{(1+i)^n}}{i} = \frac{1 - \frac{1}{(1+R/m)^n}}{R/m}$$

$$a_{\overline{30}} = \frac{1 - \frac{1}{(1+0.08/2)^{30}}}{(0.08/2)}$$

$$= \frac{1 - 0.30832}{0.04}$$

$$= 17.2920$$

Then multiply 17.2920 by the actual amount of each semiannual coupon payment.

$$\text{present value of income} = \$6 \times 17.2920 = \$103.75$$

The Column 4 formula would be used to obtain the present value of the reversion.

$$V^n = \frac{1}{(1 + i)^n} = \frac{1}{(1 + R/m)^n}$$

$$V^{30} = \frac{1}{(1 + 0.08/2)^{30}}$$

$$= \frac{1}{3.2434}$$

$$= 0.3083$$

Multiply 0.3083 by the actual redemption value.

$$\text{present value of reversion} = \$100 \times 0.3083 = \$30.83$$

The total present value of a $100 face value bond would be $134.58 ($103.75 plus $30.83).

Example—Figuring the Present Value of a Bond Selling at a Discount and Purchased on a Coupon Payment Date

A bond is selling at a discount when the present value of the bond is below the redemption value. Assume that the coupon yield of a bond is 6%, the yield to maturity is 8%, and the remaining bond life is 15 years. It is anticipated that this debt security will be redeemed at maturity at its par value of $100. What is the price (present value) of the bond?

The same procedure used to find the present value of the premium bond will be used to determine the present value of this discount bond. From the semiannual compounding interest table for a nominal annual rate of 8%, a Column 5 value of 17.2920 is obtained for $n = 30$ semiannual periods. The factor 17.2920 is multiplied by $3, because the bond's semiannual interest payments per $100 of face value are $3 each. The product of $51.876 is the present value of the income payments over a 15-year period.

For $n = 30$, Column 4 of the semiannual compounding table for a nominal annual rate of 8% contains the number 0.3083. Since the redemption value of the bond is $100, the figure of 0.3083 is multiplied by $100. The product of $30.83 is the present value of the $100 redemption amount, which is to be received at the end of 15 years.

The present value of the income payments ($51.876) is added to the present value of the redemption amount ($30.83) to get the total present value of the bond ($82.71). The discount is $17.29 (redemption value of $100 minus the purchase price of $82.71). The discount would be prorated over the 15-year life of the bond. The discount would act to increase the bond's yield from 6% to 8%.

A bond with a face value of $100 would be priced at $82.71, which is 82.71% of par. Then for a $1,000 face value bond the price would be 82.71% of $1,000, or $827.10. For bonds amounting to $1,000,000, the present value would be 0.8271 times $1,000,000 or $827,100.

BONDS PURCHASED BETWEEN COUPON PAYMENT DATES

The foregoing examples of a discount bond and a premium bond were based on the assumption that the delivery date for the purchase of the securities occurred on an interest or coupon payment date. When the delivery date for the purchase of a bond takes place in the interval between coupon payment dates, some adjustment is made in computing the price of the security so as to give consideration to the accured interest. This point is illustrated in the following example.

Example—Computing the Price of a Bond Purchased between Coupon Payment Dates

As was done in the case of the discount bond example, assume that a bond has a coupon rate of 6%, a yield to maturity of 8%, and a par value and redemption value of $100. However, instead of assigning a 15-year remaining life to the bond, assume that the remaining maturity of this debt obligation is arbitrarily selected as being 15 years and 3 months.

Earlier it was found that a discount bond with a 15-year maturity had a present value of 82.71% of par, or $82.71 for a bond with a par value of $100. Thus the sum of $82.71 is the present value of the bond with a remaining term of 15 years and 3 months at its next coupon date, after the payment of the current period's interest.

Since the coupon rate is 6%, the accrued interest on this (corporate) bond for a full 6-month period will be $3.00. (Accrued interest on bonds is discussed in Chapter 2.)

$$
\begin{aligned}
I &= PRT \\
&= (\$100)(0.06)(180/360) \text{ or } (\$100)\frac{(0.06)}{2} \\
&= \$3.00
\end{aligned}
$$

This interest will be paid to the buyer of the bond at the next interest payment date. Adding $3.00 and $82.71 gives a total of $85.71.

Including the current period's coupon, the sum of $85.71 is the present value of the bond as of its next interest payment date. This amount is discounted for a 3-month period in order to obtain its value now. The discounting factor is 0.9806—that is, $1/(1 + 0.04)^{\frac{3}{6}} = 1/\sqrt{1.04} = 0.9806$. The discounting of $85.71 provides an amount of $84.05 (0.9806 × $85.71).

If the accrued interest that is owed to the bond seller is calculated for a 3-month period (the initial 3 months of the semiannual period preceding the next coupon date), the interest amount is found to be $1.50. The accrued interest of $1.50 belonging to the seller is deducted from the figure of $84.05 to obtain $82.55.

This residual amount of $82.55 is the price of a $100 bond having a coupon rate of 6%, a yield to maturity of 8%, and a remaining term of 15 years and 3 months.

Example—Comparison of Bonds (Premium, Discount, and Par)

Premium bonds have a purchase price that exceeds their redemption price. Discount bonds have a purchase price that is less than their redemption value. Par bonds are those bonds whose purchase price equals their redemption price. They have neither a premium nor a discount. (In practice, bonds having a slight premium or discount may still be referred to as par bonds by some persons.)

Compare the present values of par, discount, and premium bonds that all have the same yield to maturity but different coupon rates. Suppose that each bond has a remaining life of one year and a face value and a redemption value of $100.

Par Bond
   Yield to maturity 8%
   Coupon yield 8%

$$PV = \frac{4}{(1 + 0.04)} + \frac{4}{(1 + 0.04)^2} + \frac{100}{(1 + 0.04)^2}$$
$$= 3.8462 + 3.6982 + 92.4556$$
$$= 100 = \text{present value}$$

Discount Bond
   Yield to maturity 8%
   Coupon yield 6%

$$PV = \frac{3}{(1 + 0.04)} + \frac{3}{(1 + 0.04)^2} + \frac{100}{(1 + 0.04)^2}$$
$$= 2.8846 + 2.7737 + 92.4556$$
$$= 98.1139 = \text{present value}$$

Premium Bond
   Yield to maturity 8%
   Coupon yield 10%

$$PV = \frac{5}{(1 + 0.04)} + \frac{5}{(1 + 0.04)^2} + \frac{100}{(1 + 0.04)^2}$$
$$= 4.8077 + 4.6228 + 92.4556$$
$$= 101.8861 = \text{present value}$$

The investor who buys the par bond above receives a yield to maturity of 8% and a current yield of 8% ($8 interest income per year ÷ the current price of $100). The discount bond also provides a yield to maturity of 8%, but only furnishes a current yield of 6.12% ($6 ÷ $98.1139). A purchase of the premium bond would give a yield to maturity of 8% as well, but the current yield would amount to 9.81% ($10 ÷ $101.8861).

INFLUENCE OF INCOME TAX LAWS ON BONDS

Different investors may have different investment needs and objectives. Coupled with this thought is the fact that income tax consequences may influence an investor's decisions. American investors who operate outside of the United States may find that tax laws in other countries differ from those that exist here. Another complication is that fact that taxation laws have a way of changing over time.

In the preceding bond examples, each of the three securities would provide an investor with the same yield to maturity. However, if an investor wanted as much current income as possible, the premium bond would be chosen. It is noted that its current yield (9.81%) exceeds the current yield of either the par bond (8%) or the discount bond (6.12%).

Income tax laws commonly apply lower tax rates to capital gains than to ordinary income. For individual investors, income tax laws usually require that their interest income be treated as ordinary income. Where a difference in tax treatment exists between capital items and ordinary items, ordinary income such as interest income is relatively more attractive to lower tax bracket investors than to those in higher tax brackets. Investors who are subject to higher tax rates tend to focus more on capital gains than on ordinary income in cases where capital gains are accorded more favorable treatment by the tax laws.

An investor who is willing to take part of a return in the form of a capital gain would opt for buying the discount bond if intending to keep it to maturity. The investor's gain in this case, disregarding transaction and other related costs, would be the difference between the redemption price (100) and the purchase price (98.1139). Neither the par bond nor the premium bond would provide an opportunity for taking a capital gain if the intent were to hold either bond to maturity. On the other hand, if the tax laws were to require that the discount be amortized and treated as ordinary income over the remaining life of the bond, then the motive of buying the discount bond so as to capture a favorably treated capital gain would no longer exist.

For an investor purchasing the premium bond, income tax laws might provide alternatives. One option might be for the laws to allow the investor to record a loss (usually a capital one) when submitting the bond for redemption at maturity. The loss, exluding related costs, would be the difference between the purchase price (101.8861) and the redemption price (100).

Another possibility might be for the tax laws to permit the investor to amortize the bond's premium as an ordinary loss over the remaining life of the security. From an individual taxpayer's standpoint, it is generally better to have an ordinary loss than a capital loss. If the tax rates on ordinary income happen to be greater than the tax rates on capital gains, then a dollar of offsetting ordinary loss would save the taxpayer more money than a dollar of offsetting capital loss. In addition, there may be times when the tax laws might limit the amount of capital loss that can be used effectively in any one year while not restricting the use of ordinary losses.

An investor may elect to sell a discount bond or a premium bond before maturity. If this is done, the redemption price of the security will not be of any consequence in determining gain or loss. If the discount bond is sold at a price below the purchase price of 98.1139, the investor will record a loss on the transaction. Disregarding the possibility of discount amortization, the sale of the discount bond above the purchase price of 98.1139 would result in a gain.

Since the premium bond carries a purchase price of 101.8861, the sale of the security in excess of that price would give the investor a gain. Without concern for any possible premium amortization, the sale of the bond below the purchase price would result in a loss.

BEHAVIOR OF PAR BOND PRESENT VALUE

When a bond's yield to maturity is equivalent to its coupon yield, the present value (purchase price) of the security is equal to the redemption price at maturity. In this case the par bond's present value will not change as the life of the bond is allowed to increase. Although the lengthening of the maturity provides additional amounts of coupon income which tend to increase the present value of the bond, this increase is offset by a similar amount of decrease in the present value of the bond reversion, or lump sum redemption amount.

Example—Finding Par Bond Present Values as Maturity Increases

The increase in coupon income present values as maturity increases and offsetting decrease in reversion present values is demonstrated for a bond in the following examples. Assume that a bond has a coupon yield of 8% ($4 per semiannual period for each $100 of bond face value). The yield to maturity is 8% (4% per semiannual period). The redemption price of the bond is 100, and suppose initially that the security has a life of one semiannual period. The present value (PV) of the bond may be calculated as follows.

$$
\begin{aligned}
PV_1 &= \frac{4}{(1 + 0.04)} + \frac{100}{(1 + 0.04)} \\
&= 4(0.9615) + 100(0.9615) \\
&= 3.8460 + 96.15 \\
&= 100
\end{aligned}
$$

Consider what happens if the life of the bond is now increased to one year (two semiannual periods), with the other bond terms unchanged. The present value (PV) would be

$$
\begin{aligned}
PV_2 &= \frac{4}{(1 + 0.04)} + \frac{4}{(1 + 0.04)^2} + \frac{100}{(1 + 0.04)^2} \\
&= 4(0.9615) + 4(0.9246) + 100(0.9246) \\
&= 3.8460 + 3.6984 + 92.46 \\
&= 100
\end{aligned}
$$

The increase in the maturity of the bond from one period to two semiannual periods does not change the present value of the bond. The additional coupon income of 3.6984 is offset by the drop in the present value of the redemption amount from 96.15 to 92.46 (a difference of 3.69). There is a slight difference in 3.6984 and 3.69 because of rounding.

Allow the life of the bond to be expanded to 1.5 years, or three semi-annual periods, again without changing the other bond terms. The present value (PV) becomes

$$PV_3 = \frac{4}{(1 + 0.04)} + \frac{4}{(1 + 0.04)^2} + \frac{4}{(1 + 0.04)^3} + \frac{100}{(1 + 0.04)^3}$$
$$= 4(0.9615) + 4(0.9246) + 4(0.8890) + 100(0.8890)$$
$$= 3.8460 + 3.6984 + 3.5560 + 88.90$$
$$= 100$$

As a result of increasing the life of the bond by one semiannual period, the coupon income is increased by the interest payment of 3.5560 in the third period. However, the present value of the redemption amount or reversion drops from 92.46 to 88.90 (a decrease of 3.56), thereby offsetting the 3.5560 (or 3.56) increase in the present value of the coupon income. The present value of the total stream of income plus the reversion still amounts to 100.

If the extension of the life of the bond were continued, the present value of the bond would not change so long as the yield to maturity remained equal to the coupon yield. The additional present value generated by coupon income would continue to be offset by the reduction in the present value of the redemption amount or reversion.

Looking at the same situation from a different viewpoint, when the redemption value of a bond is equal to the present value or purchase price of the bond, the coupon yield will be equal to the yield to maturity. The present value of such a bond having a maturity of a finite number of periods can be found by dividing the periodic income (rP) by the periodic interest rate (i). For a bond with a face value of \$100, a coupon yield of 4% per semiannual period, and a yield to maturity per semiannual period of 4%, the present value (PV) would be

$$PV = \frac{rP}{i} = \frac{(0.04)(100)}{0.04} = \frac{4}{0.04} = 100$$

PERPETUITIES

If a stream of equal payments is going to be paid or received at equal intervals for an indefinite time (forever), the flow of payments or receipts is known as a perpetuity. The present value (PV) of this annuity can be found using the relationship

$$PV = \frac{\text{Coupon yield} \times \text{Face value}}{\text{Yield}}$$

Example—Computing the Present Value of a Perpetuity

Assume that a bond with a $100 face value has annual coupon payments of $6 (6%) and a yield of 4%. The bond has an indefinite life (forever). What is the present value of this perpetuity?

$$PV = \frac{\text{Coupon}}{\text{Yield}}$$
$$= \frac{\$6}{0.04}$$
$$= \$150$$

On the basis of semiannual quantities, the present value of the perpetuity would still be 150. Consider the following computation.

$$PV = \frac{\text{Coupon}}{\text{Yield}}$$
$$= \frac{\$3}{0.02}$$
$$= \$150$$

For an annuity having semiannual interest payments of $3 and a semiannual interest rate of 2%, the present value of the payments and the present value of a $100 reversion would be as shown below.

Number of Semiannual Periods	Present Value of Interest Payments	Present Value of Reversion
700	$149.9998568	$0.0000955
800	$149.9999802	$0.0000132
900	$149.9999973	$0.0000018
1,000	$149.9999996	$0.0000003

It can be seen that as the income stream is lengthened the present value of the interest payments approaches $150. As the reversion is placed farther out into the future, its present value decreases toward zero. For example, at the end of 500 years (1,000 semiannual periods), a $100 reversion has a present value of $3 × 10^{-7}, which is very much less than one cent.

BEHAVIOR OF DISCOUNT BOND PRESENT VALUE

Although it has been shown that for a given coupon rate and a given yield to maturity the present value (PV) of a par bond does not change as the maturity is increased, the same is not true of a discount bond. As the maturity increases for a given coupon rate and a given yield to maturity, the present value of a discount bond decreases.

Example — Determining Discount Bond Present Values as Maturity Increases

Consider the following example, in which a $100 discount bond has a coupon rate of 8% and a yield to maturity of 9%. For a life of one semiannual period the bond has a present value of $99.52, calculated as follows.

$$PV = \frac{\$4}{(1 + .045)} + \frac{\$100}{(1 + .045)}$$
$$= \$3.83 + \$95.69$$
$$= \$99.52$$

Allow the maturity of the bond to be increased to two semiannual periods.

$$PV = \frac{\$4}{(1 + .045)} + \frac{\$4}{(1 + .045)^2} + \frac{\$100}{(1 + .045)^2}$$
$$= \$3.83 + \$3.66 + \$91.57$$
$$= \$99.06$$

The present value of the bond declines from $99.52 to $99.06. Although there is an increase of $3.66 in the stream of interest payments, there is a drop of $4.12 in the value of the reversion, causing a net decline of $0.46 in the total present value of the security.

In the following calculation the maturity of the discount bond is lengthened to three semiannual periods.

$$PV = \frac{\$4}{(1 + .045)} + \frac{\$4}{(1 + .045)^2} + \frac{\$4}{(1 + .045)^3} + \frac{\$100}{(1 + .045)^3}$$
$$= \$3.83 + \$3.66 + \$3.51 + \$87.63$$
$$= \$98.63$$

The decline of $3.94 in the present value of the reversion is greater than the increase of $3.51 in the present value of the income stream, so the present value of the bond drops another $0.43.

As the maturity of the discount bond continues to increase, the present value of the security will continue to drop. This will occur because the decline in the value of the reversion will continue to exceed the increase in the value of the income stream brought about by the additional coupon payments.

BEHAVIOR OF PREMIUM BOND PRESENT VALUE

Unlike a discount bond, the present value (PV) of a premium bond increases as maturity increases for a given coupon rate and a given yield to maturity. The behavior of a premium bond's present value is examined in the following example.

Example—Figuring Premium Bond Present Values as Maturity Increases

The supposition is made in this example that a $100 premium bond has a coupon rate of 8% and a yield to maturity of 7%. The premium bond has a maturity of one semiannual period and a present value of $100.48, calculated as follows.

$$PV = \frac{\$4}{(1 + .035)} + \frac{\$100}{(1 + .035)}$$
$$= \$3.86 + \$96.62$$
$$= \$100.48$$

When the maturity of the premium bond is extended to two semiannual periods, the computation becomes

$$PV = \frac{\$4}{(1 + .035)} + \frac{\$4}{(1 + .035)^2} + \frac{\$100}{(1 + .035)^2}$$
$$= \$3.86 + \$3.73 + \$93.35$$
$$= \$100.94$$

Although the present value of the reversion declines $3.27, the increase in the income stream due to an additional interest payment ($3.73) is enough to raise the present value of the bond by $0.46 to $100.94.

The following computation is based on a maturity of three semiannual periods.

$$PV = \frac{\$4}{(1 + .035)} + \frac{\$4}{(1 + .035)^2} + \frac{\$4}{(1 + .035)^3} + \frac{\$100}{(1 + .035)^3}$$
$$= \$3.86 + \$3.73 + \$3.61 + \$90.19$$
$$= \$101.39$$

The present value of the security rises by $0.45 because the decline in the present value of the reversion of $3.16 is outpaced by the addition of $3.61 to the income stream.

The continued extension of the premium bond's maturity will result in additional increments to the total present value of the security. This will be the case because the increase in the present value of the coupon payments will continue to exceed the drop in the present value of the reversion.

REINVESTMENT OF BOND COUPON PAYMENTS

As coupon payments are received, the bondholder has the option of spending the interest payments or reinvesting them. If the payments are spent, the investor's income from coupon reinvestment is zero. For a bondholder who reinvests the interest receipts, the additional income generated from the reinvestment process depends upon the reinvestment rate.

Take the case of a bondholder who owns a security with a coupon yield of 8%, a yield to maturity of 8%, and a maturity of 10 years. This investor will receive semiannual payments of $4 per $100 of bond face value for 20 semiannual periods. The total return from the reinvestment of the $4 coupon payments can be found by treating the payments as the amount of an annuity. If the reinvestment rate is also 8%, the compound interest table for a nominal annual rate of 8%and a semiannual compounding frequency can be consulted. Column 2 shows that an annuity of $1.00 payments over 20 semiannual periods (10 years) has a future value of 29.7781. For a series of $4 payments, the total return would be $119.11 ($4 times 29.7781). Of this total, $80 ($4 times 20 semiannual periods) represents the amount of coupon income that is reinvested, and $39.11 ($119.11 minus $80) represents the interest earned on the reinvestment of coupon payments (interest on interest).

This bond situation may be thought of as a two-account arrangement. In one account is the $100 of bond face value or principal, which earns interest at the nominal annual rate of 8%. As the interest payments of $4 are received at the end of each semiannual period, they are placed in a second account.

The second account represents an investment or savings arrangement that is outside of the original bond investment. The life of this savings arrangement begins when the first bond interest payment is received and ends when the last bond interest payment is made. In this second account each interest payment is allowed to earn interest at the nominal annual rate of 8% compounded semiannually over whatever remaining life the savings arrangement has after each individual payment is received.

The yield to maturity for the bond under discussion is 8% per year, which is the same as the annual coupon rate. Because the coupon rate is equal to the yield to maturity, there is no bond premium or bond discount. This security is a par bond. If this investment instrument had been a premium bond or a discount bond, the yield to maturity would have been less than or more than the coupon rate. Although the reinvestment rate for this par bond was allowed to be the same as the yield to maturity, a different reinvestment rate could have been selected.

Example—Comparison of External Bond Coupon Reinvestment with Internal Compounding

Rather than investing $100 in a 10-year bond where the interest payments paid out by the issuer have to be reinvested externally on a semiannual basis by the bondholder (lender), assume that $100 is put into a savings arrangement for 10 years where the unpaid semiannual interest payments are reinvested for the lender internally (within the original investment). Assume that the funds earn interest at the nominal annual rate of 8% compounded semiannually.

Column 1 of the compound interest tables can be used to find the total amount of the investment, which includes the principal, the interest on principal, and the interest on interest for the savings arrangement. The future value of the investment after n semiannual periods would be (see Chapter 5)

$$S = \text{Principal} + \text{Interest on Principal} + \text{Interest on Interest}$$
$$= P(1 + i)^n = P(1 + R/m)^n$$

Under the conditions in this example, the amount would be

$$S = \$100(1 + 0.08/2)^{20}$$
$$= \$219.11$$

The Column 1 factor for semiannual compounding and $n = 20$ periods would be 2.1911 for an initial investment of $1.00. For an investment of $100 the total growth amount would be $219.11 ($100 times 2.1911). The amount of interest on principal plus interest on interest would be $119.11 ($219.11 minus $100). The interest on principal is $80 ($4 per semiannual period for 20 periods). The interest on interest would come to $39.11 ($119.11 minus $80).

It may be seen that the total amount ($119.11) of interest on principal plus interest on interest obtained for this savings arrangement is the same as the figure for interest on principal plus interest on interest found for the reinvestment of interest payments of a 10-year par bond with a yield to maturity of 8% and a coupon rate of 8%.

Example—Handling a Bond Reinvestment Rate That Differs from the Yield to Maturity (Par Bond)

The reinvestment rate of a bond may be assumed to be the same as or different from the yield to maturity. When the supposition is made that the reinvestment rate is different from the yield to maturity, the nominal annual rate of the bond is modified. The modified rate can be determined as outlined below.

Suppose that a 10-year bond has a yield to maturity of 8%, a coupon rate of 8%, and a reinvestment rate of 6%. What would be the total future value of a $100 face value bond, and what would be the modified nominal annual interest rate?

The semiannual interest payments of $4 would amount to $80 over the 20 semiannual periods. As each payment is received, it is reinvested at 6%, compounded semiannually. The future value of such an annuity of 20 payments of $1.00 each would be 26.8704 (see Chapter 6). For interest payments of $4 each, the interest on principal plus the interest on interest amounts to $107.48. Since the interest on principal is $80, the interest on interest is $27.48. The total future value for the sum of principal, interest on principal, and interest on interest is $207.48 ($100 + $80 + $27.48) per $100 of bond face value. For $1.00 of bond face value, the total future value is $2.0748.

The computation of the modified nominal annual interest rate is as follows.

$$(1 + R/m)^n = S$$
$$(1 + R/2)^{20} = 2.0748$$
$$20 log(1 + R/2) = log 2.0748$$
$$= 0.31698 (\text{from logarithm tables})$$
$$= 0.31698/20$$
$$= 0.01585$$
$$1 + R/2 = \text{antilog } 0.01585$$
$$1 + R/2 = 1.0372 (\text{from logarithm tables})$$
$$R = 0.0744, or 7.44\%$$

The yield to maturity of 8% and the reinvestment rate of 6% produce a modified nominal annual interest rate of 7.44%.

Example—Verifying the Modified Nominal Annual Rate (Par Bond)

If a 10-year bond with a face value of $100 is given a coupon rate, a yield to maturity, and a reinvestment rate of 7.44%, the sum of the prinicipal, interest on principal, and interest on interest can be calculated. The semi-annual interest payments of $3.72 for 20 semiannual periods would amount to $74.40. The future value of 20 semiannual payments of $1.00 each, with an interest rate of 7.44%, would be 28.92766. Therefore, the total amount of interest on principal and interest on interest for $3.72 semiannual interest payments would be $107.61 ($3.72 times 28.92766). The interest on interest would be $33.21 ($107.61 minus $74.40). For the $100 bond, the sum of principal, interest on principal, and interest on interest would be $207.61 ($100 + $74.40 + $33.21). This sum compares well with the total ($207.48) obtained earlier for a 10-year $100-face value bond having a yield to maturity of 8% and a reinvestment rate of 6%. The totals should be the same, but there is a slight difference of 13 cents due to rounding.

The modified nominal annual rate of 7.44% has been found for a bond that has a coupon yield of 8% equal to the yield to maturity of 8%, indicating that there is no discount and no premium. The modified rate for a discount bond will now be examined.

Example—Obtaining the Modified Nominal Annual Rate for a Discount Bond

Suppose that a $100-face value bond with a 10-year maturity has a coupon rate of 9%. Let the bond sell for the discount price of 93.77% of par, so that the yield to maturity is 10%. Allow the reinvestment rate to be 8%.

The interest payments of $4.50 per semiannual period total $90 at the end of 20 periods. The table for a nominal annual rate of 8%(reinvestment rate) and semiannual compounding has a Column 2 factor of 29.7781 for $n = 20$. The multiplication of $4.50 by 29.7781 provides a total of $134.00 as interest on principal and interest on interest. Since interest on principal is $90, interest on interest is $44.

For a bond with a $100 face value, the sum of the principal (reversion), interest on principal, and interest on interest is $234 at the end of 10 years. For each dollar of bond face value, the sum of these three components is $2.34.

A modified rate for this discount bond can be found by solving for R:

$$P(1 + R/m)^n = S$$
$$\$93.77(1 + r/2)^{20} = \$234$$
$$(1 + R/2)^{20} = \$234/\$93.77$$
$$= 2.4955$$

When this equation is solved for R, using logarithms as before, it is found that for this discount bond the modified nominal annual interest rate $R = 9.36\%$.

Example — Determining the Modified Nominal Annual Rate for a Premium Bond

If a modified rate (R) were being sought for a premium bond, the premium would be reflected in the initial principal amount (P) just as the discount was handled for the discount bond. Assuming a bond maturity of 10 years, a coupon rate of 9%, a yield to maturity of 8.4% (which implies a bond price of 104.01% of $100 par value), and a reinvestment rate of 8%, the equation $P(1 + R/m)^n = S$ per dollar of bond value would become

$$1.0401(1 + R/2)^20 = 2.34$$
$$(1 + R/2)^20 = 2.34/1.0401$$
$$= 2.2498$$

When this last equation is solved (using logarithms) for R, the modified rate of the premium bond turns out to be 8.28%. As would be expected, the modified rate rests between the yield to maturity of 8.4% and the reinvestment rate of 8%.

VOLATILITY OF BOND PRICES

For a given change in yield to maturity, bond prices (present values) usually exhibit increased amounts of change, or volatility, as the coupon yield decreases and as the maturity increases. Both of these effects will be investigated. The behavior of changes in bond prices as the coupon yield decreases will be examined first.

Bond Price Volatility as Coupon Yield Decreases

At a given yield to maturity and a given bond maturity, the total present value (price) of a bond is equal to the present value of the interest payments plus the present value of the reversion, or redemption value. The ratio (expressed as a percent) of the present value of the interest payments to the total present value of the bond, plus the ratio (expresssed as a percent) of the present value of the reversion to the total present value of the bond is equal to 100%.

As the coupon yield decreases, the ratio of the present value of the interest payments to the total present value of the bond will decrease while the ratio of the present value of the reversion to the total present value of the bond will increase. As the interest payments become relatively less important in determining the total present value (price) of a bond, the reversion becomes relatively more important in the determination of the bond's price.

As the coupon yield decreases, the amount received from interest payments will decrease. If the reversion and maturity are fixed, this causes the total present value of the bond to decrease. For a bond with a zero% coupon the present value of interest payments will be zero. In this case the total present value of the bond will be represented by the present value of the reversion or redemption amounts. (See Chapter 7 for a discussion of zero coupon bonds.)

Compare a bond with a 14% coupon and a bond with a 2% coupon. Suppose that both securities have a maturity of 15 years and the yield to maturity for both bonds changes from 10% to 12%. The redemption value of each bond is $100.

As the yield to maturity increases on the bond with the 14% coupon and on the bond with the 2% coupon, the total present value of the bonds declines by 13% and 19%, respectively. The percentage decline (24.8%) in the present value of the reversion of both bonds is greater than the percentage decline (10.5%) in the present value of the interest payments of both bonds.

At a yield to maturity of 10%, the present value of the interest payments accounts for 82.3% of the 14%-coupon bond's total present value. The present value of the reversion is responsible for the remaining 17.7% of this bond's total present value.

At the same yield to maturity of 10%, the present value of the interest payments constitutes only 39.9% of the total present value of the bond with the 2% coupon. The remaining 60.1% of this bond's total present value is accounted for by the present value of the reversion, or redemption amount.

The reversion is relatively more important in the case of the security with the 2% coupon than the security with the 14% coupon (60.1% of total present value versus 17.7% of total present value). Also, the reversion of the 2%-coupon bond is more volatile than this bond's stream of interest payments (a 24.8% decline in reversion present value versus a 10.5% decline in interest present value for a change in yield to maturity from 10% to 12%). Because the reversion is relatively more important in the case of the lower coupon bond and because the reversion of this bond is more volatile than its stream of interest payments, the total present value (price) of the 2% bond experiences greater volatility than does the total present value of the 14% bond as the yield to maturity changes.

Recall that a rise in yield to maturity from 10% to 12% causes a 19% price decline for the 2%-coupon security and a 13% price decline for the 14%-coupon security. If the yield to maturity for both bonds is allowed to drop from 12% to 10%, the price of the 2%-coupon bond would go up 23.5% whereas the price of the 14%-coupon bond would increase 14.9%.

Bond Price Volatility as Maturity Increases

As the maturity of a bond increases, the volatility of the price of the bond in response to a change in the yield to maturity also tends to increase. First assess the behavior of a single bond so as to understand better the value changes that occur as the maturity and the yield to maturity increase for a bond with a given reversion (100) and a given coupon. After this is done, price changes for additional maturities will be viewed.

Consider that a bond with a coupon of 9% has its maturity increased from 10 years to 15 years while its yield to maturity is increased from 10% to 12%. As these increases are effected, the total present value (price) of the bond drops 15.4%. Although the present value of the interest payments increases 10.4%, the present value of the reversion undergoes a 53.8% decline. The ratio of the present value of the reversion to the total present value of the bond decreases from 40.2% to 21.9%. The ratio of the present value of the interest payments to the total present value of the bond increases from 59.8%to 78.1%.

The present values of interest payments and reversion each account for roughly half of the bond's total present value prior to the increases in maturity and the yield to maturity. The drop of 53.8% in the present value of the reversion after the increases have occurred constrasts sharply with the increase of 10.4% in the present value of the interest payments after the increases in maturity and the yield to maturity have taken place.

As the maturity of a bond increases, the increased number of interest payments serves to increase the total present value of these payments. However, the impact of each additional coupon payment is less than that of the preceding payment. This happens because the present value of a lump sum decreases with an increase in the amount of time that it takes to make or to receive the payment.

The same effect applies to the redemption amount as the maturity of the bond is extended. The reversion is pushed farther out into the future, causing its present value to become smaller. The change in the reversion impacts the total present value of the bond more and causes it to undergo a drop of 15.4%.

Some price changes are given in Table 9–1 at various maturities for a bond with a reversion of 100 and a coupon of 9%, as the security's yield to maturity moves from 10% to 12%. As an example, the first entry shows that when the subject bond is assigned a maturity of 5 years, the price of the bond drops 7.47% as the yield to maturity rises from 10% to 12%. For the same change in yield to maturity, the bond declines 15.97% in price when the security is given a maturity of 25 years.

The price increases for the same 9%-coupon bond are given in Table 9–2 for different maturities as the yield to maturity falls from 12% to 10%.

Table 9–1. Price Changes for a 9%-Coupon Bond as Yield to Maturity Increases (from 10% to 12%).

Maturity of Bond	Change in Bond Price (Percent)
5 years	− 7.47
10 years	−11.70
15 years	−14.04
20 years	−15.30
25 years	−15.97

Table 9–2. Price Changes for a 9%-Coupon Bond as Yield to Maturity Decreases (from 12% to 10%).

Maturity of Bond	Change in Bond Price (Percent)
5 years	+ 8.07
10 years	+13.25
15 years	+16.33
20 years	+18.07
25 years	+19.00

CALLABLE BONDS

Bonds that carry a call provision allow the issuer the option of requiring bondholders to have their securities redeemed prior to maturity. If, for instance, a company sells bonds when interest rates are relatively high, the firm may wish to refinance the debt if rates should subsequently move to lower levels, so it would call in the existing bonds. The bondholder enjoying the collection of high interest payments will probably not be inclined to look too kindly upon the call feature when the issuer exercises this option to call the investor's securities.

One means of making the call option less objectionable to a prospective bond buyer would be for the issuer to provide the investor with call protection (perhaps five years). After the passage of the protected period, the issuer might offer to pay the investor a premium for a certain period of time for the option to call the bonds for redemption. After the expiration of the premium period, the issuer would usually be able to call the bonds by just paying par for them.

Of course, during periods of rising interest rates the issuing firm might find its bonds selling at a discount. If the firm has managed to generate some excess cash, it might be advantageous for the issuer to purchase some of its own bonds in the open market. This would be particularly true if the bond issue were a relatively small issue with a sinking fund feature at par and the issuer noted from its bondholder list that an investor (termed a collector in this case) was trying to corner the market in the bonds.

Example—Calculating Bond Price Based on Yield to Call

The call premium and the yield to call are treated in this example. A $100-par value bond has a coupon of 9% and is callable in four years at 106% of par (the call premium is 6% of par). Recent movements in the bond market have given the security a yield to call of 8%. What is the price (present value) of the bond?

The present value (price) of this callable bond based on its yield to call is found in the same manner as was the present value of a bond when the yield to maturity determined the present values of the interest payment stream and the reversion.

Column 5 of the semiannual compounding table for a nominal annual rate of 8% contains a present value of 6.7327 for a series of 8 semiannual $1.00

payments. Since the $100 bond has a coupon yield of 9%, the semiannual interest payments are $4.50 each. The multiplication of $4.50 by 6.7327 gives a present value of $30.30 for the interest payments.

The Column 4 factor of 0.7307 for a lump sum of $1.00 is found for $n = 8$ in the semiannual compounding table with a nominal annual rate of 8%. The present value of the reversion is $77.45. It is computed by multiplying 0.7307 by the reversion of $106. The addition of the present values of $30.30 and $77.45 provide a sum of $107.75, which is the total present value or price of the bond based on the yield to call.

10 A QUICK APPROACH TO UNDERSTANDING REAL ESTATE INVESTMENTS

ESTIMATING REAL ESTATE VALUE

The three basic approaches to estimating the market value of real estate are the comparable sales or market approach, the cost method, and the income capitalization technique.

The market approach is widely used in appraising residential properties. The cost method is well suited to the appraisal of structures such as public buildings. The income capitalization technique is applied to income-producing types of real estate, such as commercial properties. It is common in the valuation of commercial properties, for instance, to find an appraiser estimating value on the basis of the market approach, the cost method, and the income capitalization technique.

The market approach in the case of residential real estate, for example, attempts to ascertain the relatively current sale prices of properties in the same market area that are comparable to the subject property (a competitive market analysis). Where differences exist in physical characteristics, a comparable property (or comp, as it is called) is adjusted to that the subject property. If, for example, the comparable property has a desirable feature that the subject property does not have or has a physical characteristic that is superior to a similar feature in the subject property, then a deduction is made from the value of the comparable property.

Conversely, an addition is made to the value of a comparable property in instances where the subject property has an amenity or an attractive physical characteristic that the comparable real estate does not have or has a similar feature that is better than that possessed by the comparable property.

149

Value adjustments between the subject real estate and a comparable property can also be made for differences relating to location, financing terms, conditions of sale, and time (the time of sale of a comparable property versus the appraisal time of the subject real estate).

The cost method requires the determination of the cost of reproducing or replacing an improvement (for example, a building). After this cost figure has been estimated, a deduction is taken from the cost figure for depreciation (physical deterioration) and obsolescence (both functional and external or economic). An addition is then made for land value and for site improvements (for instance, paving and landscaping).

The income capitalization approach seeks to determine a property's income and then uses a capitalization rate to convert this income into a present value for the property.

INCOME CAPITALIZATION TECHNIQUE

Real estate appraisers commonly use the following relationship when dealing with the technique of income capitalization.

$$\text{Present value} = \frac{\text{Net operating income}}{\text{Capitalization rate}}$$

The acronym IRV is usually used to denote this relationship. The I symbolizes the net operating income, R stands for capitalization rate, and V represents present value. Using these symbols, the equation reads

$$V = \frac{I}{R}$$

If two of the three quantities in the equation are known, the unknown quantity can be found. The equation can be rearranged to read

$$I = RV$$

or

$$R = \frac{I}{V}$$

If it is desired to find the present value of an income property, the net operating income (I) and the capitalization rate (R) have to be known. Consider a case in which a capitalization rate of 11% is applied to an income property such as apartment complex. The property's net operating income can be found by utilizing the following net operating income statement. (The figures are annual amounts.)

Gross scheduled income	$272,000
Deduct vacancy and collection losses	− 16,320
Add other income	+900
Gross operating income	$256,580
(or effective gross income)	
Deduct operating expenses	− 92,000
Net operating income	$164,580

Using the IRV relationship, the present value of the total property would be

$$V = I/R$$
$$= \$164,580/0.11$$
$$= \$1,496,182$$

The market value of the subject income property using the income capitalization technique is estimated to be $1,496,182.

The question might arise in the reader's mind as to what would happen, for instance, to the estimate of present value if a constant net operating income of $164,580 were to be discounted for a number of annual periods at 11%. The answer is that the value estimate will not change so long as the value of the property at the end of the final discounting period is assumed to be equal to the present value of the property as determined by the income capitalization technique.

As an illustration, assume that the net operating income of $164,580 is discounted for a two-year period and a three-year period at a rate of 11 percent to obtain the present value (PV).

$$\text{two-year PV} = \frac{\$164,580}{(1 + .11)} + \frac{\$164,580}{(1 + .11)^2} + \frac{\$1,496,182}{(1 + .11)^2}$$
$$= \$148,270 + \$133,577 + \$1,214,335$$
$$= \$1,496,182$$

$$\text{three-year PV} = \frac{\$164,580}{(1 + .11)} + \frac{\$164,580}{(1 + .11)^2} + \frac{\$164,580}{(1 + .11)^3} + \frac{\$1,496,182}{(1 + .11)^3}$$
$$= \$148,270 + \$133,577 + \$120,339 + \$1,093,995$$
$$= \$1,496,181 (\text{rounding difference of } \$1)$$

The additional income of $120,339 in the third year is offset by the lower reversion value in the third year ($1,214,335 − $1,093,995). This type of offsetting will continue as the discounting is extended for additional annual periods.

This real estate discounting situation may be compared to the discounting of a par bond. For the sake of illustration, assign to a par bond both a selling price and a redemption value of $1,496,182. Allow this bond to have annual compounding and to make annual coupon payments of $164,580 (11% coupon rate times a par value of $1,496,182).

Since the purchase price is equal to the redemption value, the yield to maturity will be equal to the coupon rate of 11%. As the maturity of this bond is extended, the present value, or price of the bond, will not change. The additional coupon income from each additional year will be offset by corresponding decreases in the discounted amount of the bond's redemption value.

If the supposition is made that the property with an annual net operating income of $164,580 is bought for $1,496,182 and is sold for a higher price, the discounted yield would be greater than 11 percent. This would be similar in concept to purchasing a bond at a discount. On the other hand, if this same piece of real estate costs $1,496,182 and is sold for a lesser amount, the discounted yield would be less than 11 percent. This would be analogous to buying a bond at a premium, whereby the purchase price exceeds the redemption value.

DIFFERENCE BETWEEN NET OPERATING INCOME AND NET INCOME

The net operating income should not be confused with the net income. If interest expense and depreciation expense are deducted from net operating income, the remaining quantity will be the taxable income. By applying the investor's tax rate to the taxable income, the income tax expense is gotten. The net income (or income after taxes) is figured by deducting the income tax expense from the taxable income.

If the property produces a loss instead of taxable income, the investor's tax rate is applied to the loss so as to get the amount of tax savings. This would imply that the investor had other income that the loss could offset, and that the tax laws would permit the real estate loss to be used to offset that other income.

LOAN-TO-VALUE RATIO

The loan-to-value ratio permits finding the loan amount when the property value is known or the property value when the loan amount is known. Consider again the apartment complex. The property value has been estimated at $1,496,182 (say, $1,496,000) from the IRV relationship, so a 70% ratio would indicate a loan amount for the property of $1,047,200 (say, $1,047,000).

$$\text{Loan-to-value ratio} = \frac{\text{Loan}}{\text{Value}}$$

$$0.70 = \frac{\text{Loan}}{\$1,496,000}$$

$$\text{Loan} = \$1,047,200$$

DEBT SERVICE

In order to calculate the service on a debt, it is necessary to know the loan rate and the maturity as well as the loan amount. If payments of principal and interest are made monthly and there is an annual interest rate of 10% and an amortization period of 20 years, the annual mortgage or loan constant would be 11.58%. (See Chapter 11 for a detailed explanation of the mortgage constant.) The annual debt service on the loan made against the apartment complex would then be $121,243.

$$\text{Annual debt service} = (\text{Loan amount}) \times (\text{Annual mortgage constant})$$
$$= (\$1,047,000)(0.1158)$$
$$= \$121,243$$

CASH FLOW BEFORE TAXES

This calculation shows the allocation of net operating income (NOI) among the suppliers of capital (debt capital and equity capital).

The debt service amount represents the lender's share of net operating income. The remainder of the net operating income, or the cash flow before taxes, constitutes that portion of NOI that belongs to the provider of equity, or so-called risk capital.

Net operating income	$164,580
Deduct debt service	$121,243
Cash flow before taxes	$ 43,337

RETURN ON EQUITY (CASH-ON-CASH RETURN)

The return on equity, or cash-on-cash return, is obtained by dividing the cash flow before taxes ($43,337 for the apartment complex) by the equity investment. With a property valuation of $1,496,000 and a loan amount of $1,047,000, the equity portion of the investment would be the difference between these two sums, which is $449,000.

$$\text{Return on equity} = \frac{\text{Cash flow before taxes}}{\text{Equity}}$$
$$= \frac{\$43,337}{\$449,000}$$
$$= 0.097, or\ 9.7\%$$

RETURN ON TOTAL CAPITAL

The total amount of capital includes both equity funds and borrowed funds. The return on total capital is the ratio of the net operating income to the total investment. The calculation is one of the variations of the IRV relationship. Earlier, a return rate of 11% was taken to obtain a figure for total investment.

$$\text{Return on total capital} = \frac{\text{Net operating income}}{\text{Total investment}}$$

$$R = I / V$$

$$\text{Return on total capital} = \frac{\$164,580}{\$1,496,000}$$

$$= 0.11, \text{ or } 11\%$$

DEBT SERVICE COVERAGE RATIO

When the net operating income is divided by the annual debt service, the debt service coverage ratio is determined. This ratio is viewed closely by lenders since it is a measure of debt payment cushion.

$$\text{Debt service coverage ratio} = \frac{\text{Net operating income}}{\text{Debt service}}$$

$$= \frac{\$164,580}{\$121,243}$$

$$= 1.36$$

If the debt service were to equal the net operating income, the debt service coverage ratio would be 1. The net operating income would just cover the debt service, so there would be no cushion.

MAXIMUM LOAN AMOUNT

The maximum loan that a lender will make for a given project may depend on certain criteria. One criterion might be that the project meet a minimum debt service coverage ratio.

The determination of the maximum loan amount based on a minimum debt service coverage ratio may be viewed as a two-step problem. The first step requires finding the amount of debt service for a given net operating income and a given debt service coverage ratio. The second step entails the computation of the loan amount based on known values for the amount of debt service and the annual loan (mortgage) constant.

Step 1:

$$\text{Debt service} = \frac{\text{Net operating income}}{\text{Debt service coverage ratio}}$$

Step 2:

$$\text{Maximum loan amount} = \frac{\text{Debt service}}{\text{Loan constant}}$$

These two equations can be combined to form the following relationship.

$$\text{loan amount} = \frac{\underset{\text{Net operating income}}{\text{Maximum}} \div \text{Debt service coverage ratio}}{\text{Loan constant}}$$

For a net operating income of $164,580, a debt service coverage ratio of 1.30, and an annual loan (mortgage) constant of 11.58%, or .1158, the calculation would be

$$\begin{aligned}
\text{Maximum loan amount} &= \frac{\$164,580 \div 1.30}{.1158} \\
&= \frac{\$126,600}{.1158} \\
&= \$1,093,264
\end{aligned}$$

or, say, $1,093,000.

OPERATING EXPENSE RATIO

While the type of property that is being managed influences the operating expense ratio, this measure still gives some indication as to the quality of a project's management and its ability to control costs.

$$\begin{aligned}
\text{Operating expense ratio} &= \frac{\text{Operating expenses}}{\text{Gross operating income}} \\
&= \frac{\$92,000}{\$256,580} \\
&= 0.359, \, or \, 35.9\%
\end{aligned}$$

(The operating expenses and gross operating income for the apartment complex were given in the net operating income statement.)

BREAK-EVEN RATIO

By taking into account the annual debt service as well as the operating expenses, the break-even ratio can be computed.

$$\text{Break-even ratio} = \frac{\text{Operating expenses} + \text{Debt service}}{\text{Gross scheduled income}}$$
$$= \frac{\$92,000 + \$121,243}{\$272,000}$$
$$= 0.784, \text{ or } 78.4\%$$

In addition to cash flows and tax benefits such as depreciation, there are other benefits that can be derived from real estate ownership. Included among them are appreciation and equity buildup.

APPRECIATION

Real estate has long been considered a good hedge against inflation. During periods of rising prices, property values may more than keep pace with the rate of inflation. Many factors can influence the appreciation that a property experiences. Not least among these elements would be the location of the property and the possible legal uses to which the property might be put.

Although it may be argued that appreciation is not realized or captured until a property is sold, some investors still may view it as an addition to the yearly return they receive from a property. It may not be unusual, during periods of relatively high inflation, for an investor to sacrifice cash flow (that is, to buy a piece of real estate with either a negative cash flow or a small positive cash flow) in order to benefit from the property's potential to appreciate in value.

Example—Calculating the Appreciation in Property Value

Suppose that a parcel of real estate has a current value of $225,000. If an annual rate of inflation of 4% is anticipated over each of the next five years and it is assumed that the property's value will keep pace with the inflation rate, what will be the anticipated value of the property at the end of five years?

The equation $S = P(1 + R/m)^n$ can be used to secure the future growth value.

$$S = \$225,000(1 + 0.04/1)^5$$
$$= \$225,000(1.21665)$$
$$= \$273,747$$

The appreciated value of the property at the end of 5 years would be $273,747 (say, $273,700) if the appreciation rate stays at 4%.

EQUITY BUILDUP VERSUS FINANCIAL LEVERAGE

Equity buildup is viewed as another one of the benefits of real estate ownership. It has an association with the term *financial leverage*. In a closed-end transaction where additional amounts of debt are not being infused, leverage and equity exhibit contrary behavior. That is, as leverage (debt) decreases, equity increases.

It is the incurrence of debt that gives rise to the creation of financial leverage. If a borrower can earn a return on the borrowed money that is higher than what has to be paid for interest and other related borrowing costs, the leverage is said to be positive. If the borrower's cost for borrowed funds exceeds the return from the employment of these funds, the leverage is negative.

Consider the following relationship.

$$\text{Purchase price} = \text{Debt} + \text{Equity}$$

The left side of the equation represents the purchase price of a property. It is a fixed or constant quantity. Both of the terms on the right side of the equation (debt and equity) represent the sources of purchase funds. Each quantity is in a state of flux over the life of a loan during which payments provide for the periodic reduction of principal as well as for the payment of interest. As periodic payments are made, the debt term in the equation continues to decline over the life of the loan, as does the amount of financial leverage. Each time that the debt or leverage is reduced, the investor's equity increases. This buildup of equity continues over the term of the loan. The equation holds because the equity increases by the same amount that the debt decreases.

When the loan has been fully repaid, the debt becomes zero, as does the amount of leverage. All of the purchase price is now accounted for by equity investment. The equation becomes

$$\text{Purchase price} = \text{Equity}$$

The equation now looks as it would have at the time that the property was acquired if no loan had been made (zero leverage) and the purchase had been consummated solely with equity capital (that is, on a free and clear basis).

Example—Computing the Present Value of a Property (Level Income Stream)

Column 5 and Column 4 can be used to find the present value of an income-producing property in the same way that the columns are used to find the present value of a bond having a stream of interest payments and a reversion.

Consider an income-producing piece of real estate that has an annual net operating income of $40,000. Assume that the only operating expenses that are considered are fixed expenses and variable expenses. No provision is made for a reserve for replacements. Let the annual debt service, or mortgage payments, be $25,000 so that the cash flow before income taxes is $15,000. Suppose that the cash flow before taxes will be stable over an ownership period of five years, after which it is anticipated that the property can be sold for $450,000. If the investor discounts the reversion and the stream of annual cash flows before taxes at an interest rate of 8%, what is the present value of the property?

Column 5 of the annual compounding interest table with a nominal annual rate of 8%, carries a value for $n = 5$ years of 3.9927, for $1.00 payments or receipts. Since each yearly cash flow before taxes is $15,000, 3.9927 is multiplied by $15,000 to obtain a present value of $59,891 for the cash flows. Column 4 of the same table reflects a figure of 0.6806 for $n = 5$ years, which is the present value of a lump sum of $1.00. The multiplication of 0.6806 by the reversion or future anticipated selling price of $450,000 renders a present value of $306,270. The addition of $59,891 and $306,270 gives the property a total present value of $366,161 (say, $366,000).

Example—Seeking the Present Value of a Property (Uneven Income Stream)

Make the assumption that over a three-year holding period an income-producing property is expected to have uneven cash flows because of lease expirations. The annual cash flows are projected to be $12,400, $11,200, and $13,000 for the first, second, and third years, respectively. It is anticipated that the property can be sold for $400,000 at the end of three years. What is the present value of the property?

Since the cash flows are not level, Column 5 of the compound interest tables cannot be used to get a figure for computing the present value of the series of payments. Only Column 4 of the annual compounding table will be used since each payment can be treated as a future lump sum. A nominal annual rate of 8% is chosen to discount the cash flows (see Chapter 7). The present value equation would be

$$PV = \frac{12,400}{(1 + 0.08)} + \frac{11,200}{(1 + 0.08)^2} + \frac{13,000}{(1 + 0.08)^3} + \frac{400,000}{(1 + 0.08)^3}$$

$$= 12,400(0.9259) + 11,200(0.8573) + 13,000(0.7938)$$

$$+ 400,000(0.7938)$$

$$= 11,481 + 9,602 + 10,319 + 317,520$$

$$= 348,922$$

The present value of the property would be $348,922 (say, $349,000).

NET PRESENT VALUE (NPV)

Where there is a positive cash flow before income taxes, the cash flow after taxes is found by deducting taxes from the cash flow before taxes. A discounted stream of cash flows after taxes can be used in net present value (NPV) analysis. This type of analysis is one means of determining whether an investment should be made.

In doing NPV analysis, the future periodic cash flows after taxes from a proposed income property investment have to be determined, and the future selling price of the property after taxes has to be projected. These future benefits are then discounted at a rate that is acceptable to the investor so as to arrive at a present value. The present value of the future cash flows after taxes and the reversion after taxes are compared with the present value (cost) of the investment or outlay.

If the present value of the future stream of benefits is greater than the present value of the outlay, the NPV (the difference between these two present values) will be positive. In this case the rate of return on the investment will exceed the desired yield (the discount rate that has been chosen), and the indication will be that the investment should be made.

Should the present value (cost) of the investment exceed the present value of the future periodic cash flows after taxes and the reversion after taxes, then the net present value will be negative. Under these circumstances the indication will be that the investment should not be made.

Example—Calculating the Net Present Value (NPV)

Assume that an income property can be purchased at the present time for $310,000. The monthly cash flows after income taxes are projected at level amounts of $420 over a time horizon of seven years. An equity investment of $90,000 is required at the time of purchase. The expectation is that the equity will be $115,000 after taxes when the property is sold in seven years. The desired yield is 8%. Is the net present value positive or negative?

Reference is made to Column 5 of the 8% monthly compounding table. For $n = 84$ months, the factor is 64.1593. A stream of monthly payments of $1.00 over a time frame of 84 months (seven years) has a present value of $64.1593 when discounted at a nominal annual rate of 8% compounded monthly. The present value of an 84-month flow of $420 monthly payments is $26,947 ($420 times 64.1593).

For $n = 84$ months in the same monthly table, Column 4 shows that a lump sum reversion of $1.00 to be received at the end of seven years has a present value of $0.5723. An equity reversion of $115,000 to be received at the end of seven years would have a present value of $65,815 ($115,000 times 0.5723).

The present value of the monthly cash flows after income taxes plus the present value of the equity reversion after income taxes is $92,762 ($26,947 plus $65,815).

Since the present value of the flow of future benefits ($92,762) exceeds the equity investment ($90,000), the net present value of $2,762 ($92,762 minus $90,000) is positive, indicating that the rate of return on the investment is more than the desired rate of 8%. On the basis of yield, the investment should be made.

GROSS RENT OR GROSS INCOME MULTIPLIER

Income data can be used in several ways to estimate property values. The income capitalization approach and the discounted cash flow method have been discussed already. The gross rent multiplier or gross income multiplier technique will be considered next.

The gross rent multiplier (GRM), also called the gross income multiplier (GIM), is similar in concept to the price-earnings ratio P-E ratio, which is used as one of the tools in determining the prices of common stocks (see Chapter 1). For instance, if a financial analyst determines that a company's stock should sell for 12 times its current annual earnings of $3 per share, then the analyst would be placing a market value on the stock of $36 per share based on earnings.

$$\text{Price-Earnings ratio} = \frac{\text{Price per share}}{\text{Earnings per share}}$$

$$12 = \frac{\text{Price per share}}{\$3}$$

$$\text{Price per share (Value)} = \$36$$

Example—Using a Gross Rent Multiplier (GRM) to Estimate Property Value

The gross rent multiplier is usually applied to smaller income properties. An estimate of the GRM for a subject property can be determined by taking the sale prices of comparable properties in the same area and dividing them by either the monthly gross rental income or the annual gross rental income.

Assume that comparable income properties have an average GRM of 12 based on annual gross rental income, or an average GRM of 144 based on monthly gross rental income. If the subject property has an annual gross rental income of $11,400, the property would be valued at $136,800.

$$\text{GRM} = \frac{\text{Property Value}}{\text{Annual gross rental income}}$$

$$12 = \frac{\text{Value}}{\$11,400}$$

$$\text{Value} = \$136,800$$

The property valuation of $136,800 can also be obtained by using monthly data.

$$GRM = \frac{\text{Property Value}}{\text{Monthly gross rental income}}$$

$$144 = \frac{\text{Value}}{\$950}$$

$$\text{Value} = \$136,800$$

11 HOW TO FIGURE MONTHLY PAYMENTS FOR A HOME, AUTOMOBILE, OR BOAT WHEN THE PURCHASE IS FINANCED

Column 6 of the compound interest tables is of particular interest to people who purchase such things as homes, automobiles, and boats on credit and then make principal and interest payments on the debt at regular intervals. Column 6, although not a column of present values as are Columns 4 and 5, is nevertheless directly involved with present values since each entry gives payment size. Hence it may be viewed as a column of loan constants.

Example—Finding the Monthly Payments for Principal and Interest for a Car Purchase

Financing for five years in the amount of $19,000 is obtained for the purchase of a car. If the nominal annual rate is 8%, what is the amount of the buyer's monthly payments for principal and interest?

Column 6 of the compound interest tables is useful in determining payments when purchases are financed. Since monthly payments are involved, the monthly compounding table for the nominal rate of 8% is used. For $n = 60$ months (5 years), the figure is 0.0203. Monthly payments of 2.03 cents would have to be made over the next five years to pay off a loan with a present value of $1.00. Since the present value of the car loan is $19,000. The amount of the buyer's monthly payments is $385.70 (0.0203 × $19,000).

165

Example—Figuring the Total Amount of Interest Paid on a Car Loan

In the foregoing example it was determined that automobile financing in the amount of $19,000 for five years required monthly payments for principal and interest of $385.70.

Over a five-year period, these monthly payments total $23,142. When the loan amount of $19,000 is subtracted from the payment total of $23,142, the total amount of interest paid is found to be $4,142, which is almost 22% of the loan amount.

Example—Choosing Between a Lower Financing Rate and a Rebate on the Purchase of an Automobile

Suppose that an automobile purchase will require $12,000 worth of financing for three years (36 months). The buyer has two financing options from which to select.

The buyer can pay the regular annual interest rate of 8% on 36 monthly payments and receive a cash rebate from the manufacturer of $900, or take an annual financing rate of 2% without any cash rebate. Which option should the buyer choose? (The assumption is made that the rebate would be spent if taken.)

The monthly compound interest table for a nominal annual interest rate of 8% contains a Column 6 factor of 0.0313 for $n = 36$ months. Using a financing figure of $12,000, the monthly payments would be $375.60 (0.0313 × $12,000).

Total payments over a period of 36 months would be $13,522. The total amount of interest that the buyer would pay under this option would be $1,522 ($13,522 − $12,000).

It can be found that the monthly compound interest table for a nominal yearly interest rate of 2% has a Column 6 value of 0.0286 for $n = 36$ months. Monthly payments for an initial principal of $12,000 would be $343.20 (0.0286 times $12,000).

Over a payment period of 36 months, total payments would be $12,355. Interest over this period would amount to $355 ($12,355 minus $12,000).

Under the option with the rebate, the buyer's total interest expense would be $1,522. Total interest under the alternative option without a rebate would be $355. The difference in interest expense would be $1,167.

By taking the 2% financing option instead of the 8% credit package, the automobile buyer would be saving $1,167 in interest. Since this amount exceeds the $900 rebate given with the 8% loan alternative, it would in this case be to the purchaser's advantage to select the option with the lower interest cost.

Example—Financing a Boat Purchase with Monthly Payments

A boat buyer agrees to make monthly principal and interest payments for seven years to finance $28,000 of a boat purchase. What will be the size of each monthly payment if the nominal annual interest rate is 8%.

A column 6 value from the monthly compounding table for a nominal rate of 8% is obtained for $n = 84$ months (7 years). The number is 0.0156, indicating that less than two cents must be paid each month for seven years for each dollar of the boat purchase that is financed. The multiplication of $28,000 by 0.0156 provides the actual monthly payment figure of $436.80.

Factors Affecting Monthly Payments of Principal and Interest for a Home, Car, or Boat Purchase

The amount of monthly payments for principal and interest is of major concern to most buyers of homes, automobiles, boats, and other large ticket items. The elements that determine the size of the monthly payments are the amount of money borrowed, the interest rate charged, and the length of time for which the loan is made.

For a given loan period, or maturity, monthly payments increase as either the amount of money borrowed increases or as the interest rate increases. For a given amount of money and a given rate of interest, monthly payments increase as the maturity of a loan is shortened and decrease as the duration of a loan is lengthened. Therefore, if wishing to reduce the monthly payments on a home, car, or boat, a buyer can reduce the amount of money borrowed, or try to get a lower interest rate, or increase the maturity of the loan. The ability to implement all three of these actions at the same time would, of course, have a greater inpact on reducing the monthly payments than just doing one of these things.

Points

The expression *basis point* should not be confused with the term *points*. The word *points* usually arises in connection with real estate loans. It refers to a way of changing the true yield on a loan. One point would amount to one percent of the principal amount of a loan. Three points would constitute three percent of the loan principal.

Points are generally paid to the lender up front, that is at the time that a loan is made. The effect of the payment of points is to pay the lender interest on an amount of money greater than the amount that is actually being loaned.

Suppose that a lender loans $5,000 to a borrower for one year at an annual interest rate of 13%. The interest of $650 ($5,000 × 0.13) is to be paid at maturity. The lender is restricted from charging the borrower more than 13%. The use of points is considered legal, so the lender decides to increase the yield on the loan by charging two points (i.e., 2% of the loan amount). If the borrower pays $100 (which is 2% of the $5,000) at the time the loan is made, the lender in effect is loaning only $4,900. If the interest amount $650 is divided by $4,900, the interest rate that the lender is charging for the loan is 13.27%.

As a rule of thumb, a charge of one point by the lender increases the interest rate on a fixed 30-year real estate mortgage (loan) by $\frac{1}{8}$%. The impact of points on 30-year mortgage (loan) at different rates of interest is shown in Table 11–1. (Over the years many people have used the word mortgage to mean a loan. Technically, however, a mortgage is not a loan but a pledge of security against a loan.)

Table 11–1 reveals, for example, that a one point charge by a lender on a 30-year loan raises the rate of interest from 8% to 8.106%, whereas a charge of one point raises a 10% rate to 10.120%. A charge of two points on a 30-year real estate loan would increase a 14% interest rate to 14.305% and a four-point charge would move a 15% rate to 15.657%.

Table 11–1. Effect of Loan Points on Interest Rates (in percent, on a 30-year loan).

Nominal Annual Interest Rate	1 Point	2 Points	3 Points	4 Points	5 Points
7%	7.100	7.201	7.305	7.409	7.516
8%	8.106	8.214	8.324	8.435	8.549
9%	9.113	9.227	9.344	9.463	9.584
10%	10.120	10.242	10.366	10.492	10.620
11%	11.127	11.257	11.388	11.522	11.659
12%	12.135	12.272	12.412	12.554	12.699
13%	13.143	13.288	13.436	13.587	13.741
14%	14.151	14.305	14.462	14.622	14.785
15%	15.160	15.332	15.488	15.657	15.829

Example—Calculating the Monthly Payments for a Home Purchase

Assume that a person buys a new home that requires $100,000 of the purchase price to be financed. The annual mortgage rate is fixed at 8%. What would be the monthly payments of principal and interest for a 30-year mortgage?

Where the nominal annual interest rate is 8% and $n = 360$ months (30 years), the table for monthly compounding contains a Column 6 payment of 0.0073 for each $1.00 of principal. Since $100,000 is to be financed, $100,000 is multiplied by 0.0073. The resulting figure of $730 represents the level monthly payments the home buyer must make to the lender in order to provide for the repayment of the $100,000 of principal plus the interest on the borrowing.

Loan Repayment Schedule

The loan repayment schedule for the first year of loan life for the home purchase is shown in Table 11–2. The initial loan amount is $100,000, the interest rate is 8% per annum, and the loan life is 30 years. The level monthly payments of principal and interest are considered to be $733.76 instead of $730. (If the Column 6 factor of 0.0073 is carried out to more decimal places, a figure of 0.0073376 is obtained. When multiplied by $100,000, this figure gives monthly payments of $733.76).

If the loan repayment table were completed for 360 months (30 years) using the same format reflected in the table, Column B would show a figure of zero at the beginning of Month 361. The loan would be completely repaid after 360 months. The total interest for 360 months would be the sum of the monthly interest figures contained in Column C. Using the factor of 0.0073376, the total interest amount would be $164,154. The sum of the figures in Column D would be $100,000, which is the total principal amount of the loan. In Column E the loan balance at the end of Month 360 would be zero. (In practice, the final payment might have to be adjusted in order to achieve an ending balance of zero.)

Examining the number in Column C, it can be seen that interest decreases with each succeeding month. This occurs because the loan balance (Column B) on which interest is calculated decreases each month. It may be observed in Column D that the amount by which the loan principal is reduced each month increases.

Table 11–2. Loan Repayment Schedule (First Year).

A	B	C	D	E
	Loan Balance		Reduction	Loan Balance
	at Start of	Interest	of Loan	at End of
	Period	on Loan	Principal	Period
Period	(Dollars)	(Dollars)	(Dollars)	(Dollars)
Month 1	100,000.00	666.67	67.09	99,932.91
Month 2	99,932.91	666.22	67.54	99,865.37
Month 3	99,865.37	665.77	67.99	99,797.38
Month 4	99,797.38	665.32	68.44	99,728.94
Month 5	99,728.94	664.86	68.90	99,660.04
Month 6	99,660.04	664.40	69.36	99,590.68
Month 7	99,590.68	663.94	69.82	99,520.86
Month 8	99,520.86	663.47	70.29	99,450.57
Month 9	99,450.57	663.00	70.76	99,379.81
Month 10	99,379.81	662.53	71.23	99,308.58
Month 11	99,308.58	662.06	71.70	99,236.88
Month 12	99,236.88	661.58	72.18	99,164.70

The monthly payment is a fixed amount. Its purpose is to pay interest on a declining loan balance and to repay a portion of loan principal. If the amount of interest that is paid declines each month, then an increasing portion of each monthly payment becomes available for the repayment of loan principal.

The procedure used in obtaining the numbers in the loan repayment table may be demonstrated by using the figures for Month 3. In Column B the loan balance at the start of the period is $99,865.37. This amount is multiplied by the decimal 0.0066667, which corresponds to the monthly interest rate of 0.66667% (8%/12 months). The product of the multiplication is a monthly interest amount of $665.77 (Column C).

The interest of $665.77 is deducted from the level monthly payment of $773.76 to arrive at the portion of principal that is repaid ($67.99 in Column D). The repaid amount of principal is a residual number, meaning that interest is taken out of the monthly payment first. Whatever amount remains after interest has been deducted from the monthly payment becomes the sum allocated to the repayment of principal. The amount of $67.99 is subtracted from the period's beginning loan balance ($99,865.37 in Column B). The difference ($99,797.38) is recorded in Column E as the loan balance at the end of Month 3. This loan balance rolls over into the next period (Month 4) to become that period's starting principal balance (Column B).

AMOUNTS OF MONTHLY PAYMENTS AND TOTAL INTEREST EXPENSE FOR A FINANCED DWELLING FOR SELECTED INTEREST RATES

The rounded monthly payments of principal and interest and the rounded amounts of total interest expense over the life of a loan are shown in Table 11–4. This section considers loans for the purchase of a dwelling such as a house, condominium, or town house. All of these tables are based on a loan period of 30 years. Tables are constructed for fixed annual interest rates ranging from 7% to 15%.

The monthly mortgage (loan) constants used in Table 11–4 are listed in Table 11–3.

The factors for $n = 360$ months in Column 6 of the compound interest tables can be used as loan constants. However, the loan constants in Table 11–3 are carried seven digits to the right of the decimal point, whereas the factors in the table for a nominal rate of 8% contain only four digits. Therefore using Table 11–3 will give more precise data. (In Table 11–6, monthly and annual loan constants for more interest rates are presented, which have been carried to seven and five decimal places, respectively.)

It can be observed in Table 11–3 that the mortgage (loan) constant increases as the interest rate increases for a fixed period of 30 years.

Also, it may be of interest to note that for each fixed nominal interest rate shown the loan constant would become larger as the period of the loan becomes shorter. For example, the loan constant for a fixed rate of 7%

Table 11–3.   Monthly Mortgage Constants for a 30-Year Loan.

Fixed Annual Interest Rate	Monthly Mortgage (Loan) Constant
7%	0.0066530
8%	0.0073376
9%	0.0080462
10%	0.0087757
11%	0.0095232
12%	0.0102861
13%	0.0110620
14%	0.0118487
15%	0.0126444

Table 11–4a. Payment Table For Purchase of a Dwelling–Annual Interest Rate 7% (30-Year Loan).

Loan Amount (Dollars)	Amount of Monthly Payments (Dollars)	Total Interest Expense Over 30 Years (Dollars)
25,000	166	34,760
50,000	333	69,880
75,000	499	104,640
100,000	665	139,400
125,000	832	174,520
150,000	998	209,280
175,000	1,164	244,040
200,000	1,331	279,160
225,000	1,497	313,920
250,000	1,663	348,680
275,000	1,830	383,800
300,000	1,996	418,560
350,000	2,329	488,440
400,000	2,661	557,960
450,000	2,994	627,840
500,000	3,327	697,720
600,000	3,992	837,120
700,000	4,657	976,520
800,000	5,322	1,115,920
900,000	5,988	1,255,680
1,000,000	6,653	1,395,080

Table 11–4b.   Payment Table For Purchase of a Dwelling–Annual Interest Rate **8%** (30-Year Loan).

Loan Amount (Dollars)	Amount of Monthly Payments (Dollars)	Total Interest Expense Over 30 Years (Dollars)
25,000	183	40,880
50,000	367	82,120
75,000	550	123,000
100,000	734	164,240
125,000	917	205,120
150,000	1,101	246,360
175,000	1,284	287,240
200,000	1,468	328,480
225,000	1,651	369,360
250,000	1,834	410,240
275,000	2,018	451,480
300,000	2,201	492,360
350,000	2,568	574,480
400,000	2,935	656,600
450,000	3,302	738,720
500,000	3,669	820,840
600,000	4,403	985,080
700,000	5,136	1,148,960
800,000	5,870	1,313,200
900,000	6,604	1,477,440
1,000,000	7,338	1,641,680

Table 11–4c. Payment Table For Purchase of a Dwelling–Annual Interest Rate **9%** (30-Year Loan).

Loan Amount (Dollars)	Amount of Monthly Payments (Dollars)	Total Interest Expense Over 30 Years (Dollars)
25,000	201	47,360
50,000	402	94,720
75,000	603	142,080
100,000	805	189,800
125,000	1,006	237,160
150,000	1,207	284,520
175,000	1,408	331,880
200,000	1,609	379,240
225,000	1,810	426,600
250,000	2,012	474,320
275,000	2,213	521,680
300,000	2,414	569,040
350,000	2,816	663,760
400,000	3,218	758,480
450,000	3,621	853,560
500,000	4,023	948,280
600,000	4,828	1,138,080
700,000	5,632	1,327,520
800,000	6,437	1,517,320
900,000	7,242	1,707,120
1,000,000	8,046	1,896,560

Table 11–4d. Payment Table For Purchase of a Dwelling–Annual Interest Rate **10%** (30-Year Loan).

Loan Amount (Dollars)	Amount of Monthly Payments (Dollars)	Total Interest Expense Over 30 Years (Dollars)
25,000	219	53,840
50,000	439	108,040
75,000	658	161,880
100,000	878	216,080
125,000	1,097	269,920
150,000	1,316	323,760
175,000	1,536	377,960
200,000	1,755	431,800
225,000	1,975	486,000
250,000	2,194	539,840
275,000	2,413	593,680
300,000	2,633	647,880
350,000	3,071	755,560
400,000	3,510	863,600
450,000	3,949	971,640
500,000	4,388	1,079,680
600,000	5,265	1,295,400
700,000	6,143	1,511,480
800,000	7,021	1,727,560
900,000	7,898	1,943,280
1,000,000	8,776	2,159,360

Table 11–4e. Payment Table For Purchase of a Dwelling–Annual Interest Rate **11%** (30-Year Loan).

Loan Amount (Dollars)	Amount of Monthly Payments (Dollars)	Total Interest Expense Over 30 Years (Dollars)
25,000	238	60,680
50,000	476	121,360
75,000	714	182,040
100,000	952	242,720
125,000	1,190	303,400
150,000	1,428	364,080
175,000	1,667	425,120
200,000	1,905	485,800
225,000	2,143	546,480
250,000	2,381	607,160
275,000	2,619	667,840
300,000	2,857	728,520
350,000	3,333	849,880
400,000	3,809	971,240
450,000	4,285	1,092,600
500,000	4,762	1,214,320
600,000	5,714	1,457,040
700,000	6,666	1,699,760
800,000	7,619	1,942,840
900,000	8,571	2,185,560
1,000,000	9,523	2,428,280

Table 11–4f. Payment Table For Purchase of a Dwelling–Annual Interest Rate **12%** (30-Year Loan).

Loan Amount (Dollars)	Amount of Monthly Payments (Dollars)	Total Interest Expense Over 30 Years (Dollars)
25,000	257	67,520
50,000	514	135,040
75,000	771	202,560
100,000	1,029	270,440
125,000	1,286	337,960
150,000	1,543	405,480
175,000	1,800	473,000
200,000	2,057	540,520
225,000	2,314	608,040
250,000	2,572	675,920
275,000	2,829	743,440
300,000	3,086	810,960
350,000	3,600	946,000
400,000	4,114	1,081,040
450,000	4,629	1,216,440
500,000	5,143	1,351,480
600,000	6,172	1,621,920
700,000	7,200	1,892,000
800,000	8,229	2,162,440
900,000	9,257	2,432,520
1,000,000	10,286	2,702,960

Table 11–4g. Payment Table For Purchase of a Dwelling–Annual Interest Rate **13%** (30-Year Loan).

Loan Amount (Dollars)	Amount of Monthly Payments (Dollars)	Total Interest Expense Over 30 Years (Dollars)
25,000	277	74,720
50,000	553	149,080
75,000	830	223,800
100,000	1,106	298,160
125,000	1,383	372,880
150,000	1,659	447,240
175,000	1,936	521,960
200,000	2,212	596,320
225,000	2,489	671,040
250,000	2,766	745,760
275,000	3,042	820,120
300,000	3,319	894,840
350,000	3,872	1,043,920
400,000	4,425	1,193,000
450,000	4,978	1,342,080
500,000	5,531	1,491,160
600,000	6,637	1,789,320
700,000	7,743	2,087,480
800,000	8,850	2,386,000
900,000	9,956	2,684,160
1,000,000	11,062	2,982,320

Table 11–4h. Payment Table For Purchase of a Dwelling–Annual Interest Rate **14%** (30-Year Loan).

Loan Amount (Dollars)	Amount of Monthly Payments (Dollars)	Total Interest Expense Over 30 Years (Dollars)
25,000	296	81,560
50,000	592	163,120
75,000	889	245,040
100,000	1,185	326,600
125,000	1,481	408,160
150,000	1,777	489,720
175,000	2,074	571,640
200,000	2,370	653,200
225,000	2,666	734,760
250,000	2,962	816,320
275,000	3,258	897,880
300,000	3,555	979,800
350,000	4,147	1,142,920
400,000	4,739	1,306,040
450,000	5,332	1,469,520
500,000	5,924	1,632,640
600,000	7,109	1,959,240
700,000	8,294	2,285,840
800,000	9,479	2,612,440
900,000	10,664	2,939,040
1,000,000	11,849	3,265,640

Table 11–4i. Payment Table For Purchase of a Dwelling–Annual Interest Rate 15% (30-Year Loan).

Loan Amount (Dollars)	Amount of Monthly Payments (Dollars)	Total Interest Expense Over 30 Years (Dollars)
25,000	316	88,760
50,000	632	177,520
75,000	948	266,280
100,000	1,264	355,040
125,000	1,581	444,160
150,000	1,897	532,920
175,000	2,213	621,680
200,000	2,529	710,440
225,000	2,845	799,200
250,000	3,161	887,960
275,000	3,477	976,720
300,000	3,793	1,065,480
350,000	4,426	1,243,360
400,000	5,058	1,420,880
450,000	5,690	1,598,400
500,000	6,322	1,775,920
600,000	7,587	2,131,320
700,000	8,851	2,486,360
800,000	10,116	2,841,760
900,000	11,380	3,196,800
1,000,000	12,644	3,551,840

would be 0.0070678 for a loan of 25 years and 0.0077530 for a 20-year loan period. Both of these constants may be contrasted with the 30-year mortgage (loan) constant of 0.0066530 for a fixed annual rate of 7%.

The first part of Table 11–4 which shows the payments on a 30-year loan for the purchase of a dwelling, gives information based on an annual interest rate of 7%. A mortgage (loan) amount of $150,000, for instance, would require monthly payments of $998 for principal and interest. This assumes a fixed nominal annual interest rate of 7% over the whole 30-year period. The monthly payment figure is found by multiplying the loan amount of $150,000 by the loan constant, 0.0066530. (The actual calculated figure is $997.95, which rounds to $998.)

The total amount of the 360 monthly payments would be $359,280. Of this sum, $150,000 would be a repayment of the loan principal and the remaining figure of $209,280 would represent the total interest paid.

Interpolation may be used to obtain the size of the monthly payments for loan amounts not shown in each of the tables. This statement may be illustrated as follows.

Suppose that a borrower has made a home loan for $320,000 for 30 years at a fixed annual interest rate of 7%. In the 7% table a loan amount of $320,000 is not shown. However, monthly payments appear for loan amounts of $300,000 and $350,000. They are $1,996 and $2,329, respectively.

The difference in monthly payments is $333 ($2,329 − $1,996) for the $50,000 difference in loan amounts ($350,000 − $300,000).

The increase in monthly payments for each additional $1,000 of loan principal is $6.66 ($333/50). Thus, for an additional $20,000 of loan principal, the increase in monthly payments would be 20 × $6.66 or $133,20 (say, $133). If $133 is added to $1,996 (the monthly payments for a $300,000 loan), the monthly payments for a $320,000 loan are found to be $2,129.

The accuracy of the interpolation can be checked by multiplying the loan amount of $320,000 by the loan constant 0.0066530. When this is done, a monthly payment size of $2,129 (actually, $2,128.96) is obtained. The need to use interpolation would arise in cases where the loan constant was unknown.

It is also possible to use interpolation (in a manner similar to that shown above) to find the total amount of interest expense from the tables presented. For instance, for a $320,000 loan at a fixed interest rate of 7% for 30 years, the total interest expense over the life of the loan would be found to be $446,512 by interpolation and $446,440 by using a known loan constant (0.0066530) to get the monthly payments of $2,129.

Table 11–5 gives the (rounded) total interest that a home buyer would pay for each dollar borrowed, for various loan maturities and interest rates. For example, for a fixed annual interest rate of 11%, a loan maturity of 15 years, and monthly payments, a borrower would have to pay interest of $1.05 for each dollar of indebtedness incurred. If a home purchaser made a $120,000 loan for 15 years under these terms, the total interest expense over 15 years would be approximately $126,000 (120,000 × $1.05). At a fixed interest rate of 13% for 25 years with monthly payments, the total interest on a $95,000 loan would be about $226,100 (95,000 × $2.38).

MONTHLY AND ANNUAL MORTGAGE (LOAN) CONSTANTS FOR VARIOUS MATURITIES AND INTEREST RATES

Table 11–6 contains mortgage (loan) constants (both monthly and annual) per dollar of beginning loan amount for loan periods of 15, 20, 25, and 30 years. Constants are provided for fixed annual interest rates (monthly compounding) ranging from 7% to 15%, in increments of 0.25%.

The constants are used to determine the required payments of principal and interest on a loan made for the purchase of a large item such as a home.

Consider the fact that the monthly mortgage constant for a fixed annual interest rate of 11% (monthly compounding) for a loan period of 25 years is 0.0098011 per dollar of starting loan principal. In order to repay $1.00 of beginning loan amount and to pay interest on the loan at an annual rate of 11%, it is necessary for the borrower to pay the lender almost one cent each month for 25 years.

The initial loan principal of $1.00 is reduced, or amortized, each month over a period of 25 years so that the amount of loan principal becomes zero at the time that the loan reaches maturity. The annual interest rate of 11% is applied to a loan balance that declines each month.

For a fixed annual interest rate of 11% (monthly compounding) for 25 years, the annual mortgage constant of 0.11761 is found by multiplying the monthly mortgage constant (0.0098011) by 12 months. The annual constant says that each year over the life of the loan (25 years in this case), the borrower is required to pay to the lender 11.761 cents for each dollar borrowed at the time the loan is made. Each year, principal and interest payments would amount to 11.761% of the initial loan amount.

For a home loan made for $135,000 for 25 years, the borrower will have monthly payments of $1,323 (0.0098011 × $135,000) for principal and

Table 11–5. Total Interest (in dollars) Per Dollar of Loan Amount For Monthly Compounding at Selected Annual Interest Rates.

Loan Maturity	7%	8%	9%	10%	11%	12%	13%	14%	15%
15 Years	0.62	0.72	0.83	0.93	1.05	1.16	1.28	1.40	1.52
20 Years	0.86	1.01	1.16	1.32	1.48	1.64	1.81	1.98	2.16
25 Years	1.12	1.32	1.52	1.73	1.94	2.16	2.38	2.61	2.84
30 Years	1.40	1.64	1.90	2.16	2.43	2.70	2.98	3.27	3.55

183

Table 11–6a.   Monthly and Annual Mortgage Constants For Selected Fixed Annual Interest Rates, and Maturities (Monthly Compounding, **15-Year Loan**).

Fixed Annual Interest Rate (Percent)	Monthly Mortgage (Loan) Constant	Annual Mortgage (Loan) Constant
7.00	0.0089883	0.10786
7.25	0.0091286	0.10954
7.50	0.0092701	0.11124
7.75	0.0094128	0.11295
8.00	0.0095565	0.11468
8.25	0.0097014	0.11642
8.50	0.0098474	0.11817
8.75	0.0099945	0.11993
9.00	0.0101427	0.12171
9.25	0.0102919	0.12350
9.50	0.0104423	0.12531
9.75	0.0105936	0.12712
10.00	0.0107461	0.12895
10.25	0.0108995	0.13079
10.50	0.0110540	0.13265
10.75	0.0112095	0.13451
11.00	0.0113660	0.13639
11.25	0.0115235	0.13828
11.50	0.0116819	0.14018
11.75	0.0118413	0.14210
12.00	0.0120017	0.14402
12.25	0.0121630	0.14596
12.50	0.0123252	0.14790
12.75	0.0124884	0.14986
13.00	0.0126524	0.15183
13.25	0.0128174	0.15381
13.50	0.0129832	0.15580
13.75	0.0131499	0.15780
14.00	0.0133174	0.15981
14.25	0.0134858	0.16183
14.50	0.0136550	0.16386
14.75	0.0138250	0.16590
15.00	0.0139959	0.16795

Table 11–6b. Monthly and Annual Mortgage Constants For Selected Fixed Annual Interest Rates, and Maturities (Monthly Compounding, **20-Year Loan**).

Fixed Annual Interest Rate (Percent)	Monthly Mortgage (Loan) Constant	Annual Mortgage (Loan) Constant
7.00	0.0077530	0.09304
7.25	0.0079038	0.09485
7.50	0.0080559	0.09667
7.75	0.0082095	0.09851
8.00	0.0083644	0.10037
8.25	0.0085207	0.10225
8.50	0.0086782	0.10414
8.75	0.0088371	0.10605
9.00	0.0089973	0.10797
9.25	0.0091587	0.10990
9.50	0.0093213	0.11186
9.75	0.0094852	0.11382
10.00	0.0096502	0.11580
10.25	0.0098164	0.11780
10.50	0.0099838	0.11981
10.75	0.0101523	0.12183
11.00	0.0103219	0.12386
11.25	0.0104926	0.12591
11.50	0.0106643	0.12797
11.75	0.0108371	0.13005
12.00	0.0110109	0.13213
12.25	0.0111857	0.13423
12.50	0.0113614	0.13634
12.75	0.0115381	0.13846
13.00	0.0117158	0.14059
13.25	0.0118943	0.14273
13.50	0.0120738	0.14489
13.75	0.0122541	0.14705
14.00	0.0124352	0.14922
14.25	0.0126172	0.15141
14.50	0.0128000	0.15360
14.75	0.0129836	0.15580
15.00	0.0131679	0.15802

Table 11–6c. Monthly and Annual Mortgage Constants For Selected Fixed Annual Interest Rates, and Maturities (Monthly Compounding, **25-Year Loan**).

Fixed Annual Interest Rate (Percent)	Monthly Mortgage (Loan) Constant	Annual Mortgage (Loan) Constant
7.00	0.0070678	0.08481
7.25	0.0072281	0.08674
7.50	0.0073899	0.08868
7.75	0.0075533	0.09064
8.00	0.0077182	0.09262
8.25	0.0078845	0.09461
8.50	0.0080523	0.09663
8.75	0.0082214	0.09866
9.00	0.0083920	0.10070
9.25	0.0085638	0.10277
9.50	0.0087370	0.10484
9.75	0.0089114	0.10694
10.00	0.0090870	0.10904
10.25	0.0092638	0.11117
10.50	0.0094418	0.11330
10.75	0.0096209	0.11545
11.00	0.0098011	0.11761
11.25	0.0099824	0.11979
11.50	0.0101647	0.12198
11.75	0.0103480	0.12418
12.00	0.0105322	0.12639
12.25	0.0107174	0.12861
12.50	0.0109035	0.13084
12.75	0.0110905	0.13309
13.00	0.0112784	0.13534
13.25	0.0114670	0.13760
13.50	0.0116565	0.13988
13.75	0.0118467	0.14216
14.00	0.0120376	0.14445
14.25	0.0122293	0.14675
14.50	0.0124216	0.14906
14.75	0.0126147	0.15138
15.00	0.0128083	0.15370

Table 11–6d. Monthly and Annual Mortgage Constants For Selected Fixed Annual Interest Rates, and Maturities (Monthly Compounding, **30-Year Loan**).

Fixed Annual Interest Rate (Percent)	Monthly Mortgage (Loan) Constant	Annual Mortgage (Loan) Constant
7.00	0.0066530	0.07984
7.25	0.0068218	0.08186
7.50	0.0069922	0.08391
7.75	0.0071641	0.08597
8.00	0.0073377	0.08805
8.25	0.0075127	0.09015
8.50	0.0076891	0.09227
8.75	0.0078670	0.09440
9.00	0.0080462	0.09655
9.25	0.0082268	0.09872
9.50	0.0084085	0.10090
9.75	0.0085915	0.10310
10.00	0.0087757	0.10531
10.25	0.0089610	0.10753
10.50	0.0091474	0.10977
10.75	0.0093348	0.11202
11.00	0.0095232	0.11428
11.25	0.0097126	0.11655
11.50	0.0099029	0.11884
11.75	0.0100941	0.12113
12.00	0.0102861	0.12343
12.25	0.0104790	0.12575
12.50	0.0106726	0.12807
12.75	0.0108669	0.13040
13.00	0.0110620	0.13274
13.25	0.0112577	0.13509
13.50	0.0114541	0.13745
13.75	0.0116511	0.13981
14.00	0.0118487	0.14218
14.25	0.0120469	0.14456
14.50	0.0122456	0.14695
14.75	0.0124448	0.14934
15.00	0.0126444	0.15173

interest. During each of the 25 years, $15,877 (0.11761 times $135,000) will be paid by the borrower for principal and interst on the loan. Because of the rounding, the figure of $15,877 differs slightly from the sum of $15,876 found by multiplying the monthly payment of $1,323 by 12 months.

Example—Determining the Remaining Balance of a Loan Prior to Maturity (Method 1)

Assume that the buyer of a home helps finance its purchase with a $100,000 loan at an annual interest rate of 8% for 30 years, and then decides to sell the house after living in it for 10 years. What would be the unpaid principal balance of the loan at the end of 10 years?

At least two methods may be employed for finding the outstanding balance of a loan prior to its normal maturity. The first technique to be examined uses Columns 2 and 3 of the compound interest tables.

For an annual interest rate of 8% the table for monthly compounding contains the payment figure of 0.0007 in Column 3 for $n = 360$ months (30 years), and the amount of 182.9460 in Column 2 for $n = 120$ months (10 years). The monthly payment of $0.0007, invested at the nominal annual interest rate of 8%, is required to accumulate a future value of $1.00 over a 30-year period. Hence monthly payments of $0.0007 over 30 years will repay a principal of $1.00, if interest is being charged at the annual rate of 8 the principal is $100,000, the monthly payments need to be of size $70 (100,000 × $0.0007). The figure $182.9460 is the amount to which a series of monthly payments of $1.00 will grow (with interest at 8% over a period of 10 years. Since the payments are actually $70, the amount of $182.9460 is multiplied by 70 to get the amount ($12,806) to which a series of monthly payments of $70 will grow with interest over 10 years.

Thus $12,806 is the amount by which the principal is reduced after 10 years. The remaining balance of the debt is found to be $87,194 by deducting $12,806 from the initial loan balance of $100,000.

Greater accuracy can be achieved by taking the Column 3 and Column 2 factors to more decimal places. If the Column 3 number is taken to be 0.000671, and the Column 2 figure to be 182.94604, the principal reduction figure becomes $12,276. The deduction o $12,276 from $100,000 leaves a remaining principal balance of $87,724.

The figure of $87,724 is more accurate than the principal balance of $87,194 calculated with factors containing fewer decimal places. Borrowers and lenders should keep in mind that using fewer decimal places can produce results that are significantly different from those obtained using more precise values. In real situations that involve large sums of money, more decimal places are retained throughout the calculation.

BALLOON LOAN PAYMENT

This first method for finding the remaining principal balance of a loan at some time prior to the end of the normal life of the loan involves the same procedure that is used for finding the balloon payment that must be made with a balloon loan. The purchaser of a home who makes a $100,000 loan at an annual interest rate of 8% for 30 years could agree to pay the lender the remaining principal balance after 10 years. With such an understanding the borrower would make monthly payments of $733.76 for 10 years and then a balloon payment of $87,724 at the end of 10 years. After the balloon payment, the loan would terminate. If desired, however, the borrower and the lender could agree to an extension of the loan at the end of the 10-year period.

Example—Determining the Remaining Balance of a Loan Prior to Maturity (Method 2)

The second method for finding the remaining balance of a loan prior to maturity involves Column 5 and 6 of the compound interest tables. Consider again the situation with a $100,000 home loan, an annual interest rate of 8%, and an initial maturity of 30 years. If the home is sold after 10 years, what is the remaining loan balance at the time of the sale?

The first step in finding the remaining balance of the loan is to ascertain the size of the monthly payments for a loan maturity of 30 years. Column 6 of the table for an annual interest rate of 8% and monthly compounding shows a payment size of $0.0073 for a present value or loan amount of $1.00 with a maturity of $n = 360$ months. For greater accuracy, the column 6 value will be extended to seven decimal places to get 0.0073376.

The present value of the loan in this example is $100,000, so monthly payments of $733.76 (0.0073376 × 100,000) will be needed to amortize this loan.

If payments of $733.76 will amortize a loan amount (present value) of $100,000 in 30 years, then a payment size of $733.76 will amortize a loan amount (present value) of some unknown size in 20 years of remaining loan life.

Therefore for the second step Column 5 of the monthly compounding table is consulted. For $n = 240$ months (20 years), $119.5543 is the present value of a stream of $1.00 payments made every month for 20 years. Hence, monthly payments of $733.76 for 20 years have a present value of $87,724 ($119.5543 × 733.76).

The figure of $87,724 is the amount of principal that would be amortized if the loan payments were continued during the last 20 years of the loan and so this is the outstanding loan balance after ten years. This value agrees with the remaining loan balance of $87,724 obtained by the first method.

CONTRASTING MORTGAGES AND BONDS

Some similarities and differences may be noted between mortgages and bonds. A mortgage (or, more correctly, a loan) on a dwelling provides periodic payments of principal (or investment recapture) plus interest (investment income) to the lender. In general, bonds also provide the holder with a level stream of periodic payments. If desired, a mortgage lender could sell a mortgage to another lender in the same way that a bondholder (lender) could sell a bond to another investor.

Two major segments of the financial markets are the money market and the capital market. Short-term financial instruments compose the money market, whereas the capital market is comprised of longer term investment instruments. Mortgages and bonds are both part of the capital market.

One difference between the two investments is that mortgages usually involve monthly payments whereas bonds generally provide for semiannual payments. Another difference lies in the character of the payments. A portion of each mortgage payment represents a return of investment (principal repayment) plus a return on investment (interest). The calculation of the present value of a mortgage does not include a reversion in the stream of future benefits because some portion of the investment is repaid in each of the periodic payments. Since periodic bond payments consist of interest only, the present value computation of a bond contains a reversion (return of principal) in the flow of future benefits.

Just as the resale of bonds can involve discounts and premiums, (see Chapter 9), so may the resale of mortgages occur at discounts and premiums. If a bond has a 9% coupon while other bonds of similar quality and maturity are selling in the secondary market at a yield to maturity of 8%, then the bond would be expected to trade at a premium. For a secondary market yield to maturity of 10% and a bond coupon of 9%, the expectation would be for the bond to sell at a discount. Similarly, for a mortgage carrying a fixed annual interest rate of 9%, the mortgage would probably be resold at a premium if mortgages of similar quality and maturity were selling in the secondary market at a yield to maturity of 8%. A 9% fixed rate mortgage would be expected to trade at a discount in a secondary market environment of a 10% yield to maturity.

Example—Obtaining the Present Value of a Mortgage Selling at a Premium

Suppose that a $100 mortgage carries a fixed annual interest rate of 9% over a period of 30 years. What would be the price of the mortgage at the beginning of the thirty years at a yield to maturity of 8%?

Take as given that the 9% nominal annual interest rate table for monthly compounding carries a Column 6 figure of 0.0080462 for n = 360 months (30 years). The $100 mortgage would have monthly payments of principal and interest of $0.80462 ($100 × 0.0080462). Since the current market yield to maturity is 8 using the monthly compounding table for a nominal annual rate of 8% for n = 360 months. Column 5 contains a present value of $136.2835 for a stream of $1.00 monthly payments. For a stream of monthly payments of $0.80462, the present value would be $109.66 (136.2835 × $0.80462). A $100 mortgage with a fixed annual interest rate of 9% for 30 years would have a yield to maturity of 8% when priced at $109.66.

Example—Seeking the Present Value of a Mortgage Selling at a Discount

In this instance suppose that a 30-year $100 mortgage with a fixed yearly interest rate of 9% is to be priced to provide a yield to maturity of 10%. What would be the price (present value) of the mortgage at the beginning of the thirty years?

Column 6 of a monthly compounding table for a nominal annual rate of 9% would have a factor of 0.0080462 for n = 360 months (30 years), giving the mortgage monthly payments of $0.80462 ($100 × 0.0080462).

Column 5 of a monthly compounding table for a nominal annual rate of 10% shows a factor of 113.9508 for n = 360 months (or the factor can be calculated using the Column 5 methods in Chapter 8). The present value of a stream of 360 monthly payments of $0.80462 would be $91.69 (113.9508 × $0.80462). The price of a 30-year $100 mortgage with a fixed annual rate of 9% and a yield to maturity of 10% would be $91.69.

DETERMINING PAYMENT SIZE OF AN ANNUITY WHEN THE PRESENT VALUE IS KNOWN: RECIPROCAL RELATIONSHIP BETWEEN COLUMN 5 AND COLUMN 6

Since Column 5 lists the present value of n periodic payments of one unit each and Column 6 gives the size of n periodic payments that total to a present value of one unit, it is easily shown that Columns 5 and 6 are reciprocals of each other. Recall that Columns 2 and 3 are also reciprocals of each other (Chaper 6). As in that case, some slight discrepancies in the reciprocal relationship might appear in the tables, due to rounding. In the annual compounding table for a nominal annual rate of 8%, Column 5 contains the present value 4.6229 for $n = 6$ years. The reciprocal of this number if 0.02163, which appears in Column 6 for $n = 6$. If the reciprocal of 0.2163 is taken, the figure 4.6232 is obtained; the difference of 0.0003 between this value and the original 4.6229 is due to rounding and can be eliminated by taking 0.2163 to more decimal places.

The relationship between Column 5 and Column 6 may be better understood by comparing the manner in which the values of each column can be computed. Consider three annual periods (A1, A2, and A3).

Figure 11–1.   Time Line.

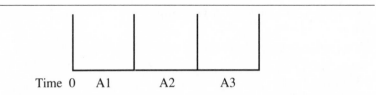

Time 0   A1   A2   A3

Three annual payments of $1.00 each, subject to a nominal rate of 8%, would have a present value (Column 5) of

$$PV_3 = \frac{1}{(1 + i)} + \frac{1}{(1 + i)^2} + \frac{1}{(1 + i)^3}$$

$$= \frac{1}{1 + 0.08} + \frac{1}{(1 + 0.08)^2} + \frac{1}{(1 + 0.08)^3}$$

$$= 0.9259 + 0.8573 + 0.7938$$

$$= 2.5770$$

Suppose that three annual payments of size $X_1 = X_2 = X_3 = X$ are made at a nominal annual rate of 8% so that they amortize a present value of $1.00. The payment size (Column 6) can be gotten from the following calculation.

$$PV_3 = \frac{X_1}{(1 + i)} + \frac{X_2}{(1 + i)^2} + \frac{X_3}{(1 + i)^3}$$

$$1 = \frac{X}{(1 + 0.08)} + \frac{X}{(1 + 0.08)^2} + \frac{X}{(1 + 0.08)^3}$$

$$= 0.9259X + 0.8573X + 0.7938X$$

$$= 2.5770X$$

$$= 0.3880$$

The present value of a $1.00 payment make n periods in the future (Column 4) is $V^n = 1/(1 + i)^n$. Here the present value (PV) equation for Column 6 could be viewed as

$$PV = X_1 V^1 + X_2 V^2 + X_3 V^3$$

since the first payment, X_1, is made after one period ($n = 1$), the second payment after two periods, and the third payment after three periods.

Column 5 is a column of present values. The stream of payments for each n is assumed to be composed of individual payments of $1.00 each. Since the payment size and the interest rate are known, the initially unknown present value can be computed. In Column 5 the payment size is fixed at $1.00 but there are no restrictions on the present values.

The payment size that belongs in Column 6 is unknown and has to be calculated. The payments are assumed to be equal. There are no other restrictions on the payments except that the present value of the stream of payments is fixed at $1.00 for each n. By knowing the present value and the interest rate, the payment size can be computed for each n.

For $n = 6$, the table for annual compounding (8% interest rate) contains a Column 5 present value of 4.6229 and a Column 6 payment size of 0.2163. A present value of $4.6229 is obtained from six annual payments of $1.00 each. From this it can be seen that a present value of $1.00 will produce a payment size that is $1/4.6229 \times$ the payment size of $1.00 in Column 5. Therefore each of the six payments in Column 6 will be $0.2163 ($1/4.6229 $\times$ $1.00).

The relationship between Columns 5 and 6 can be expressed as a direct proportion.

$$\frac{\text{Present value in Column 6}}{\text{Present value in Column 5}} = \frac{\text{Payment size in Column 6}}{\text{Payment size in Column 5}}$$

The payment size in Column 6 can be found by the following procedure.

$$\text{Payment size in Column 6} = \frac{\begin{matrix}\text{Present value} \\ \text{in Column 6}\end{matrix} \times \begin{matrix}\text{Payment size} \\ \text{in Column 5}\end{matrix}}{\text{Present value in Column 5}}$$

$$= \frac{1 \times 1}{4.6229}$$

$$= .216314$$

The present value in Column 5 would be

$$\text{Present value in Column 5} = \frac{\begin{matrix}\text{Present value} \\ \text{in Column 6}\end{matrix} \times \begin{matrix}\text{Payment size} \\ \text{in Column 5}\end{matrix}}{\text{Payment size in Column 6}}$$

$$= \frac{1 \times 1}{.216314}$$

$$= 4.6229$$

VALUE OF THE ANNUITY: RELATIONSHIP BETWEEN COLUMN 3 AND COLUMN 6

In addition to the relationship that Column 6 has with Column 5, there is also a relationship between Column 3 and Column 6. Column 3 may be viewed as containing the payments necessary to repay $1.00 of loan principal. Column 6 may be regarded as listing the payments required to repay an initial amount of $1.00 of loan principal plus the interest on the declining principal balance.

According to the table for monthly compounding for a nominal annual rate of 8 monthly payments of almost two cents each plus the interest that accumulates on these payments once they are paid would equal $1.00 at the end of four years. Forty-eight monthly payments of $0.0177 each would total $0.8496; the remaining $0.1504 would be provided by the interest on the payments.

It should be kept in mind that the interest amount of $.1504 on these payments of $.0177 has nothing to do with the interest required in Column 6 on an initial loan principal of $1.00 which declines to zero at the end of 48 months. The sole concern of Column 3 is to provide for the repayment of $1.00 of initial loan principal over a 48-month period.

For a nominal annual interest rate of 8%, the monthly interest rate is $R/m = i = 0.08/12 = 0.0067$ (0.67%). If the monthly interest rate of 0.0067 is added to the Column 3 factor of 0.0177, the Column 6 monthly payment size of 0.0244 for $n = 48$ months will be obtained. The relationship between Column 3 and Column 6 can be expressed as Column 3 factor $+ i =$ Column 6 factor where (i) is the periodic interest rate.

The monthly payment of $0.0244 for each $1.00 initially borrowed would provide for giving the lender a return of the original investment ($1.00) plus a return on the investment at the nominal annual interest rate of 8%.

DETERMINING THE PAYMENT SIZE OF AN ANNUITY WHEN THE PRESENT VALUE IS KNOWN: COLUMN 6 FORMULA

Column 5 present values can be computed using the formula (see Chapter 8)

$$a_{\overline{n}} = \frac{1 - \frac{1}{(1+i)^n}}{i}$$

Since the payment sizes in Column 6 are reciprocals of the present values in Column 5, this formula can be rearranged to calculate the Column 6 figures.

$$\frac{1}{a_{\overline{n}}} = \frac{i}{1 - \frac{1}{(1+i)^n}}$$

Using the Column 6 formula, what would be the quarterly payments of principal and interest on a three-year loan of $50,000 at a fixed annual rate of 8%?

$$\frac{1}{a_{\overline{n}|}} = \frac{i}{1 - \frac{1}{(1+i)^n}}$$

$$= \frac{R/m}{1 - \frac{1}{(1+R/m)^h}}$$

$$= \frac{0.08/4}{1 - \frac{1}{(1+0.08/4)^{12}}}$$

$$= \frac{0.02}{1 - 0.7885}$$

$$= \frac{0.02}{0.2115}$$

$$= 0.0946$$

The quarterly payments for a $1.00 loan would be $0.0946, or more than nine cents according to the Column 6 formula. The figure $0.0946 agrees with the factor found for $n = 12$ quarters in Column 6 of the quarterly compounding table where the nominal annual rate is 8 principal and interest for a three-year $50,000 loan would be $4,730 (0.0946 × $50,000).

ADD-ON RATES OF INTEREST

In automobile and other types of installment financing, the nominal annual rate of interest (also called annual percentage rate, or APR) on a loan may be converted into an add-on interest rate if desired. Column 6 of the compound interest tables may be employed to convert a nominal annual interest rate to an annual add-on interest rate.

Example—Converting an Annual Percentage Rate (APR) to an Add-On Rate

Assume that a four-year loan has an annual percentage rate (nominal annual rate of interest) of 8%. The payments are monthly and the compounding is monthly. What would be the annual add-on interest rate?

For a nominal annual interest rate of 8%, Column 6 of the monthly compounding table has a factor of 0.0244 for $n = 48$ months (4 years). If the factor is carried out to six decimal places, the number becomes 0.024413.

A total amount of $1.1718 ($0.024413 per month for 48 months) would have to be paid to a lender in order to return the principal of $1.00 and provide $0.1718 in interest. Over a four-year period, the interest payment would amount to 17.18% of the principal. The add-on interest rate is the average per year of the total interest rate. In this case it is 4.30% (17.18% ÷ 4 years).

If given a figure of 4.30% as the annual add-on interest rate, how would a borrower determine what monthly payment would be required for a four-year loan of $1.00 in order to pay interest and repay principal?

Since the annual add-on interest rate is 4.30%, the monthly interest is 0.3583% (4.30% ÷ 12), or $0.003583 being that the principal is $1.00. If $1.00 of principal is repaid over 48 months, the principal repayment per month becomes $0.020833 ($1.00 ÷ 48). The total monthly payment per dollar of loan principal would thus be $0.024416 ($0.003583 plus $0.020833). This figure matches the factor of 0.0244 found in Column 6 of the monthly compounding table.

Example — Using an Add-on Interest Rate to Find Monthly Payments for a Car Purchase

Suppose that an automobile is bought using installment financing. The amount of the financing is $13,000, and the principal and interest are to be paid monthly over a three-year period. The annual add-on interest rate is 6.52%. How much will the purchaser's monthly payments be?

The interest for three years can be figured by using the general interest equation (see Chapter 2).

$$I = PRT$$
$$= (\$13,000)(0.0652)(3)$$
$$= \$2,543$$

The interest amount of $2,543 is added on to the loan principal of $13,000 to get a total sum of $15,543. Based on a total of 36 months, the monthly payments would be $431.75 ($15,543 ÷ 36 months).

The Column 6 factor for a nominal annual interest rate of 12%, monthly compounding, and $n = 36$ months would be 0.033214. If 0.033214 is

Table 11-7. Annual Add-On Interest Rates (in Percent) Corresponding to Selected Annual Percentage Rates (Monthly Compounding).

Maturity	9%	10%	11%	12%	13%	14%	15%	16%
12 Months (1 year)	4.94	5.50	6.06	6.62	7.18	7.74	8.31	8.88
24 Months (2 years)	4.82	5.37	5.93	6.49	7.05	7.62	8.18	8.76
36 Months (3 years)	4.83	5.39	5.95	6.52	7.10	7.68	8.27	8.86
48 Months (4 years)	4.86	5.44	6.01	6.60	7.19	7.79	8.40	9.01
60 Months (5 years)	4.91	5.50	6.09	6.69	7.30	7.92	8.55	9.18
72 Months (6 years)	4.96	5.56	6.17	6.79	7.42	8.06	8.71	9.36
84 Months (7 years)	5.02	5.64	6.26	6.90	7.54	8.20	8.87	9.55
96 Months (8 years)	5.08	5.71	6.35	7.00	7.67	8.35	9.03	9.73
108 Months (9 years)	5.14	5.78	6.44	7.11	7.79	8.49	9.20	9.92
120 Months (10 years)	5.20	5.86	6.53	7.22	7.92	8.63	9.36	10.10

multiplied by the loan principal of $13,000, a monthly payment figure of $431.78 is obtained. (Rounding causes the payment of $431.78 to differ from the above figure of $431.75.)

The 12% annual percentage rate provides for a return of investment as well as a return on investment computed on a declining principal balance. The 6.52% add-on rate does not make provision for a recapture of the lender's investment and is calculated on a fixed amount of initial principal. Payments of principal and interest are determined by adding on the interest to the original principal and then allocating this sum over the number of periodic payments that are to be made.

Some annual add-on interest rates have been computed for various annual percentage rates in Table 11.7. The add-on rates are based on Column 6 factors (monthly compounding) that have been calculated to six decimal places.

The table shows, for instance, that an annual add-on rate of 5.44% corresponds to an annual percentage rate of 10% where payments are made monthly for four years (48 months). An annual percentage rate of 10% would be equivalent to an annual add-on rate of 5.39% for monthly payments occurring over a period of 36 months (three years).

12 SUMMARY (PART I)

Included in the material of the previous chapters has been an analysis of the six functions of $1.00 that appear in the compound interest tables. The equations used to calculate the entries in each column are listed in Table 12.1. The periodic interest rate is i, and n is the number of periods.

For three compounding periods ($n = 3$) and ($i = 0.08$), for instance, the specific entries in the columns could be found as follows.

Column 1

$$\text{Future Value} = (1 + i)^3$$

Column 2

$$\text{Future Value} = \frac{(1 + i)^3 - 1}{i}$$

Column 3

$$\text{Payment Size} = \frac{i}{(1 + i)^3 - 1}$$

Column 4

$$\text{Present Value} = \frac{1}{(1 + i)^3}$$

Table 12–1.   Compound Interest Table Formulas.

Column	Formula
1. Future Value of 1 (Lump Sum)	$S = (1 + i)^n$
2. Future Value of 1 per Period (Amount of an Annuity)	$S_{\overline{n}} = \dfrac{(1 + i)^n - 1}{i}$
3. Sinking Fund Payment (Future Value is 1)	$\dfrac{1}{S_{\overline{n}}} = \dfrac{i}{(1 + i)^n - 1}$
4. Present Value of 1 (Lump Sum)	$V^n = \dfrac{1}{(1 + i)^n}$
5. Present Value of 1 per Period (Present Value of an Annuity)	$a_{\overline{n}} = \dfrac{1 - \dfrac{1}{(1 + i)^n}}{i}$
6. Periodic Payment to Amortize 1 (Present Value is 1)	$\dfrac{1}{a_{\overline{n}}} = \dfrac{i}{1 - \dfrac{1}{(1 + i)^n}}$

Column 5

$$\text{Present Value} = \frac{1 - \frac{1}{(1+i)^3}}{i}$$

Column 6

$$\text{Payment Size} = \frac{i}{1 - \frac{1}{(1+i)^3}}$$

As can be seen in the equations in Table 12.1, the expression $(1 + i)^n$ serves as the basis for the future value equations as well as the present value equations. Although the expression $(1 + i)^n$ appears in both the future value and present value equations, the discounting in the present value arrangements is achieved by the use of reciprocals of $(1 + i)^n$.

As further clarification of the Column 2–Column 3 relationship, consider the following equation.

$$\$75(1 + .04)^2 + \$75(1 + .04) + \$75 = \$234.12$$

If the future value ($234.12) is unknown, the equation is a Column 2 type problem because Column 2 contains the future values of annuities when payment size is known.

Should the payment size ($75) be unknown, the equation is a Column 3 type problem since Column 3 contains payment sizes of annuities when total future value is known.

Regarding the relationship between Column 5 and Column 6, examine the following equation.

$$\$133.65 = \$50\left[\frac{1}{(1 + .06)}\right] + \$50\left[\frac{1}{(1 + .06)^2}\right] + \$50\left[\frac{1}{(1 + .06)^3}\right]$$

If this equation is solved for an unknown present value ($133.65), the equation becomes a Column 5 type problem since Column 5 is composed of the present values of annuities when payment size is known.

Solving the same equation for an unknown payment size ($50) would make the equation a Column 6 type problem in that Column 6 contains payment sizes of annuities when total present value is known.

In using the equations themselves or the compound interest tables to solve problems it is necessary to identify first whether a future value, a present value, or a payment size is being sought. Solutions to certain problems may require more than one step and the use of more than one compound interest column or equation.

If the growth, or future value, is needed for a lump sum payment or deposit that accumulates interest at a periodic rate i, then the Column 1 formula can be used to obtain that future value.

The Column 2 equation can be employed when a future value is desired for an annuity, that is, a series of level payments or deposits that accumulates interest.

When the future value (including the accumulated interest) of a series of payments or deposits is known, the Column 3 equation can be utilized to find the size of the required level periodic payments or deposits.

The Column 4 formula allows for the determination of the present value of a future lump sum payment or receipt.

The Column 5 equation can be used to determine the present value of an annuity (a series of level future payments or receipts).

Where the present value (principal) of a series of future payments is known, the Column 6 equation makes it possible to arrive at the level periodic payment size necessary to pay interest as well as provide for the repayment of principal.

The factors in the compound interest tables are based on the following assumptions:

In Column 1, a lump sum payment or deposit of one unit (e.g., $1.00) is made at the beginning of the first period.

In Column 2, periodic payments or deposits of $1.00 occur at the end of each period.

In Column 3, level periodic payments grow to a future value of $1.00

In Column 4, the lump sum payment or receipt of $1.00 happens at the end of the period.

In Column 5, periodic payments or receipts of $1.00 take place at the end of each period.

In Column 6, a present value of $1.00 is to be amortized.

In Columns 2, 3, 5, and 6, the compounding frequency is the same as the frequency of the payments, deposits, or receipts.

There are two kinds of interest: simple interest and compound interest. The dissimilarity between the two types lies in the fact that simple interest does not accumulate interest on interest that has been earned, whereas compound interest does.

A nominal (stated) rate of interest is an uncompounded rate. When a nominal annual interest rate (R) is adjusted for the compounding frequency per year (m), it becomes a periodic interest rate (i). For example, a nominal annual rate of 12% is transformed into a periodic interest rate of 1% when it is adjusted for monthly compounding. (That is, $i = R/m = 0.12/12 = 0.01$ or 1%).

An effective rate of interest is a compounded rate. It incorporates the effects of compounding, that is, interest on interest. It is the interest on interest that produces the difference between a nominal interest rate and an effective interest rate. An effective annual interest rate is generated when a periodic interest rate is compounded for one year. Effective interest rates may also be calculated for periods exceeding a year.

Compounding and the computation of effective interest rates may be done in several ways. For the calculations that follow, assume an initial principal of $100 and a nominal annual interest rate of 10% compounded quarterly, which gives a periodic interest rate of 2.5%.

Method 1

This approach reflects the basic concept of compound interest. It makes the assumption that the quarterly accruals of earned interest are not paid by the borrower to the lender. The earned interest is retained within the original investment and is converted into principal at the end of the quarterly periods so that interest on interest is generated internally. In this technique an uncompounded periodic interest rate is applied to an increasing amount of principal. Here $i = 2.5\%$ since the yearly rate of 10% is compounded quarterly. The amount of a $100 deposit at the end of each of the next four quarters can be found as follows.

$$(\$100.0000)(1.025) = \$102.5000$$
$$(\$102.5000)(1.025) = \$105.0625$$
$$(\$105.0625)(1.025) = \$107.6891$$
$$(\$107.6891)(1.025) = \$110.3813$$

The growth of an initial principal amount of $100 to $110.3813 at the end of one year (4 quarterly periods) indicates an effective annual interest rate of 10.3813%. The interest on interest of 0.3813% causes the difference between the nominal annual interest rate (10.000%) and the effective annual interest rate.

Method 2

The second method for compounding and figuring interest on interest is reflective of how the compound interest tables are used. A compounded periodic interest rate is applied to a given amount of principal P. Since this is a lump sum deposit, a Column 1 calculation is done to find S, the amount to which the principal grows.

$$S = P(1 + i)^n$$
$$= (\$100)(1 + 0.025)^4$$

$$= (\$100)(1.025)^4$$
$$= (\$100)(1.103813)$$
$$= \$110.3813$$

Again, the growth of $100 to $110.3813 over a one-year period (4 quarters) provides an effective annual interest rate of 10.3813%.

Method 3

The earning of interest on interest may be done externally, or outside of the original investment. Two accounts may be visualized for explaining this approach. In one account is an initial principal that earns interest at the end of each quarter at the quarterly rate of 2.5%.

As soon as the paid interest is received by the lender at the end of each quarter, the money is placed in the second account, which is another investment that is external to the original investment. In the second account each reinvested interest payment is allowed to earn interest at the periodic rate of 2.5%. This rate is compounded on each payment over the remaining life of the original investment. The accumulation of interest is displayed in this quarterly interest schedule.

End of Period	Account1		Account2	
Quarter 1	($100) (0.025) =	$2.50	($2.50) (1.025)^3 =	$2.6922
Quarter 2	($100) (0.025) =	2.50	($2.50) (1.025)^2 =	2.6266
Quarter 3	($100) (0.025) =	2.50	($2.50) (1.025) =	2.5625
Quarter 4	($100) (0.025) =	2.50	($2.50) =	2.5000
	Totals	$10.00		$10.3813

The total amount of interest on principal plus interest on interest is $10.3813. Since interest on the $100 of principal for one year (4 quarters) is $10, the interest on interest is $0.3813. Once again the effective annual interest rate for a nominal annual interest rate of 10% compounded quarterly is found to be 10.3813%.

It is possible to use a reinvestment rate in the second account that is not the same as the rate in the first account. When different rates are used in the two accounts, a modified interest rate reflecting the combination of the two account rates can be calculated.

An effective interest rate may also be found for periods exceeding a year. Two of the ways for doing this involve the compounding of a periodic interest rate and the compounding of an effective annual interest rate. For example, for a quarterly rate of 2.5%, the effective rate for three years would be 34.49%.

$$S = (1 + i)^n$$
$$= (1 + 0.025)^{12}$$
$$= 1.3449$$

effective rate $= 1.3449 - 1 = 0.3449$, or 34.49%

Using an effective annual interest rate of 10.3813%, the effective interest rate for a three-year period is also found to be 34.49%.

$$S = (1.103813)^3 = 1.3449$$

effective rate $= 1.3449 - 1 = 0.3449$, or 34.49%

For a loan maturity of one year and a given nominal annual interest rate, it is most advantageous for the borrower when the total amount of interest on principal is payable at the end of a loan. It is least advantageous for the borrower when the total interest is payable at the start of the loan (discount loan).

Where the partial payments of interest on principal are due at periods falling beyond the start of a loan, it is better for a borrower to make these interests payments as seldom as possible. For example, from the borrower's standpoint semiannual interest payments would be superior to quarterly payments, which in turn would be better than having to make monthly interest payments.

For a loan period of one year and a given nominal annual rate of interest, it would be most advantageous for a lender (investor) to have total interest on principal payable at the beginning of a loan (discount loan). It would be least desirable to have the total amount of interest payable at the end of the loan.

For partial interest payments occurring at points beyond the commencement of a loan, it would be more beneficial for a lender to receive these interest payments as frequently as possible. For instance, it would be more preferable for the lender if interest were received, say, on a monthly basis rather than quarterly or semiannually.

In cases where a borrower or a lender has to make a decision from among alternatives having different nominal interest rates and varying payment or compounding frequencies, the decision task can be simplified by converting the nominal rates and their respective compounding frequencies to effective interest rates. The effective interest rate provides a standard by which a comparison of alternatives can be made.

PART II
USING FINANCIAL CALCULATORS TO FURNISH INVESTING AND BORROWING SOLUTIONS AND TO CONSTRUCT COMPOUND INTEREST TABLES

13 SOLVING INVESTING AND BORROWING PROBLEMS WITH FINANCIAL CALCULATORS

Financial calculators may be used to solve investing and borrowing problems involving compound interest. However, the ability to press calculator keys is no substitute for having a genuine understanding of the concepts underlying the uses of compound interest.

An understanding of compound interest and the development of a mental framework for dealing with compound interest is best achieved through a study of the compound interest tables. This is the reason that the previous chapters have been devoted to the six columns of the tables. The more a person knows about the compound interest tables the better equipped that individual will be to solve problems and to interpret solutions involving compound interest. With this background, it is possible to analyze the solution process as investing and borrowing problems are being worked with a financial calculator. A person who has merely memorized the calculator keys to press in order to arrive at a particular type of answer does not really understand what is behind the solution.

A person with the ability to analyze compound interest will probably be able to figure out how to get an investing or borrowing solution to a problem with a financial calculator. On the other hand, a person who has concentrated only on memorizing which calculator keys to press may not only start confusing the memorized key sequences but may also encounter problems that do not exactly fit any of the patterns learned.

Different types of financial calculators having different keyboard configurations may be purchased. An attempt will not be made to describe how to get solutions to investing and borrowing problems with each type of calculator available on the market. Instead, a general approach will be described for using a financial calculator to obtain answers to problems reflecting the assumptions underlying each of the six columns of the compound interest tables.

The basic compound interest equation is $S = P(1 + i)^n$. The symbol S stands for the future value (FV) to which a principal amount P, or present value (PV), will grow when compounded at a periodic interest or growth rate i over a total number of interest or compounding periods n. The periodic growth rate i is obtained by dividing the nominal annual interest rate (R) by the number of interest or compounding periods per year (m) (that is, $i = R/m$).

Financial calculators that are designed for solving compound interest problems provide for assigning values to the following variables.

i periodic interest or growth rate
n total number of interest or compounding periods
PV   present value of an amount or amounts
FV   future value of an amount or amounts
PMT   size of a payment or payments

Table 13–1 shows which variables would be affected by problems involving each of the six columns of the compound interest tables. An (X) marks the quantities that have to be put into the calculator. A question mark (?) indicates the value to be found by the calculator. A dash ($-$) signals that a value is not involved in the problem solution.

Notice that each combination is unique. If values are put in for i, n, and PMT, for example, and the present value is found, this will be the Column 5 value, the present value of an annuity.

Table 13–1. Variables Needed and Found For Various Compound Interest Calculations.

Table Column	i	n	PV	FV	PMT
Column 1	X	X	X	?	—
Column 2	X	X	—	?	X
Column 3	X	X	—	X	?
Column 4	X	X	?	X	—
Column 5	X	X	?	—	X
Column 6	X	X	X	—	?

Problems involving each of the columns of the compound interest tables will now be presented. In the problems involving Columns 2, 3, 5 and 6, the long forms of the column equations are used so as to provide a better understanding of the solutions. The short forms are listed in Chapter 12.

Example—Determining the Future Value of a Loss with an Award of Prejudgment Interest by a Court (Column 1 Type Problem)

A court has awarded a lawyer's client prejudgment interest at a rate of 10% compounded annually on a $65,000 loss the plaintiff sustained three years ago. What would be the amount of the award, excluding attorney fees?

Given

> i 10%
>
> n 3 years
>
> PV $65,000

Find

> FV

Answer

> FV = $86,515

The amount of the plaintiff's award would be $86,515.

The equation $S = P(1 + i)^n$ would offer another means of solution for FV.

$$FV = S = (\$65,000)(1 + 0.10)^3$$

Example—Calculating Values in the Compound Interest Equation (Column 1 or Column 4)

In the preceding legal example, there are four quantities of interest: i, u, PV, and FV. Given any three, the fourth can be found. The method for finding FV given i, n, and PV has already been shown.

Calculate the present value PV.   This is, in effect, a Column 4 calculation. We want to find the present value of a lump sum whose future value (FV) is known.

Given

i	10%
n	3 years
FV	$86,515

Find

PV

Answer

PV = $65,000

The equation would be

$$\$86,515 = (PV)(1 + 0.10)^3$$

Calculate the periodic interest rate i.

Given

n	3 years
PV	$65,000
FV	$86,515

Find

i

Answer

$i = 10\%$

The equation would be

$$\$86,515 = (\$65,000)(1 + i)^3$$

Calculate the number of periods n.

Given

i	10%
PV	$65,000
FV	$86,515

Find

n

Answer

$n = 3$ years

The equation would be

$$\$86,515 = (\$65,000)(1 + 0.10)^n$$

Example—Ascertaining the Rate of Growth
(Column 1 Type Problem)

A company's annual sales have risen from $72 million to $90 million during a time frame of four years. What has been the annual rate of growth?

Given

n	4 years
PV	$\$72 \times 10^6$
FV	$\$90 \times 10^6$

Find

i

Answer

$i = 5.7\%$

The annual rate of growth is 5.7%.
   The equation would be

$$(\$90 \times 10^6) = (\$72 \times 10^6)(1 + i)^4$$

Example—Determining the Rate of Decline
(Column 1 Type Problem)

In the equation $S = P(1 + i)^n$, i is the rate of change. If there has been growth, i is positive. If there has been a decline (i.e., if S is less than P), then i is negative.
   If a firm has seen its annual sales drop from $90 million to $72 million over a period of four years, what would be the annual rate of decline?

Given

n	4 years
PV	$\$90 \times 10^6$
FV	$\$72 \times 10^6$

Find

   i

Answer

   $i = -5.4\%$

The rate of decline is 5.4% per year.
   The equation would be

$$(\$72 \times 10^6) = (\$90 \times 10^6)(1 + i)^4$$

The negative rate of growth (that is, rate of decline) can be obtained explicitly.

$$
\begin{aligned}
\$72 \times 10^6 &= (\$90 \times 10^6)(1 + i)^4 \\
(1 + i)^4 &= \$72 \times 10^6 / \$90 \times 10^6 = 0.800 \\
(1 + i) &= 0.9457 \\
i &= -0.054, \text{ or } -5.4\%
\end{aligned}
$$

Example—Finding the Effective Annual Interest Rate Charged on a Stock Margin Account (Column 1 Type Problem)

An investor bought a stock in a margin account one year ago. (That is, the investor bought a certain amount of stock while actually paying only a part of the total cost). The stock started rising after it was purchased, and the investor has not reduced the initial margin balance or the monthly interest charges that have been debited to the account.

   Although call money rates usually accompany the changes or movements in other money market rates, the assumption will be made that the investor is charged a nominal annual rate of 13% during the year. What is the investor's effective annual interest cost or borrowing rate?

   The equation $S = P(1 + i)^n$ may be used.

Given

   i 1.0833% (13% ÷ 12 months)

   n 12 months

   PV   \$1.00

Find

   FV

Answer

FV = $1.1380

If a beginning amount of $1.00 grows to $1.1380 at the end of one year, then the investor's effective annual interest rate or borrowing cost is

$$\text{Effective Annual Rate} = \frac{\$1.1380 - \$1.00}{\$1.00} = 0.1380, \text{ or } 13.80\%$$

The following substitution would be made in the growth equation to get the future value.

$$FV = (\$1.00)(1 + 0.010833)^{12}$$

Example—Obtaining the Adjusted Annual Discount Rate and Effective Annual Interest Rate for a Discount Security (Column 1 Type Problem)

An investor buys a discount security with a current maturity of 114 days at an annual discount rate of 7%. On the basis of a 365-day year, what is the security's adjusted annual discount rate and the effective annual interest rate?

Given

Annual discount rate   7%

n   114 days

Find

Adjusted annual discount rate

Effective annual discount rate

Answer

7.26%, 7.44%

Thus,

$$\begin{aligned}\text{Adjusted Annual Discount Rate} &= \frac{(365)(\text{Annual discount rate})}{360 - (\text{Annual discount rate})(\text{Current maturity})} \\ &= \frac{(365)(0.07)}{360 - (0.07)(114)} \\ &= 0.0726 \text{ or } 7.26\%\end{aligned}$$

Since the adjusted annual discount rate, 7.26%, is figured on the basis of a 365-day year, it is also the bond or coupon equivalent yield.

The effective annual interest rate is 7.44%, computed as shown.

$$1 + \text{Effective annual rate} = \left(1 + \frac{R}{m}\right)^n$$

$$= \left(1 + \frac{0.0726}{365/114}\right)^{\frac{365}{114}}$$

$$= 1.0744$$

Effective annual rate $= 1.0744 - 1 = 0.0744$ or 7.44%

A means of arriving at the equation for the adjusted annual discount rate is as follows. Where P is the par amount of principal,

$$I = PRT$$

$$= (1)(0.07)\left(\frac{114}{360}\right)$$

Where P is the discounted amount of principal,

$$R = \frac{I}{PT}$$

$$= \frac{(1)(0.07)(\frac{114}{360})}{\left[1 - \frac{(1)(0.07)(114)}{360}\right](\frac{114}{360})}$$

$$= \frac{0.07}{\left[360 - (0.07)(114)\right]/360} \times \frac{365}{360}$$

$$= \frac{(365)(0.07)}{360 - (0.07)(114)}$$

Example—Verifying the Effective Annual Interest Rate Paid On Bank Savings Deposits (Column 1 Type Problem)

A bank advertises that it pays an annual rate of 9.20% compounded daily on one-year savings deposits. It stipulates further that this rate provides an effective annual yields of 9.78%. Is 9.78% the correct effective annual yield, or has there been a printing error by the newspaper?

Given

    i   0.02556% (9.20% ÷ 360 days)

    n   365 days

    PV $1.00

Find

    FV

Answer

    FV = $1.0978

    Effective Annual Rate = 1.0978 − 1 = 0.0978, or 9.78%

The advertisement is correct since 9.78% is the effective annual yield. The equation to find the final value would be

$$FV = (\$1.00)(1 + 0.0002556)^{365}$$

Attention is drawn to the fact that in this example the nominal annual rate of 9.20% is divided by 360 days in order to get the periodic interest rate of 0.02556% (the decimal 0.0002556). However, a total of 365, rather than 360, days is used as the value of the exponent *n*. The time values the bank uses, if different from these, would need to be given. Different time values would cause a difference in effective rates.

Example—Computing the Effective Annual Interest Rate Charged on Credit Card Unpaid Debit Balances (Column 1 Type Problem)

A consumer has a credit card from a company that charges an interest rate of 1.25% per month on unpaid monthly balances. What effective annual rate of interest does the consumer pay on the unpaid debit balances?

    The monthly rate of 1.25% corresponds to a nominal annual interest rate of 15% (1.25% times 12 months).

Given

    i   1.25% (15% ÷ 12 months)

    n   12 months

    PV $1.00

Find
    FV

Answer
    FV = $1.1608

    Effective Annual Rate = 1.1608 − 1 = 0.1608, or 16.08%

The effective annual interest rate is 16.08%.
    The equation $S = P(1 + i)^n$ used in the solution would be

$$FV = (\$1.00)(1 + 0.0125)^{12}$$

Example—Seeking the Modified Nominal Annual Rate of a Bond (Column 1 Type Problem)

A ten-year $100 bond has a total future value of $207.48, or $2.0748 per dollar of bond par value. The presumption is made that the $4 semiannual coupon payments are reinvested at a rate of 6%. What is the modified nominal annual rate of this par bond whose yield to maturity is 8%?
    The Column 1 equation would become

$$P(1 + i)^n = S$$

$$\$100\left(1 + \frac{R}{2}\right)^{20} = \$207.48$$

$$(1 + ?)^{20} = \$2.0748$$

Given
    n 20 semiannual periods
    PV $1.00
    FV $2.0748

Find
    i

Answer
    i = 3.72% per semiannual period (7.44% per year)

The modified nominal annual rate of the bond is 7.44%. *Note:* The present value of $1.00 may have to be entered in some calculators as a negative figure.

Example—Calculating the Future Value of a Series of Bonus Payments Used to Provide for an Addition to a Home (Column 2 Type Problem)

A homeowner's annual bonus is going to be invested each year for the next three years in order to accumulate funds that can be applied toward the construction of an addition to the house. How much money will have accumulated at the end of the three years if it is assumed that the homeowner's estimated annual net bonus of $6,000 can earn a yearly return of 7.5% compounded annually?

Given

i 7.5%

n 3 years

PMT $6,000

Find

FV

Answer

FV = $19,384

The homeowner will have $19,384 at the end of three years.

The long form of the Column 2 equation would be

$$(\$6,000)(1 + 0.075)^2 + (\$6,000)(1 + 0.075) + \$6,000 = FV$$

Example—Obtaining Other Values in the Long Form of the Column 2 Equation

The previous example had four quantities of interest: i, n, PMT, and FV. Given any three of them, the fourth can be found. We have already calculated FV given i, n, and PMT.

Calculate the payment value PMT.

Given

i 7.5%

n 3 years

FV $19,384

Find

PMT

Answer

PMT = $6,000

The equation would be

$$\text{PMT}(1 + 0.075)^2 + \text{PMT}(1 + 0.075) + \text{PMT} = \$19,384$$

Note that this is the same as a Column 3 equation: finding the payment size of an annuity when the future value is known.

Calculate the interest rate i.

Given

n	3 years
PMT	$6,000
FV	$19,384

Find

i

Answer

$i = 7.5\%$

(Note: Some calculators may require that either the value of PMT or FV be put in with a minus sign before they will do the computation.)

The equation would be

$$\$6,000(1 + i)^2 + \$6,000(1 + i) + \$6,000 = \$19,384.$$

Calculate the number of payments n.

Given

i	7.5%
PMT	$6,000
FV	$19,384

Find

n

Answer

$n = 3$ years

(See the foregoing note regarding a change of signs.)

The equation would be

$$\$6,000(1 + 0.075)^{n-1} + \$6,000(1 + 0.075)^{n-2} + \$6,000 = \$19,384$$

Example—Figuring the Breakeven Reinvestment Rate of a Coupon Bond Based on a Zero Coupon Bond Yield (Column 2 Type Problem)

A ten-year $100 zero coupon bond provides its owner with a return of 9% compounded semiannually.

A second $100 bond with a ten-year life is a par bond that has a coupon rate of 9.50% and semiannual payments of $4.75. What reinvestment rate will give this debt obligation a return from interest on principal and interest on interest that will be equivalent to the return on the zero coupon bond?

If a hypothetical ten-year $100 par bond had a coupon rate of 9% and a reinvestment rate of 9%, it would provide its holder with a return of 9% compounded semiannually (the same as the return on the zero coupon bond). Therefore, the first step in finding a reinvestment rate for the par bond with the 9.50% coupon involves a determination of the total return from interest on principal and interest on interest on this hypothetical par bond with a 9 percent coupon.

Step 1

Given

    i 4.5% (9% ÷ 2 semiannual periods)
    n 20 semiannual periods
    PMT $4.50

Find

    FV

Answer

    FV = $141.17

The long form of the Column 2 equation would be

$$\$4.50(1 + .045)^{19} + \$4.50(1 + .045)^{18} + \cdots + \$4.50 = ?$$

The second step requires seeking a reinvestment rate for a series of $4.75 payments that will produce a return from interest on principal and interest on interest of $141.17.

Step 2

Given

    n 20 semiannual periods
    PMT $4.75
    FV $141.17

Find

> i

Answer

> i = 3.98% per semiannual period (or 7.96% per year)

Note: Some financial calculators may require that the amount of $141.17 in the second step be entered as a negative quantity.

The long form equation for Step 2 would be

$$\$4.75(1 + ?)^{19} + \$4.75(1 + ?)^{18} + \cdots + \$4.75 = \$141.17$$

An annual reinvestment rate of 7.96% will give the bond with a 9.50% coupon a return that is equivalent to the return of the zero coupon bond. A reinvestment rate of more than 7.96% will provide the 9.50% coupon bond with a return that exceeds the return of the zero coupon bond, and a reinvestment rate of under 7.96% will give the 9.50% coupon bond a return that is less than that supplied by the zero coupon bond.

Example — Ascertaining the Size of Equal Deposits Needed for the Future Purchase of Home Appliances (Column 3 Type Problem)

A consumer wants to be able to pay cash one year from now for home appliances worth $2,700. In order to have $2,700 at the end of twelve months how much money will the consumer have to place in a savings arrangement each month? A yearly earning rate of 7% compounded monthly is anticipated on the savings.

Given

> i 0.583% (7% ÷ 12 months)
> n 12 months
> FV $2,700

Find

> PMT

Answer

> PMT = $217.88

Each of the consumer's monthly deposits will have to be $217.88.

The Column 3 equation could be written as follows.

$$\text{PMT}(1 + 0.00583)^{11} + \text{PMT}(1 + 0.00583)^{10} + \cdots + \text{PMT} = \$2,700$$

Example—Finding the Purchase Price of a Company's Zero Coupon Bonds (Column 4 Type Problem)

A promising high technology company is offering to pay an annual rate of 12% compounded semiannually to a small group of investors if they will purchase the firm's five-year debt obligations. The debt would be sold as discount bonds. How much would the investors pay now for each $1,000 of zero coupon bonds that they purchase?

Given

    i 6% (12% ÷ 2 semiannual periods)
    n 10 semiannual periods
    FV $1,000

Find

    PV

Answer

    PV = $558.39

The investors would pay $558.39 for each $1,000 of debt they decide to buy.

    The set up for the Column 4 equation would be

$$\text{PV} = (\$1,000)\left[\frac{1}{(1 + 0.06)^{10}}\right]$$

Example—Computing Other Quantities in the Column 4 Equation

The Column 4 equation involves four quantities: i, n, FV, and PV. Given any three of these, the fourth value can be found. Finding PV given i, n, and FV has already been done for the preceding example.
Find the future value FV.

$$\$558.39 = FV\left[\frac{1}{(1 + 0.06)^{10}}\right]$$

$$\text{FV} = \$1,000$$

Note that this is the same as a Column 1 calculation: finding the future value of a lump sum.

Find the interest rate i.

$$\$558.39 = \$1,000\left[\frac{1}{(1 + i)^{10}}\right]$$

$$i = 6.0\%$$

Find the number of periods n.

$$\$558.39 = \$1,000\left[\frac{1}{(1 + 0.06)^n}\right]$$

$$n = 10 \text{ semiannual periods}$$

Example—Finding the Compensation to be Paid to an Injured Employee (Column 5 Type Problem)

An employee is to be compensated now for a work-related injury. The payment is to reflect a rate of $250 per week for a total of 26 weeks. How much will the injured worker receive if the payments are discounted at an annual rate of 5%?

Given

i	.096% (5% ÷ 52 weeks)
n	26 weeks
PMT	$250

Find

PV

Answer

PV = $6,417

The employee will receive $6,417 now.

The equation for Column 5 would appear as follows.

$$PV = \$250\left[\frac{1}{(1 + .00096)}\right] + \$250\left[\frac{1}{(1 + .00096)^2}\right] + \cdots$$

$$+ \$250\left[\frac{1}{(1 + .00096)^{26}}\right]$$

Example—Figuring a Death Settlement Payment to Be Made to the Spouse of a Deceased Person (Column 5 Type Problem)

The spouse of a person who was killed in an accident is to get a settlement payment now. The payment will be based on a stream of ten annual payments of $75,000 each.

How much will the spouse get if the payments are discounted at an annual rate of 6%?

Given

i 6%

n 10 years

PMT $75,000

Find

PV

Answer

PV = $552,007

A payment of $552,007 will be made to the spouse.

The following equation contains the problem data.

$$PV = \$75,000\left[\frac{1}{(1 + .06)}\right] + \$75,000\left[\frac{1}{(1 + .06)^2}\right] + \cdots$$

$$+ \$75,000\left[\frac{1}{(1 + .06)^{10}}\right]$$

Example—Determining the Present Value of a Series of Rental Payments (Column 5 Type Problem)

A firm obtained a five-year lease on some warehouse space four years ago. Although the lease still has one year to run, the company (lessee) has decided to prepay a full year's rent to the lessor so as to terminate its obligation for the facility under the lease. Both parties agree that the monthly rental payments of $5,400 will be discounted at an annual rate of 6%. What amount of money will the lessee pay to the lessor? (The assumption will be made that the rental payments are due at the beginning of each month).

Given

      i 0.5% (6% ÷ 2 months)

     n 12 months

    PMT $5,400

Find

    PV

Answer

    PV = $62,742.23

The answer of $62,742.23 presumes that the rental payments are made at the end of each month (ordinary annuity). The adjustment for rental payments occurring at the start of each month (annuity due) can be made by multiplying $62,742.23 by the base (1 + 0.005). When this is done, the amount to be paid by the lessee to the lessor becomes $63,055.94.

    For rental payments made at the end of each month the problem would be reflected in the Column 5 equation.

$$PV = \$5,400\left[\frac{1}{(1 + 0.005)}\right] + \$5,400\left[\frac{1}{(1 + 0.005)^2}\right] + \cdots$$
$$+ \$5,400\left[\frac{1}{(1 + 0.005)^{12}}\right]$$

    The Column 5 equation is adjusted for rental payments taking place in advance, or at the beginning of each month.

$$PV = \$5,400 + \$5,400\left[\frac{1}{(1 + 0.005)}\right] + \cdots + \$5,400\left[\frac{1}{(1 + 0.005)^{11}}\right]$$

Example—Finding the Present Value of a Deferred Annuity (Column 5 Type Problem)

An individual wishes to purchase an insurance contract that will pay $400 at the end of each month for a total period of ten years. The purchaser stipulates that the payments are to begin after a deferred period of five years.

How much will this person have to pay to the insurance company now in order to buy the contract if an annual interest rate of 6% is used for discounting purposes?

A solution to finding the present value of a 10-year deferred annuity can be obtained by finding the present value of a 15-year annuity and then subtracting from this quantity the present value of a 5-year annuity.

Step 1

Given

> i 0.5% (6% ÷ 12 months)
>
> n 180 months
>
> PMT $400

Find

> PV

Answer

> PV = $47,401

The present value of a 15-year annuity is $47,401.

The Column 5 equation would be

$$PV = \$400\left[\frac{1}{(1 + .005)}\right] + \$400\left[\frac{1}{(1 + .005)^2}\right] + \cdots$$
$$+ \$400\left[\frac{1}{(1 + .005)^{180}}\right]$$

Step 2

Given

> i 0.5% (6% ÷ 12)
>
> n 60 months
>
> PMT $400

Find

> PV

Answer

> PV = $20,690

The 5-year annuity has a present value of $20,690.

$$PV = \$400\left[\frac{1}{(1 + .005)}\right] + \$400\left[\frac{1}{(1 + .005)^2}\right] + \cdots$$

$$+ \$400\left[\frac{1}{(1 + .005)^{60}}\right]$$

Step 3   When the present value of the 5-year annuity ($20,690) is deducted from the present value of the 15-year annuity ($47,401), the present value of the 10-year deferred annuity is found to be $26,711. Therefore, the cost of the insurance contract to the buyer would be $26,711.

Example—Computing the Price of a Bond Purchased on a Coupon Payment Date (A Combination of Column 5 and Column 4)

A 20-year $1,000 bond carries a coupon of 11% and the security has semiannual interest payments and semiannual compounding. What is the bond's price, or present value, if its yields to maturity is 12%?

Given

i	6% (12% ÷ 2 semiannual periods)
n	40 semiannual periods
FV	$1,000
PMT	$55 semiannually ($1,000 times 5.5%)

Find
    PV

Answer
    PV = $924.77

The bond has a price or present value of $924.77.
    The present value can be obtained by combining the equations for Column 4 and Column 5.

$$PV = \$55\left[\frac{1}{(1 + 0.06)}\right] + \$55\left[\frac{1}{(1 + 0.06)^2}\right] + \cdots$$

$$+ \$55\left[\frac{1}{(1 + 0.06)^{40}}\right] + \$1,000\left[\frac{1}{(1 + 0.06)^{40}}\right]$$

Example—Obtaining the Size of Coupon Payments and the Coupon Rate of a Bond (a Combination of Column 6 Type Problem and a Column 4 Type Problem)

A $1,000 par value bond has a remaining life of ten years, a price of 96 $\frac{7}{8}$, and a yield to maturity of 10%. What is the size of the semiannual coupon payments and what is the annual coupon rate?

Given

i	5% (10% ÷ 2 semiannual periods)
n	20 semiannual periods
PV	$968.75
FV	$1,000

Find

   PMT

Answer

   PMT = $47.49 (say, $47.50)

The semiannual payments per $1,000 par value bond are $47.50. The annual coupon payments of $95.00 provide an annual coupon rate of 9.50%.

The problem data are reflected in the following equation.

$$\$968.75 = PMT\left[\frac{1}{(1 + .05)}\right] + PMT\left[\frac{1}{(1 + .05)^2}\right] + \cdots$$
$$+ PMT\left[\frac{1}{(1 + .05)^{20}}\right] + \$1,000\left[\frac{1}{(1 + .05)^{20}}\right]$$

(The last term represents the Column 4 part of the equation.)

Example—Determining the Price of a Government Bond Bought between Coupon Payment Dates Using the Actual Number of Days (A Combination of Column 5 and Column 4)

A $1,000 par value government bond is bought between interest payment dates. There are 182 days in the current interest period. The interval between the last interest payment date and the delivery date of the purchase contains 47 days. The time between the delivery date and the next coupon date is 135 days.

The security provides a coupon rate of 7% and a yield to maturity of 8%. What is the present value (price) of this debt obligation if its remaining life is 14 years and 135 days?

Given

i	4% (8% ÷ 2 semiannual periods)
n	28 semiannual periods
FV	$1,000
PMT	$35 semiannually ($1,000 times 3.5%)

Find

PV

Answer

PV = $916.68

The present value of a bond having a maturity of 14 years is $916.68.

Including the current semiannual period's interest of $35, the present value of the security at its next coupon date will be $951.68 ($35 + $916.68).

The sum of $951.68 is discounted for 135 days to find its value as of the delivery date of the purchase. The 8% annual yield to maturity is adjusted for semiannual compounding to get a value of 4%. There are 182 days in the current semiannual period.

$$(\$951.68)\left(\frac{1}{(1 + 0.04)^{135/182}}\right) = (\$951.68)(0.9713) = \$924.37$$

The value of $924.37 contains accrued interest for 47 days that belongs to the seller of the bond. The accrued interest would be

$$\begin{aligned} I &= PRT \\ &= (\$1,000)(0.07)\left(\frac{47}{2 \times 182}\right) \\ &= \$9.04 \end{aligned}$$

The calculation could also be thought of as

$$\begin{aligned} I &= (\$1,000)\left(\frac{0.07}{2}\right)\left(\frac{47}{182}\right) \\ &= \$9.04 \end{aligned}$$

The price of the bond, excluding accrued interest, would be $915.33 ($924.37 − $9.04).

Example—Figuring the Price of a Corporate Bond Bought between Coupon Payment Dates Using a 360-Day Year (A Combination of Column 5 and Column 4)

Assume that a corporate bond is purchased between coupon payment dates. Also assume that the bond has a par value of $1,000, a coupon rate of 9%, a yield to maturity of 10%, and a remaining life of 12 years and 161 days.

The period between coupon dates contains 180 days. There are 19 days in the interval between the delivery date of the purchase and the last coupon date, and 161 days separate the delivery date from the next start of interest payment period. What is the present value (price) of this bond?

Given

i	5% (10% ÷ 2 semiannual periods)
n	24 semiannual periods
FV	$1,000
PMT	$45 semiannually ($1,000 × 4.5%)

Find

PV

Answer

PV = $931.01

A bond with a maturity of 12 years has a present value of $931.01.

At its next interest payment date, the bond will have a present value of $976.01. This figure includes the current semiannual period's interest of $45 plus the amount of $931.01.

The value of the bond at the delivery date of the purchase is found by discounting the amount of $976.01 for 161 days. The following computation reflects a current semiannual period of 180 days and a yield to maturity of 10%, adjusted for semiannual compounding to get the rate of 5%.

$$\cdot \ (\$976.01)\left(\frac{1}{(1 + 0.05)^{161/180}}\right) = (\$976.01)(0.9573) = \$934.33$$

The accrued interest belonging to the seller would be computed as shown for 19 days.

$$I = PRT$$
$$= (\$1,000)(0.09)\left(\frac{19}{360}\right)$$
$$= \$4.75$$

This calculation could also be viewed as

$$I = (\$1,000)\left(\frac{0.09}{2}\right)\left(\frac{19}{180}\right)$$
$$= \$4.75$$

The deduction of the accrued interest of $4.75 from the discounted figure of $934.33 provides a bond price of $929.58.

Example—Ascertaining the Price of a Piece of Income-Producing Real Estate (A Combination of Column 5 and Column 4)

A piece of income property has a yearly cash flow (before taxes) of $46,000. It is estimated that the property can be sold for $3,260,000 after a 10-year holding period. What is the present value of this parcel of real estate if an annual rate of 10% is used to discount the flow of future values?

Given

i	10%
n	10 years
FV	$3,260,000
PMT	$46,000

Find

PV

Answer

PV = $1,539,521

The property has a present worth of $1,539,521 or, say, $1,540,000.

The present value can be obtained by combining the equations for Columns 4 and 5.

$$PV = \$46,000\left[\frac{1}{(1 + 0.10)}\right] + \$46,000\left[\frac{1}{(1 + 0.10)^2}\right] + \cdots$$
$$+ \$46,000\left[\frac{1}{(1 + 0.10)^{10}}\right] + \$3,260,000\left[\frac{1}{(1 + 0.10)^{10}}\right]$$

(The discounting of the lump sum reversion of $3,260,000 in the last term represents the Column 4 part of the equation.)

Example—Calculating the Size of Equal Monthly Payments Necessary to Purchase an Automobile (Column 6 Type Problem)

An individual intends to purchase an automobile that will require a $15,000 loan for 48 months (four years). If the loan can be gotten at an annual percentage rate (APR) of 6%, what will be the size of the monthly payments for interest and principal repayment?

Given

i 0.5% (6% ÷ 12 months)
n 48 months
PV $15,000

Find

PMT

Answer

PMT = $352.28

The payments will be $352.28 per month.

The payment size in this problem can be obtained from the Column 6 equation.

$$\$15,000 = PMT\left[\frac{1}{(1 + 0.005)}\right] + PMT\left[\frac{1}{(1 + 0.005)^2}\right] + \cdots$$
$$+ PMT\left[\frac{1}{(1 + 0.005)^{48}}\right]$$

Example—Figuring the Monthly Payments Required to Finance a Boat Purchase (Column 6 Type Problem)

The portion of a boat purchase that has to be financed is $37,000. This amount will be paid on a monthly basis for eight years at a nominal annual rate of 9.25%. How much will the boat buyer's monthly payments be?

Given

  i 0.77% (9.25% ÷ 12 months)
  n 96 months
  Pv $37,000

Find

  PMT

Answer

  PMT = $546.68

Monthly payments will be in the amount of $546.68. The equation for Column 6 would be

$$\$37,000 = PMT\left(\frac{1}{(1 + 0.0077)}\right) + PMT\left(\frac{1}{(1 + 0.0077)^2}\right) + \cdots$$
$$+ PMT\left(\frac{1}{(1 + 0.0077)^{96}}\right)$$

Example—Determining the Monthly and Annual Mortgage (Loan) Constants (Column 6 Type Problem)

A lender is offering 25-year home financing at a fixed annual interest rate of 12%. What are the monthly and annual mortgage (loan) constants per dollar of loan amount?

Given

  i 1% (12% ÷ 12 months)
  n 300 months
  PV $1.00

Find

  PMT

Answer

  PMT = 0.0105322

The monthly mortgage (loan) constant is 0.0105322, or 1.05322% per month per dollar of loan amount, and the annual constant is 0.12639 or 12.639% per year per dollar of loan value (that is, 0.0105322 × 12 months).

The Column 6 equation is

$$\$1.00 = PMT\left(\frac{1}{(1 + 0.01)}\right) + PMT\left(\frac{1}{(1 + 0.01)^2}\right) + \cdots$$

$$+ PMT\left(\frac{1}{(1 + 0.01)^{300}}\right)$$

The monthly constant (0.0105322) means that over 1¢ per month for 300 months (25 years) would be needed to repay $1.00 of borrowed money (loan value) plus the interest. Over a period of 300 months, $3.16 would be paid for each dollar borrowed, resulting in a total interest expense of $2.16.

Example — Finding the Size of Equal Monthly Payments Required for the Present Purchase of a Dwelling (Column 6 Type Problem)

The purchaser of a dwelling (such as a house, condominium, or town house), makes a 30-year loan for $140,000 at a fixed nominal annual interest rate of 9%. How much are the monthly payments for principal and interest?

Given

i 0.75% (9% ÷ 12 months)

n 360 months

PV $140,000

Find

PMT

Answer

PMT = $1,126.47

The monthly payments for just principal and interest are $1,126.47.
    The Column 6 equation is

$$\$140,000 = PMT\left(\frac{1}{(1 + 0.0075)}\right) + PMT\left(\frac{1}{(1 + 0.0075)^2}\right) + \cdots$$

$$+ PMT\left(\frac{1}{(1 + 0.0075)^{360}}\right)$$

Example—Seeking Other Quantities in the Long Form of the Equation for Column 6

Given any three of the four quantities (i, n, PV, and PMT) in the Column 6 equation, the fourth can be found. For the preceding home loan example, we have already calculated the payment size when the other three quantities are known.

Calculate the present value PV.

Given

$$i \quad 0.75\%$$
$$n \quad 360 \text{ months}$$
$$\text{PMT} \quad \$1,126.47$$

Find

$$PV = \$1,126.47\left[\frac{1}{(1 + 0.0075)} + \frac{1}{(1 + 0.0075)^2} + \cdots \right.$$

$$\left. + \frac{1}{(1 + 0.0075)^{360}}\right]$$

Answer

$$PV = \$140,000$$

This is basically a Column 5 calculation: finding the present value of an annuity.

Calculate the interest rate i.

Given

$$n \quad 360 \text{ months}$$
$$\text{PMT} \quad \$1,126.47$$
$$\text{PV} \quad \$140,000$$

Find

$$\$140,000 = \$1,126.47\left[\frac{1}{(1 + i)} + \frac{1}{(1 + i)^2} + \cdots + \frac{1}{(1 + i)^{360}}\right]$$

Answer

$$i = 0.75\%$$

The monthly interest rate would be 0.75%, and the annual rate would be 9% (0.75% times 12). (Note: The entering of a negative value for either

PMT or PV may be required by some calculators.)

Calculate the number of payments n.

Given

$$
\begin{array}{ll}
i & 0.75\% \\
\text{PMT} & \$1,126.47 \\
\text{PV} & \$140,000
\end{array}
$$

Find

$$
\$140,000 = \$1,126.47\left[\frac{1}{(1 + 0.0075)} + \frac{1}{(1 + 0.0075)^2} + \cdots \right. \\
\left. + \frac{1}{(1 + 0.0075)^n}\right]
$$

Answer

$$n = 360 \text{ months}$$

(See the foregoing note regarding negative signs.)

Example—Ascertaining the Maximum Loan Amount That a Borrower Can Service (Column 6 Type Problem)

A borrower has learned that a lender will make a home loan for 25 years at a fixed nominal annual rate of 11% compounded monthly. The borrower would not be able to allocate more than $1,150 per month for principal and interest payments. What would be the maximum loan amount that the borrower could service?

Given

$$
\begin{array}{ll}
i & 0.9167\% \ (11\% \div 12 \text{ months}) \\
n & 300 \text{ months} \\
\text{PMT} & \$1,150
\end{array}
$$

Find

   PV

Answer

   PV = $117,330

Given the terms set forth by the lender, the borrower would not be able to make the monthly payments on a loan exceeding $117,330.

Example—Determining the Increase in the Mortgage Interest Rate When a Lender Charges Points (Column 6 Type Problem)

A lender who loans money for the purchase of dwellings (home, condominium, or town house) quotes a fixed nominal annual interest rate of 12% for a 30-year mortgage (loan). However, the lender charges two points, or 2% of the initial borrowed amount at the time that the loan is made. What is the interest rate that the lender is charging after considering the points?

For each $1.00 borrowed, the lender gets two cents (2% of $1.00) at the time the loan is made. In effect, the lender only loans 98 cents for each dollar on which interest is charged.

The first step in the solution requires that a payment size be found for a $1.00 loan for 30 years (360 months). The second step entails a determination of an interest rate based on this payment size and a loan amount of $0.98.

Step 1

Given

i 1% (12% ÷ 12 months)

n 360 months

PV $1.00

Find

PMT

Answer

PMT = $0.010286

The monthly payment size for a $1.00 loan for 30 years is $0.010286.

This could be found using the Column 6 equation.

$$\$1.00 = PMT\left[\frac{1}{(1 + 0.01)} + \frac{1}{(1 + 0.01)^2} + \cdots + \frac{1}{(1 + 0.01)^{360}}\right]$$

Step 2

Given

n 360 months

PV $0.98

PMT $0.010286

Find

i

Answer

   $i = 1.02266\%$ per month

The periodic interest rate is 1.02266%, so the annual rate is 12.272% (1.02266% times 12).

The Column 6 equation for step two would be

$$\$0.98 = \$0.010286\left[\frac{1}{(1 + i)} + \frac{1}{(1 + i)^2} + \cdots + \frac{1}{(1 + i)^{360}}\right]$$

Example—Computing the Premium Price of a Mortgage (a Combination of a Column 6 Type Problem and a Column 5 Type Problem)

If a 12%, $1 million mortgage is priced to yield 11% over a 20-year period, what is the present value or price of the mortgage?

   This is a two-step problem. The size of monthly mortgage payments is determined first.

Step 1

Given

i	1% (12% ÷ 12 months)
n	240 months
PV	$\$1 \times 10^6$

Find

   PMT

Answer

   PMT = $11,011

The monthly payments are $11,011.

   The equation for Column 6 is

$$\$1 \times 10^6 = PMT\left[\frac{1}{(1 + .01)}\right] + PMT\left[\frac{1}{(1 + .01)^2}\right] + \cdots$$
$$+ PMT\left[\frac{1}{(1 + .01)^{240}}\right]$$

Step 2   This step requires that a present value be found for a yield of 11%.
Given

  i 0.9167% (11% ÷ 12)
  n 240 months
  PMT $11,011

Find

  PV

Answer

  PV = $1,066,734

The price of the mortgage is $1,066,734.
  The Column 5 equation would be written as

$$PV = \$11,011\left[\frac{1}{(1 + .009167)}\right] + \$11,011\left[\frac{1}{(1 + .009167)^2}\right] + \cdots$$

$$+ \$11,011\left[\frac{1}{(1 + .009167)^{240}}\right]$$

Example—Obtaining the Remaining Balance (or Balloon Payment) of a Loan before Maturity (a Combination of a Column 6 Type Problem and a Column 5 Type Problem)

Twelve years ago a borrower made a $215,000 loan to buy a home. The 30-year loan requires monthly payments of principal and interest and carries a fixed annual interest rate of 10.25%. What is the current remaining principal balance of the loan?

  Two steps are used to attain the desired solution. In the first step the size of the monthly payments is found for a 30-year loan.

Step 1

Given

    i 0.8542% (10.25% ÷ 12 months)
    n 360 months
    PV $215,000

Find

    PMT

Answer

    PMT = $1,926.68

The monthly payments would be $1,926.68.

The Column 6 equation would be

$$\$215,000 = PMT\left[\frac{1}{(1 + .008542)}\right] + PMT\left[\frac{1}{(1 + .008542)^2}\right] + \cdots$$

$$+ PMT\left[\frac{1}{(1 + .008542)^{360}}\right]$$

Step 2   In the second step the present value is calculated for a loan having a life of 216 months, or 18 years (30 years − 12 years), and monthly payments of $1,926.68.

Given

i	0.8542% (10.25% ÷ 12 months)
n	216 months
PMT	$1,926.68

Find

PV

Answer

PV = $189,633

The remaining principal balance of the original $215,000 loan at the end of 12 years would be $189,633. (If a borrower had made a loan for $215,000 and had agreed at that time to make a balloon payment at the end of 12 years, the amount of the balloon payment would also be $189,633.)

The set up for the Column 5 equation would be as follows.

$$PV = \$1,926.68\left[\frac{1}{(1 + .008542)}\right] + \$1,926.68\left[\frac{1}{(1 + .008542)^2}\right] + \cdots$$

$$+ \$1,926.68\left[\frac{1}{(1 + .008542)^{216}}\right]$$

Example—Figuring the Yield on a Second-Mortgage Loan under a Wraparound Loan Arrangement (Column 6 Type Problem)

A wraparound mortgage may be best understood by looking at an example. Assume that 10 years ago a property owner obtained a $70,000 first-mortgage loan at an interest rate of 9% for a term of 25 years.

Today the property owner offers to make a wraparound loan to a potential buyer of the property. This wraparound loan would be for $75,000 and would include the remaining balance of the first-mortgage loan plus a new second-mortgage loan.

The wraparound loan would carry an interest rate of 11.75% over a term of 15 years (equivalent to the remaining life of the first-mortgage loan). What yield would the wraparound lender (property owner) be receiving on the second-mortgage portion of the wraparound loan?

Step 1   The initial step involves finding the size of monthly payments required by the first-mortgage loan.

Given

   i 0.75% (9% ÷ 12 months)
   n 300 months
   PV $70,000

Find

   PMT

Answer

   PMT = $587.44

The monthly payments of the first-mortgage loan are $587.44.

Step 2   The remaining balance of the first-mortgage loan is found in the second step.

Given

   i 0.75% (9% ÷ 12 months)
   n 180 months
   PMT $587.44

Find

   PV

Answer

   PV = $57,918

The remaining balance of the first-mortgage loan is $57,918.

Step 3   The size of the monthly payments for the wraparound loan is obtained in this step.

Given

   i 0.9792% (11.75% ÷ 12 months)
   n 180 months
   PV $75,000

Find
   PMT

Answer
   PMT = $888.12

The wraparound loan would have monthly payments of $888.12.

Step 4   The monthly payments for the wraparound loan are $888.12. Since the monthly payments for the first-mortgage loan are $587.44, the monthly payments for the second-mortgage loan would be $300.68 ($888.12 − $587.44).

The wraparound loan would have a principal of $75,000 and the remaining balance of the first-mortgage loan currently is $57,918. Therefore, the principal amount of the second-mortgage loan would be the difference between these two figures, or $17,082.

The yield on the second-mortgage loan may now be calculated for a 15-year term.

Given
   n 180 months
   PMT $300.68
   PV $17,082

Find
   i

Answer
   i = 1.67% per month (or 20% per year)

The yield on the $17,082 second-mortgage loan would be 20% per annum.

The equations for steps 1–3 are not given since they are similar to those used in the previous example. The equation for step 4 is

$$\$17,082 = \$300.68\left(\frac{1}{(1+i)}\right) + \$300.68\left(\frac{1}{(1+i)^2}\right) + \cdots$$
$$+ \$300.68\left(\frac{1}{(1+i)^{180}}\right)$$

Example—Calculating Annuity Values When the Compounding Frequency Is More Than the Payment Frequency

Compounding frequency   monthly
Payment frequency   quarterly

Payment size $700
Annuity life   3 years
Nominal annual rate   6% compounded monthly

Convert Nominal Annual Rate to a Comparable Rate for Quarterly Compounding (to Agree with Quarterly Payment Frequency)

$$\left(1 + \frac{R}{m}\right)^n = \left(1 + \frac{R}{m}\right)^n$$

$$\left(1 + \frac{R}{4}\right)^4 = \left(1 + \frac{0.06}{12}\right)^{12}$$

$$1 + \frac{R}{4} = (1 + 0.005)^3$$

$$1 + \frac{R}{4} = 1.0151$$

$$R = 0.0604, \text{ or } 6.04\% \text{ compounded quarterly}$$

Future Value (FV) of an Ordinary Annuity (Column 2 Type Problem)

Given

$\quad i \quad$ 1.51% (6.04% ÷ 4 quarters)
$\quad n \quad$ 12 quarters
$\quad$ PMT $\quad$ $700

Find

$\quad$ FV

Answer

$\quad$ FV = $9,134

The ordinary annuity has a future value of $9,134.

Future Value (FV) of an Annuity Due

$$\text{Base} = \left(1 + \frac{R}{m}\right) = \left(1 + \frac{0.0604}{4}\right) = 1.0151$$

$$\text{FV of annuity due} = (\text{FV of ordinary annuity})(\text{Base})$$
$$= (\$9,134)(1.0151)$$
$$= \$9,272$$

The annuity due has a future value of $9,272.

Present Value (PV) of an Ordinary Annuity (Column 5 Type Problem)

Given

     i 1.51% (6.04% ÷ 4 quarters)

     n 12 quarters

    PMT $700

Find

    PV

Answer

    PV = $7,630

The ordinary annuity has a present value of $7,630.

Present Value (PV) of an Annuity Due

$$\text{PV of Annuity Due} = (\text{PV of ordinary annuity})(\text{Base})$$
$$= (\$7,630)(1.0151) = \$7,745.$$

The annuity due has a present value of $7,745.

Example—Computing Annuity Values When the Compounding Frequency Is Less Than the Payment Frequency

   Compounding frequency   semiannual

   Payment frequency   quarterly

   Annuity life   2 years

   Nominal annual rate   12% compounded semiannually

Convert Nominal Annual Rate to a Comparable Rate for Quarterly Compounding (to Agree with Quarterly Payment Frequency)

$$\left(1 + \frac{R}{m}\right)^n = \left(1 + \frac{R}{m}\right)^n$$

$$\left(1 + \frac{R}{4}\right)^4 = \left(1 + \frac{0.12}{2}\right)^2$$

$$\left(1 + \frac{R}{4}\right)^4 = 1.1236$$

$$1 + \frac{R}{4} = (1.1236)^{1/4}$$

$$1 + \frac{R}{4} = 1.0296$$

$$R = 0.1184, or\ 11.84\% \text{ compounded quarterly}$$

Future Value (FV) of an Ordinary Annuity (Column 2 Type Problem)

Given

     i   2.96% (11.84% ÷ 4 quarters)

     n   8 quarters

     PMT $900

Find

     FV

Answer

     FV = $7,992

The ordinary annuity has a future value of $7,992.
Future Value (FV) of an Annuity Due

$$\text{Base} = \left(1 + \frac{R}{m}\right) = \left(1 + \frac{0.1184}{4}\right) = 1.0296$$

$$\begin{aligned}
\text{FV of annuity due} &= (\text{FV of ordinary annuity})(\text{Base}) \\
&= (\$7,992)(1.0296) \\
&= \$8,229
\end{aligned}$$

The annuity due has a future value of $8,229.
Present Value (PV) of an Ordinary Annuity (Column 5 Type Problem)

Given

     i   2.96% (11.84% ÷ 4 quarters)

     n   8 quarters

     PMT $900

Find

     PV

Answer

     PV = $6,328

The ordinary annuity has a present value of $6,328.
Present Value (PV) of an Annuity Due

$$\begin{aligned}
\text{PV of annuity due} &= (\text{PV of ordinary annuity})(\text{Base}) \\
&= (\$6,328)(1.0296) \\
&= \$6,515
\end{aligned}$$

The annuity due has a future value of $6,515.

14 USING FINANCIAL CALCULATORS TO CONSTRUCT COMPOUND INTEREST TABLES

Where there is a need or a desire to construct compound interest tables, financial calculators can be used to accomplish the task. It is helpful to see explicitly what information is needed to calculate the compound interest table entries. These data were displayed in Table 13-1 and are also reproduced here. As before, the X marks quantities that have to be put into the calculator, a dash (—) signifies that a value is not involved in the problem/solution, and a question mark (?) indicates the quantity that is to be found by the calculator.

In all of the examples that follow, it is assumed that the nominal annual interest rate is 12%. Calculations are undertaken for $n = 4$ in each column for each compounding frequency (monthly, quarterly, semiannual, and annual). The computed values are carried to five decimal places.

Column quantities for other numbers of periods (n) or other interest rates can be found by exactly similar methods. The nominal annual interest

Table 14–1. Variables Needed and Found in Various Compound Interest Calculations.

Table Column	i	n	PV	FV	PMT
Column 1	X	X	X	?	—
Column 2	X	X	—	?	X
Column 3	X	X	—	X	?
Column 4	X	X	?	X	—
Column 5	X	X	?	—	X
Column 6	X	X	X	—	?

rate (R) is adjusted to the periodic interest rate (i) by taking into consideration the frequency of the compounding. When there are m compounding periods in a year, $i = R/m$.

Example—Column 1 Monthly Compounding

Given

i	1%(12% ÷ 12 months)
PV	1
n	4 months

Find

FV

Answer

FV = 1.04060

Example—Column 1 Quarterly Compounding

Given

i	3%(12% ÷ 4 quarters)
PV	1
n	4 quarters

Find

FV

Answer

FV = 1.12551

Example—Column 1 Semiannual Compounding

Given

i	6%(12% ÷ 2 semiannual periods)
PV	1
n	4 half years

Find

FV

Answer

FV = 1.26248

Example–Column 1 Annual Compounding

Given
> i 12%(12% ÷ 1 annual period)
> PV   1
> n 4 years

Find
> FV

Answer
> FV = 1.57352

Example–Column 2 Monthly Compounding

Given
> i 1%(12% ÷ 12 months)
> PMT   1
> n 4 months

Find
> FV

Answer
> FV = 4.06040

Example–Column 2 Quarterly Compounding

Given
> i 3%(12% ÷ 4 quarters)
> PMT   1
> n 4 quarters

Find
> FV

Answer
> FV = 4.18363

Example–Column 2 Semiannual Compounding

Given
> i 6%(12% ÷ 2 semiannual periods)
> PMT   1
> n 4 half years

Find
>   FV

Answer
>   FV = 4.37462

Example—Column 2 Annual Compounding

Given
>   *i*   12%(12% ÷ 1 annual period)
>   PMT   1
>   *n*   4 years

Find
>   FV

Answer
>   FV = 4.77933

Example—Column 3 Monthly Compounding

Given
>   *i*   1%(12% ÷ 12 months)
>   FV   1
>   *n*   4 months

Find
>   PMT

Answer
>   PMT = 0.24628

Example—Column 3 Quarterly Compounding

Given
>   *i*   3%(12% ÷ 4 quarters)
>   FV   1
>   *n*   4 quarters

Find
>   PMT

Answer
>   PMT = 0.23903

Example—Column 3 Semiannual Compounding

Given
    i 6%(12% ÷ 2 semiannual periods)
    FV   1
    n 4 half years
Find
    PMT
Answer
    PMT = 0.22859

Example—Column 3 Annual Compounding

Given
    i 12%(12% ÷ 1 annual period)
    FV   1
    n 4 years
Find
    PMT
Answer
    PMT = 0.20923

Example—Column 4 Monthly Compounding

Given
    i 1%(12% ÷ 12 months)
    FV   1
    n 4 months
Find
    PV
Answer
    PV = 0.96098

Example—Column 4 Quarterly Compounding

Given
    i 3%(12% ÷ 4 quarters)

     FV   1

     n   4 quarters

Find

     PV

Answer

     PV = 0.88849

Example—Column 4 Semiannual Compounding

Given

     i   6%(12% ÷ 2 semiannual periods)

     FV   1

     n   4 half years

Find

     PV

Answer

     PV = 0.79209

Example—Column 4 Annual Compounding

Given

     i   12%(12% ÷ 1 annual period)

     FV   1

     n   4 years

Find

     PV

Answer

     PV = 0.63552

Example—Column 5 Monthly Compounding

Given

     i   1%(12% ÷ 12 months)

     PMT   1

     n   4 months

Find

     PV

Answer

     PV = 3.90197

Example—Column 5 Quarterly Compounding

Given

 i 3%(12% ÷ 4 quarters)

 PMT   1

 n 4 quarters

Find

 PV

Answer

 PV = 3.71710

Example—Column 5 Semiannual Compounding

Given

 i 6%(12% ÷ 2 semiannual periods)

 PMT   1

 n 4 half years

Find

 PV

Answer

 PV = 3.46511

Example—Column 5 Annual Compounding

Given

 i 12%(12% ÷ 1 annual period)

 PMT   1

 n 4 years

Find

 PV

Answer

 PV = 3.03735

Example—Column 6 Monthly Compounding

Given

 i 1%(12% ÷ 12 months)

 PV   1

 n 4 months

Find
    PMT
Answer
    PMT = 0.25628

Example—Column 6 Quarterly Compounding

Given
    i   3%(12% ÷ 4 quarters)
    PV   1
    n   4 quarters
Find
    PMT
Answer
    PMT = 0.26903

Example—Column 6 Semiannual Compounding

Given
    i   6%(12% ÷ 2 semiannual periods)
    PV   1
    n   4 half years
Find
    PMT
Answer
    PMT = 0.28859

Example—Column 6 Annual Compounding

Given
    i   12%(12% ÷ 1 annual period)
    PV   1
    n   4 years
Find
    PMT
Answer
    PMT = 0.32923

APPENDIX A: RELATIONSHIPS BETWEEN COLUMNS OF THE COMPOUND INTEREST TABLES

It has been pointed out in Chapters 6, 7, and 11, that for a given n in the compound interest tables there is a reciprocal relationship between the values in Columns 1 and 4, Columns 2 and 3, and Columns 5 and 6. Other relationships between the factors in the columns exist as well. They are the subject of this appendix.

Figure A–1. Time Line

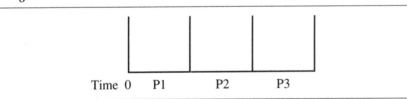

Time 0   P1   P2   P3

RELATIONSHIP BETWEEN COLUMNS 1, 2, AND 5

Suppose that there is a desire to find the relationship between the amount (future value) of an annuity (Column 2) and the present value of an annuity

257

(Column 5). Consider a case where three payments of $1.00 each will be made at the ends of periods P1, P2, and P3.

The future value (FV) of the annuity is found using the equation for Column 2 of the compound interest tables.

$$FV = (1 + i)^2 + (1 + i) + 1$$

The Column 5 present value (PV) equation for the same three payments would be

$$PV = \frac{1}{(1 + i)} + \frac{1}{(1 + i)^2} + \frac{1}{(1 + i)^3}$$

Comparing the corresponding terms in the two equations, it is seen

$$\frac{(1 + i)^2}{1/(1 + i)} = (1 + i)^3$$

$$\frac{(1 + i)}{1/(1 + i)^2} = (1 + i)^3$$

$$\frac{1}{1/(1 + i)^3} = (1 + i)^3$$

Note that $(1 + i)^3$ is the future value listed in Column 1 for $n = 3$ and a lump sum deposit of $1.00. Thus the multiplication of the Column 5 equation by the Column 1 equation produces the Column 2 equation.

$$(\text{Column 1})(\text{Column 5}) = \text{Column 2}$$

$$(1 + i)^3 \times \left(\frac{1}{(1 + i)} + \frac{1}{(1 + i)^2} + \frac{1}{(1 + i)^3} \right) = (1 + i)^2 + (1 + i) + 1$$

This relationship can be derived in a general way by examining the short form equations for Columns 1, 2, and 5, as given in Chapter 12.

$$(\text{Column 1})(\text{Column 5}) = (1+i)^n \left[\frac{1 - \frac{1}{(1+i)^n}}{i} \right] = \frac{(1 + i)^n - 1}{i} = \text{Column 2}$$

The relationship may be restated as

Column 1 = (Column 2)/(Column 5)

or

Column 5 = (Column 2)/(Column 1)

The relationship between Columns 1, 2, and 5 will be tested for different *n* values and for different frequencies using factors from the compound interest tables for a nominal annual rate of 8%.

Example 1   Given:

Monthly compounding frequency
n = 3 months

(Column 1)(Column 5) = Column 2
(1.0201)(2.9604) = 3.0199

The calculated Column 2 value of 3.0199 matches, except for a slight rounding difference, the Column 2 table figure of 3.0200.

Example 2   Given:

Quarterly compounding frequency
n = 8 quarters

(Column 1)(Column 5) = Column 2
(1.1717)(7.3255) = 8.5833

The Column 2 table value is 8.5830. Again, the only difference is caused by rounding.

Example 3   Given:

Semiannual compounding frequency
n = 14 half years

(Column 1)(Column 5) = Column 2
(1.7317)(10.5631) = 18.2921

Column 2 of the semiannual table contains a factor of 18.2919.

RELATIONSHIPS BETWEEN OTHER COLUMNS

We have established the following four relationships between the six columns in the compound interest tables:

$$\text{Column 4} = 1/(\text{Column 1})$$
$$\text{Column 3} = 1/(\text{Column 2})$$
$$\text{Column 6} = 1/(\text{Column 5})$$
$$(\text{Column 1})(\text{Column 5}) = \text{Column 2}$$

These four equations can be combined in a variety of ways to display explicitly the relationships between specific columns.

For example,

$$(\text{Column 1})(\text{Column 5}) = \text{Column 2}$$

can be written as

$$(1/\text{Column 4})(\text{Column 5}) = \text{Column 2}$$

$$\text{Column 5} = \text{Column 2} \times \text{Column 4}$$

using the fact that Column 4 $=$ 1/(Column 1).

Making the additional substitution Column 3 $=$ 1/(column 2), we find

$$\text{Column 4} = \text{Column 3} \times \text{Column 5}$$

Many other arrangements of the initial four relationships may be obtained in a like manner. A listing of these various column relationships follows.

$$\text{Column 1} = 1/\text{Column 4}$$
$$\text{Column 1} = (1/\text{Column 3})(1/\text{Column 5})$$
$$\text{Column 1} = \text{Column 2} \times \text{Column 6}$$
$$\text{Column 1} = \text{Column 2}/\text{Column 5}$$
$$\text{Column 1} = \text{Column 6}/\text{Column 3}$$
$$\text{Column 2} = 1/\text{Column 3}$$
$$\text{Column 2} = (1/\text{Column 4})(1/\text{Column 6})$$
$$\text{Column 2} = \text{Column 1}/\text{Column 6}$$

Column 2 = Column 1 × Column 5

Column 2 = Column 5/Column 4

Column 3 = 1/Column 2

Column 3 = (1/Column 1)(1/Column 5)

Column 3 = Column 4 × Column 6

Column 3 = Column 4/Column 5

Column 3 = Column 6/Column 1

Column 3 = Column 6 − i

Column 4 = 1/Column 1

Column 4 = (1/Column 2)(1/Column 6)

Column 4 = Column 3/Column 6

Column 4 = Column 3 × Column 5

Column 4 = Column 5/Column 2

Column 5 = 1/Column 6

Column 5 = (1/Column 1)(1/Column 3)

Column 5 = Column 2/Column 1

Column 5 = Column 4/Column 3

Column 5 = Column 2 × Column 4

Column 6 = 1/Column 5

Column 6 = (1/Column 2)(1/Column 4)

Column 6 = Column 1 × Column 3

Column 6 = Column 1/Column 2

Column 6 = Column 3/Column 4

Column 6 = Column 3 + i

APPENDIX B: WORKING WITH ZEROS

Sometimes financial calculations entail the use of a number of zeros. Scientific notation can be used to make the handling of the zeros less burdensome. When zeros appear to the left of a decimal point, as in $10,000,000 (ten million dollars), the number can be rewritten by moving the decimal point seven places to the left and multiplying by 10^7. In the new notation, the number would be 1×10^7, or 1.0×10^7. The whole expression would be read as *one times ten to the seven* or *one times ten to the seventh*. The 10^7 portion means that the decimal point needs to be moved seven places to the right in order to reconstruct the original number, filling in with zeros the spaces created.

The amount of $250,000,000 (250 million dollars) could be written as 2.5×10^8, indicating that the decimal point has been moved eight places to the left. The original number can be restored from scientific notation by taking the decimal point back eight places to the right. As this is done, seven zeros have to be added.

A decimal fraction such as 0.00006 (6/100,000) may be expressed as 6×10^{-5}, or 6.0×10^{-5}. The factor 10^{-5} (read *ten to the minus five*) signifies that the decimal point has been moved five places to the right. The original number is reconstructed by moving the decimal point back five places to the left, filling in the four empty spaces with zeros.

The decimal fraction 0.0043 (or 43/10,000) can be given the form 4.3×10^{-3}. The factor 10^{-3} (*ten to the minus three*) indicates that the decimal point has been shifted three places to the right. The original number can be obtained by sliding the decimal point back three places to the left, filling in the two empty spaces with zeros.

The use of scientific notation facilitates multiplication and division calculations. Exponents (powers) of the same base are added when multiplication computations are done. Division calculations require that exponents be subtracted. The advantage of scientific notation is that all the exponents have the same base, namely, 10. Some examples of calculations involving scientific notation follow.

$$
\begin{aligned}
(3,000,000)(0.091) &= (3 \times 10^6)(9.1 \times 10^{-2}) \\
&= 27.3 \times 10^4 \\
&= 273,000
\end{aligned}
$$

$$
\begin{aligned}
(2,000,000)(140) &= (2 \times 10^6)(1.4 \times 10^2) \\
&= 2.8 \times 10^8 \\
&= 280,000,000
\end{aligned}
$$

$$
\begin{aligned}
\frac{15,000,000}{2,500} &= \frac{15 \times 10^6}{2.5 \times 10^3} \\
&= 6 \times 10^3 \\
&= 6,000
\end{aligned}
$$

$$
\begin{aligned}
\frac{(55,000)(0.2\%)(400)}{440(0.1\%)} &= \frac{(55 \times 10^3)(2 \times 10^{-3})(4 \times 10^2)}{(4.4 \times 10^2)(1 \times 10^{-3})} \\
&= \frac{440 \times 10^2}{4.4 \times 10^{-1}} \\
&= 100 \times 10^3 \\
&= 100,000
\end{aligned}
$$

Some examples of 10 raised to various powers are as follows:

$$
\begin{aligned}
1 \times 10^0 &= 1 \\
1 \times 10^1 &= 10 \\
1 \times 10^2 &= 100 \\
1 \times 10^3 &= 1,000 \\
1 \times 10^4 &= 10,000 \\
1 \times 10^5 &= 100,000 \\
1 \times 10^6 &= 1,000,000 \\
1 \times 10^{-1} &= 0.1 \\
1 \times 10^{-2} &= 0.01 \\
1 \times 10^{-3} &= 0.001 \\
1 \times 10^{-4} &= 0.0001
\end{aligned}
$$

APPENDIX C: BACKGROUND MATERIAL

PERCENTAGES AND DECIMALS

Interest computations involve the use of percentages and decimals (decimal fractions). Decimals may be changed to percents, and percents converted to decimals.

The word *percent* means *per hundred*. The expression 15% means 15 for every 100 and can be written in the fractional form 15/100. If 15 is divided by 100, the decimal 0.15 is obtained. The effect of dividing 15 by 100 is to move the decimal point two places to the left. The decimal 0.15 is equivalent to 15%. The conversion is done by multiplying 0.15 by 100 and thereby moving the decimal point two places to the right.

Some other examples of percents and their decimal equivalents are

Percent	Decimal Fraction
0.004%	0.00004
0.04%	0.0004
0.4%	0.004
4.0%	0.04
40.0%	0.4

In interest compounding, the periodic interest rate i usually appears in the expression $(1 + i)^n$. When performing the computation it is necessary to express i as a decimal. Since i is almost always positive, $(1 + i)$ is usually greater than 1 and $(1 + i)^n$ is larger yet. As n increases, $(1 + i)^n$ increases. Also, as i increases, $1/(1 + i)^n$ decreases, since the denominator is getting larger.

Relative changes involve the use of percentages. A shift in annual mortgage rates, for example, from 8% to 12% represents a relative increase of 50 percent, although the absolute increase or change is 4%.

$$12\% - 8\% = 4\%$$
$$4\%/8\% = 0.50$$
$$\text{relative change} = 0.50 \times 100$$
$$= 50\%$$

A drop in annual mortgage rates from 12% to 8% is an absolute decline of 4% and a relative decrease of 33.3%.

$$12\% - 8\% = 4\%$$
$$4\%/12\% = 0.333$$
$$\text{relative change} = 0.333 \times 100$$
$$= 33.3\%$$

Confusion with regard to the base is a common error that arises when dealing with percentages. It is the original quantity (before the change occurs) that is used as the base.

The base of 8% is the proper number to use when determining the percentage increase (in the first case, in which there is movement from 8% to 12%. The base of 12% is the correct figure to use in the second case, where the rate declines from 12% to 8%.

An easy way to identify the original quantity is to remember that the number following the word *from* should be used as the base. For an increase from 30 to 35, the figure 30 follows the word *from* and is used as the base. The percentage increase would be $(5/30) \times 100 = 16.7\%$. Where there is a decrease from 80 to 60, the number 80 follows the word *from* and it is the base. The decrease would be $(20/80) \times 100 = 25\%$.

Suppose that it is known that a quantity has undergone a 25% drop to 60. The starting level, or base quantity, may be found as shown.

$$\frac{X - 60}{X} = 0.25$$
$$X - 60 = 0.25X$$
$$0.75X = 60$$
$$X = \frac{60}{0.75}$$
$$= 80$$

If the initial (80) and final (60) values had both been known, the calculation for the percentage change would be $(80 - 60)/80 = 0.25$, or 25%.

Markups and markdowns involve percentage increases and decreases and give further insight into the behavior of percentages. Assume that a retailer buys an article to sell for $15. The initial markup to cover expenses and to make a profit is 50%.

$$\$15 - \$10 = \$5$$
$$\$5/\$10 = 0.50$$
$$\text{relative increase} = 0.50 \times 100 = 50\%$$

The article sells well at $15 and the retailer marks it up another 20%. The price of the item becomes $18 (120% of $15, or 1.2 times $15).

The total markup on the product is 80%, since the original price was $10 and the final price is $18.

$$\$18 - \$10 = \$8$$
$$\$8/\$10 = 0.80$$
$$\text{relative change} = 0.80 \times 100$$
$$= 80\%$$

Another retailer has an item priced at $40. Sales are slow, and the article is marked down 25%. The revised price of the article is $30 (75% of $40, or $0.75 \times \$40$). An alternative way to get the revised price would be to subtract 25% of $40 ($10) from the original price ($40).

Later this $30 product is marked down by the retailer an additional 15%. The selling price becomes $25.50 (85% of $30).

The total markdown on the item originally priced at $40 is 36.25%.

$$\$40.00 - \$25.50 = \$14.50$$
$$\$14.50/\$40.00 = 0.3625$$
$$\text{relative change} = 0.3625 \times 100$$
$$= 36.25\%$$

Sales tax also involves percentages. The total purchase amount of an $87.00 item with a 6% sales tax would be $92.22, that is, $87.00 plus $5.22 (6% of $87.00). A one step approach to arriving at the total purchase amount of $92.22 would be to multiply 1.06 times $87.00. The total price is 106% of the original price, because of the 6% sales tax.

Situations may arise when a quantity declines to zero. The relative size of the drop is 100%.

$$12,144 - 0 = 12,144$$
$$12,144/12,144 = 1$$
$$\text{relative decline} = 100\%$$

If a number doubles in value, its increase is 100% $[(2-1)/1 \times 100\%]$, and if it triples in value, its increase is 200%. Table C–1 gives some examples of increases greater than 100%.

Table C–1. Percentage Increase.

Beginning Number	Ending Number	Percentage Increase
1	2	100
1	2.5	150
1	3	200
1	4	300
1	60	5,900
1	95	9,400
8	112	1,300
62	372	500
117	936	700
658	2,237.2	240
1,341	5,766.3	330

RULE OF 72

There is a rule of thumb call the Rule of 72 that allows a person to determine approximately how many years it would take for a number to double in value if the annual rate of increase is known. If, for instance, a number is increasing at a rate of 6% per year, the number will double in value in about 12 years (72 ÷ 6%). (Note that the rate is not converted into a decimal.) If $1.00 is increasing at a rate of 6% per year compounded annually, it will actually grow to $2.01 at the end of 12 years according to computed figures.

If a number is increasing at a rate of 8% per year, it would double in about 9 years (72 ÷ 8%). If $1.00 is growing at the rate of 8% per year compounded annually, it will actually be worth $2.00 at the end of the ninth year on the basis of calculated figures.

The Rule of 72 can also be used to approximate the annual rate of increase when the time it takes a number to double in value is known. For example, if a number doubles in six years, it will be growing at an annual rate of 12% (72 ÷ 6 years). The sum of $1.00 will actually grow to $1.97 at the end of six years if that dollar is compounded annually at a yearly rate of 12%.

For a number doubling in five years, the annual rate of growth would be 14.4% (72 ÷ 5 years). When a yearly growth rate of 14.4% compounded annually is applied to $1.00 for 5 years, that dollar becomes $1.96, according to actual calculations.

Equivalent Taxable and Nontaxable Interest Rates

The table below shows equivalent taxable interest rates for a nontaxable interest rate of 6%.

Tax Bracket (%)	Taxable Interest Rate (%)
20	7.50
30	8.57
40	10.00
50	12.00
60	15.00

A taxpayer who is in a 30% (marginal) tax bracket, for example, would keep 70% of what is earned and would pay 30% of earnings in income taxes. Therefore, a taxable interest rate of 8.57% would be comparable to a 6% tax-free interest rate for this taxpayer.

$$\text{Taxable interest rate} = \frac{\text{Nontaxable interest rate}}{(100\% - \text{tax bracket})}$$

$$= \frac{6\%}{(100\% - 30\%)}$$

$$= \frac{6}{70}$$

$$= 0.0857, \text{ or } 8.57\%$$

To solve for the nontaxable interest rate when the taxable interest rate and the tax bracket are known, the equation can be rearranged as follows.

$$\text{Nontaxable interest rate} = \left(\begin{array}{c} \text{Taxable} \\ \text{interest rate} \end{array} \right) \left(\begin{array}{c} 100\% - \\ \text{tax bracket} \end{array} \right)$$

ANNUALIZING PERIODIC INTEREST RATES

When an interest rate is stated for a period less than one year, the periodic rate can be annualized. That is, the annual rate to which this periodic rate corresponds can be found. To illustrate, a weekly rate of 0.25% would be equivalent to an annual rate of 13% (0.25% times 52 weeks per year). The monthly rate of 1.5% would correspond to an annual rate of 18% (1.5% times 12 months per year). For a quarterly rate of 2.5%, the yearly rate would be 10% (2.5% times 4 quarters per year).

RECIPROCALS

The reciprocal of a quantity is produced by dividing the number 1 by that quantity. For instance, the reciprocal of 6 is $\frac{1}{6}$. Note that the reciprocal of $\frac{1}{6}$ is 6. The reciprocal of $(1 + 0.02)^4$ is $1/(1 + 0.02)^4$, and the reciprocal of $1/(1 + 0.02)^4$ is $(1 + 0.02)^4$.

When two numbers that are reciprocals of each other are multiplied, their product is equal to 1. For example, $\frac{1}{6} \times 6 = 1$, and $1/(1 + 0.02)^4 \times (1 + 0.02)^4 = 1$.

The area of foreign exchange (or the conversion of one currency into another currency) provides examples of reciprocals. Consider the examples below where some hypothetical foreign exchange rates are assumed.

$$1 \text{ U.S. dollar} = 1.64 \text{ Swiss francs}$$

$$1 \text{ Swiss franc} = \frac{1}{1.64} = 0.61 \text{ U.S. dollars } (61 \text{ ¢})$$

1 U.S. dollar $= 140.35$ Japanese yen

1 Japanese yen $= \dfrac{1}{140.35} = 0.007$ U.S. dollars (less than 1 ¢)

1 U.S. dollar $= 1.28$ Australian dollars

1 Australian dollar $= \dfrac{1}{1.28} = 0.78$ U.S. dollars (78¢)

EXPONENTS

An exponent, or power, indicates the number of times that a base is to be used as a multiplying factor. To illustrate, the base 3 raised to the fourth power, or $(3)^4$, requires that the base be used as a factor four times during the multiplication procedure. That is, $3 \times 3 \times 3 \times 3 = 81$. Where there is multiplication of a common base, the exponents are added. The multiplication of $(3)^2$ by $(3)^5$ may be written as $(3)^7$.

$$(3)^2 = 9$$
$$(3)^5 = 243$$
$$9 \times 243 = 2,187$$

and

$$(3)^7 = 2,187$$
$$3 \times 3 \times 3 \times 3 \times 3 \times 3 \times 3 = 2,187$$

When division is being performed with a common base, the exponent of the denominator is subtracted from the exponent of the numerator.

$$\frac{(3)^7}{(3)^2} = (3)^5$$

$$\frac{2,187}{9} = 243$$

That is

$$\frac{3 \times 3 \times 3 \times 3 \times 3 \times 3 \times 3}{3 \times 3} = 3 \times 3 \times 3 \times 3 \times 3$$

The expression $(1 + i)^n$ would be handled in a similar manner. The base $(1 + i)$ is raised to a power n. The solution of $(1 + 0.02)^4$, for example, requires that the base (1.02) be multiplied as shown.

$$1.02 \times 1.02 \times 1.02 \times 1.02 = 1.0824$$

Likewise, $(1 + 0.05)^3$ would be $1.05 \times 1.05 \times 1.05 = 1.1576$, and $(1 + 0.09)^2$ would be $1.09 \times 1.09 = 1.1881$.

LOGARITHMS

The logarithm of a number is defined to be the exponent of the power of the base (e.g., 10) that equals that number. That is, if $x = 10^y$, then the logarithm of x is y. Correspondingly, x is the antilogarithm of y. The number y (i.e., the logarithm) is usually a decimal number, with two parts called the characteristic and the mantissa. The characteristic is the integer portion and the mantissa is the remaining portion, which appears as a decimal fraction. Mantissas are given in logarithm tables, and logarithm characteristics can be determined by inspection. (Although logarithms with other numbers as a base may be used, the base 10 is most usual. Logarithm tables are generally constructed using 10 as the base.)

The base 10 raised to the second power would to $(10)^2 = 100$. The number 2 may be looked upon as a power, exponent, or logarithm. The value 100 is the number that produces the logarithm 2 (i.e., 2.0000, where the characteristic is 2 and the mantissa is .0000), with 100 being referred to as the antilogarithm. The equation $(10)^2 = 100$ may be written as $\log_{10} 100 = 2$, or simply $\log 100 = 2$, where a base of 10 is understood. The antilogarithm is displayed as antilog $2 = 100$.

Although logarithm tables are not contained in this book, tables having a base of 10, or a calculator with log and antilog functions, may be used for problem solving.

The following steps can be used to calculate $(1.02)^{20}$, which has the form $(1 + i)^n$.

$$(1.02)^{20} = X$$
$$20 \log 1.02 = \log X$$
$$20(0.00860) = \log X \text{ (from logarithm tables)}$$

THE BOOK OF INTEREST AND MONEY   273

$$0.1720 = \log X$$
$$\text{antilog } 0.1720 = X$$
$$1.4859 = X \text{ (from logarithm tables)}$$
$$(1.02)^{20} = 1.4859$$

The value of 1.4859 for $(1.02)^{20}$ coincides with the value of 1.4859 which results from the use of the compound interest tables.

In using logarithms to find the value of $(1.02)^{20}$, the role of the base 10 can be better understood by looking at the following calculation sequence.

$$\log 1.02 = 0.00860 \text{(from logarithm tables)}$$
$$10^{0.00860} = 1.02, \text{ or } (1.02)^{1}$$
$$20 \log 1.02 = (20)(0.00860) = 0.1720$$
$$10^{0.1720} = 1.4859$$

Starting with

$$(10)^{0.00860} = (1.02)^{1}$$

multiply the exponents on both sides of the equation by 20 (this is equivalent to raising both sides to the power 20):

$$(10)^{0.1720} = (1.02)^{20}$$

Therefore,

$$(1.02)^{20} = 1.4859$$

APPENDIX D:
COMPOUND INTEREST TABLES

The quantities listed in each column of the compound interest tables are the following:

Column 1: Determination of the future value or amount to which a known single payment will grow (Future Value of a Lump Sum).

Column 2: Determination of the future value or amount to which a series of known equal payments will grow (Future Value of an Annuity).

Column 3: Determination of the size of a series of equal payments required to reach a known future value (Payment Size of an Annuity When Total Future Value is Known).

Column 4: Finding the present value or worth of a known single payment to be made in the future (Present Value of a Lump Sum).

Column 5: Finding the present value or worth of a series of known equal payments to be made in the future (Present Value of an Annuity).

Column 6: Finding the size of a series of equal future payments when their present value is known (Payment Size of an Annuity When Total Present Value is Known).

Monthly Compounding (Nominal Annual Rate 8%).

n (months)	Column 1 Future Value of 1 (Lump Sum)	Column 2 Future Value of 1 Per Period (Amount of an Annuity)	Column 3 Sinking Fund Payment	Column 4 Present Value of 1 (Lump Sum)	Column 5 Present Value of 1 Per Period (Present Value of an Annuity)	Column 6 Periodic Payment to Amortize 1
1	1.0067	1.0000	1.0000	0.9934	0.9934	1.0067
2	1.0134	2.0067	0.4983	0.9868	1.9802	0.5050
3	1.0201	3.0200	0.3311	0.9803	2.9604	0.3378
4	1.0269	4.0402	0.2475	0.9738	3.9342	0.2542
5	1.0338	5.0671	0.1974	0.9673	4.9015	0.2040
6	1.0407	6.1009	0.1639	0.9609	5.8625	0.1706
7	1.0476	7.1416	0.1400	0.9546	6.8170	0.1467
8	1.0546	8.1892	0.1221	0.9482	7.7652	0.1288
9	1.0616	9.2438	0.1082	0.9420	8.7072	0.1148
10	1.0687	10.3054	0.0970	0.9357	9.6429	0.1037
11	1.0758	11.3741	0.0879	0.9295	10.5724	0.0946

Monthly Compounding (Nominal Annual Rate 8%).

years						
12	(1)	1.0830	12.4499	0.0803	0.9234	11.4958	0.0870
24	(2)	1.1729	25.9332	0.0386	0.8526	22.1105	0.0452
36	(3)	1.2702	40.5356	0.0247	0.7873	31.9118	0.0313
48	(4)	1.3757	56.3499	0.0177	0.7269	40.9619	0.0244
60	(5)	1.4898	73.4769	0.0136	0.6712	49.3184	0.0203
72	(6)	1.6135	92.0253	0.0109	0.6198	57.0345	0.0175
84	(7)	1.7474	112.1133	0.0089	0.5723	64.1593	0.0156
96	(8)	1.8925	133.8686	0.0075	0.5284	70.7380	0.0141
108	(9)	2.0495	157.4295	0.0064	0.4879	76.8125	0.0130
120	(10)	2.2196	182.9460	0.0055	0.4505	82.4215	0.0121
180	(15)	3.3069	346.0382	0.0029	0.3024	104.6406	0.0096
240	(20)	4.9268	589.0204	0.0017	0.2030	119.5543	0.0084
300	(25)	7.3402	951.0264	0.0011	0.1362	129.5645	0.0077
360	(30)	10.9357	1490.3594	0.0007	0.0914	136.2835	0.0073

Quarterly Compounding (Nominal Annual Rate 8%).

n (quarters)	Column 1 Future Value of 1 (Lump Sum)	Column 2 Future Value Per Period (Amount of an Annuity)	Column 3 Sinking Fund Payment	Column 4 Present Value of 1 (Lump Sum)	Column 5 Present Value Per Period (Present Value of an Annuity)	Column 6 Periodic Payment to Amortize 1
1	1.0200	1.0000	1.0000	0.9804	0.9804	1.0200
2	1.0404	2.0200	0.4950	0.9612	1.9416	0.5150
3	1.0612	3.0604	0.3268	0.9423	2.8839	0.3468
years						
4 (1)	1.0824	4.1216	0.2426	0.9238	3.8077	0.2626
8 (2)	1.1717	8.5830	0.1165	0.8535	7.3255	0.1365
12 (3)	1.2682	13.4121	0.0746	0.7885	10.5753	0.0946
16 (4)	1.3728	18.6393	0.0537	0.7284	13.5777	0.0737
20 (5)	1.4859	24.2974	0.0412	0.6730	16.3514	0.0612
24 (6)	1.6084	30.4219	0.0329	0.6217	18.9139	0.0529
28 (7)	1.7410	37.0512	0.0270	0.5744	21.2813	0.0470
32 (8)	1.8845	44.2270	0.0226	0.5306	23.4683	0.0426
36 (9)	2.0399	51.9944	0.0192	0.4902	25.4888	0.0392
40 (10)	2.2080	60.4020	0.0166	0.4529	27.3555	0.0366
60 (15)	3.2810	114.0515	0.0088	0.3048	34.7609	0.0288
80 (20)	4.8754	193.7720	0.0052	0.2051	39.7445	0.0252
100 (25)	7.2446	312.2323	0.0032	0.1380	43.0984	0.0232
120 (30)	10.7652	488.2582	0.0020	0.0929	45.3554	0.0220

Semiannual Compounding (Nominal Annual Rate 8%).

n (half years)	Column 1 Future Value of 1 (Lump Sum)	Column 2 Future Value of 1 Per Period (Amount of an Annuity)	Column 3 Sinking Fund Payment	Column 4 Present Value of 1 (Lump Sum)	Column 5 Present Value of 1 Per Period (Present Value of an Annuity)	Column 6 Periodic Payment to Amortize 1
1	1.0400	1.0000	1.0000	0.9615	0.9615	1.0400
years						
2 (1)	1.0816	2.0400	0.4902	0.9246	1.8861	0.5302
4 (2)	1.1699	4.2465	0.2355	0.8548	3.6299	0.2755
6 (3)	1.2653	6.6330	0.1508	0.7903	5.2421	0.1908
8 (4)	1.3686	9.2142	0.1085	0.7307	6.7327	0.1485
10 (5)	1.4802	12.0061	0.0833	0.6756	8.1109	0.1233
12 (6)	1.6010	15.0258	0.0666	0.6246	9.3851	0.1066
14 (7)	1.7317	18.2919	0.0547	0.5775	10.5631	0.0947
16 (8)	1.8730	21.8245	0.0458	0.5339	11.6523	0.0858
18 (9)	2.0258	25.6454	0.0390	0.4936	12.6593	0.0790
20 (10)	2.1911	29.7781	0.0336	0.4564	13.5903	0.0736
30 (15)	3.2434	56.0849	0.0178	0.3083	17.2920	0.0578
40 (20)	4.8010	95.0255	0.0105	0.2083	19.7928	0.0505
50 (25)	7.1067	152.6671	0.0066	0.1407	21.4822	0.0466
60 (30)	10.5196	237.9907	0.0042	0.0951	22.6235	0.0442

279

Annual Compounding (Nominal Annual Rate 8%).

n (years)	Column 1 Future Value of 1 (Lump Sum)	Column 2 Future Value of 1 Per Period (Amount of an Annuity)	Column 3 Sinking Fund Payment	Column 4 Present Value of 1 (Lump Sum)	Column 5 Present Value of 1 Per Period (Present Value of an Annuity)	Column 6 Periodic Payment to Amortize 1
1	1.0800	1.0000	1.0000	0.9259	0.9259	1.0800
2	1.1664	2.0800	0.4808	0.8573	1.7833	0.5608
3	1.2597	3.2464	0.3080	0.7938	2.5771	0.3880
4	1.3605	4.5061	0.2219	0.7350	3.3121	0.3019
5	1.4693	5.8667	0.1705	0.6806	3.9927	0.2505
6	1.5869	7.3359	0.1363	0.6302	4.6229	0.2163
7	1.7138	8.9228	0.1121	0.5835	5.2064	0.1921
8	1.8509	10.6366	0.0940	0.5403	5.7466	0.1740
9	1.9990	12.4876	0.0801	0.5002	6.2469	0.1601
10	2.1589	14.4866	0.0690	0.4632	6.7101	0.1490
15	3.1722	27.1521	0.0368	0.3152	8.5595	0.1168
20	4.6610	45.7620	0.0219	0.2145	9.8181	0.1019
25	6.8485	73.1059	0.0137	0.1460	10.6748	0.0937
30	10.0627	113.2832	0.0088	0.0994	11.2578	0.0888

INDEX

281